Boston For Dumm[ies]
1st Edition

D0837605

Boston Transit

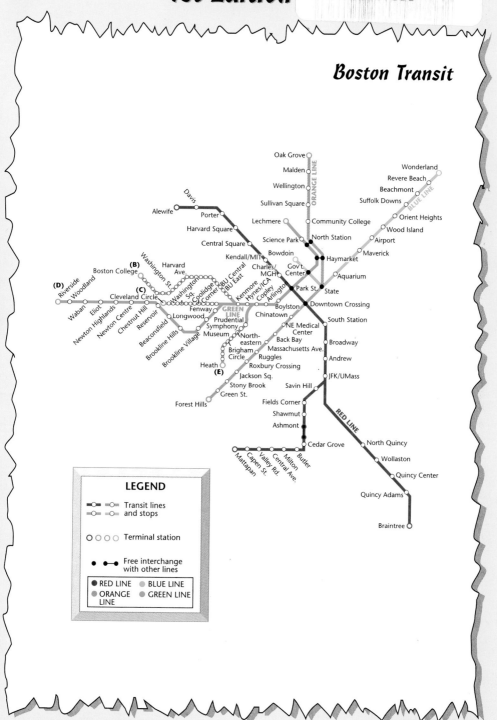

LEGEND

- Transit lines and stops
- ○ ○ ○ ○ Terminal station
- ● ●━● Free interchange with other lines

- ● RED LINE
- ● BLUE LINE
- ● ORANGE LINE
- ● GREEN LINE

Boston For Dummies,®
1st Edition

ATTRACTION	TRANSIT STOP
Beacon Hill	● Charles/MGH
Boston Common	● ● Park Street
	● ● Boylston
Boston Public Library	● Copley
Boston Tea Party Ship & Museum	● South Station
Children's Museum	● South Station
The Computer Museum	● South Station
Faneuil Hall	● ● Government Center
	● ● State
Fenway Park	● Kenmore, Fenway
Fogg Art Museum.	● Harvard Square
Franklin Park Zoo	● Forest Hills
	(then bus 16 to main entrance)
Harvard Museum of Natural History	● Harvard Square
Harvard Square/Harvard University	● Harvard Square
Institute of Contemporary Art	● Hynes/ICA
Isabella Stewart Gardner Museum	● Museum
John F. Kennedy Library and Museum	● JFK/UMass (shuttle bus)
John F. Kennedy National Historic Site	● Coolidge Corner
John Hancock Observatory	● Copley......... ● Back Bay
Mapparium	● Symphony
	● Massachusetts Ave.
Massachusetts Archives	● JFK/UMass.
Massachusetts Institute of Technology (MIT)	● Central Square or Kendall
Museum of Afro-American History	● Charles/MGH
Museum of Fine Arts	● Museum......... ● Ruggles
Museum of Science	● Science Park
Museum of Transportation	● Reservoir (then bus no. 51)
New England Aquarium	● Aquarium
Old North Church	● ● Haymarket
Paul Revere House.	● ● Government Center
Peabody Museum of Archaeology & Ethnology	● Harvard Square
Prudential Center Skywalk	● Copley......... ● Back Bay
Public Garden	● Arlington
Sports Museum of New England	● ● North Station
Symphony Hall	● Symphony

Hungry Minds™

For Dummies™: Bestselling Book Series for Beginners

 TM

References for the Rest of Us!®

BESTSELLING BOOK SERIES

Do you find that traditional reference books are overloaded with technical details and advice you'll never use? Do you postpone important life decisions because you just don't want to deal with them? Then our *For Dummies®* business and general reference book series is for you.

For Dummies business and general reference books are written for those frustrated and hard-working souls who know they aren't dumb, but find that the myriad of personal and business issues and the accompanying horror stories make them feel helpless. *For Dummies* books use a lighthearted approach, a down-to-earth style, and even cartoons and humorous icons to dispel fears and build confidence. Lighthearted but not lightweight, these books are perfect survival guides to solve your everyday personal and business problems.

> *"More than a publishing phenomenon, 'Dummies' is a sign of the times."*
>
> — *The New York Times*

> *"...you won't go wrong buying them."*
>
> — *Walter Mossberg, Wall Street Journal, on For Dummies books*

> *"A world of detailed and authoritative information is packed into them..."*
>
> — *U.S. News and World Report*

Already, millions of satisfied readers agree. They have made For Dummies the #1 introductory level computer book series and a best-selling business book series. They have written asking for more. So, if you're looking for the best and easiest way to learn about business and other general reference topics, look to For Dummies to give you a helping hand.

Hungry Minds™

1/01

Boston

FOR

DUMMIES®

by Marie Morris

Hungry Minds™

HUNGRY MINDS, INC.

New York, NY ◆ Cleveland, OH ◆ Indianapolis, IN

Boston For Dummies, 1st Edition

Published by:
Hungry Minds, Inc.
909 Third Avenue
New York, NY 10022
www.hungryminds.com
www.dummies.com

Library of Congress Control Number: 200108625

ISBN: 0-7645-6261-4

ISSN: 1531-7560

Printed in the United States of America

10 9 8 7 6 5 4 3 2 1

1B/SQ/QT/QR/IN

Distributed in the United States by Hungry Minds, Inc.

Distributed by CDG Books Canada Inc. for Canada; by Transworld Publishers Limited in the United Kingdom; by IDG Norge Books for Norway; by IDG Sweden Books for Sweden; by IDG Books Australia Publishing Corporation Pty. Ltd. for Australia and New Zealand; by TransQuest Publishers Pte Ltd. for Singapore, Malaysia, Thailand, Indonesia, and Hong Kong; by Gotop Information Inc. for Taiwan; by ICG Muse, Inc. for Japan; by Intersoft for South Africa; by Eyrolles for France; by International Thomson Publishing for Germany, Austria and Switzerland; by Distribuidora Cuspide for Argentina; by LR International for Brazil; by Galileo Libros for Chile; by Ediciones ZETA S.C.R. Ltda. for Peru; by WS Computer Publishing Corporation, Inc., for the Philippines; by Contemporanea de Ediciones for Venezuela; by Express Computer Distributors for the Caribbean and West Indies; by Micronesia Media Distributor, Inc. for Micronesia; by Chips Computadoras S.A. de C.V. for Mexico; by Editorial Norma de Panama S.A. for Panama; by American Bookshops for Finland.

For general information on Hungry Minds' products and services please contact our Customer Care department; within the U.S. at 800-762-2974, outside the U.S. at 317-572-3993 or fax 317-572-4002.

For sales inquiries and resellers information, including discounts, premium and bulk quantity sales and foreign language translations please contact our Customer Care department at 800-434-3422, fax 317-572-4002 or write to Hungry Minds, Inc., Attn: Customer Care department, 10475 Crosspoint Boulevard, Indianapolis, IN 46256.

For information on licensing foreign or domestic rights, please contact our Sub-Rights Customer Care department at 650-653-7098.

For information on using Hungry Minds' products and services in the classroom or for ordering examination copies, please contact our Educational Sales department at 800-434-2086 or fax 317-572-4005.

Please contact our Public Relations department at 212-884-5174 for press review copies or 212-884-5000 for author interviews and other publicity information or fax 212-884-5400.

For authorization to photocopy items for corporate, personal, or educational use, please contact Copyright Clearance Center, 222 Rosewood Drive, Danvers, MA 01923, or fax 978-750-4470.

Hungry Minds™ is a trademark of Hungry Minds, Inc.

About the Author

Marie Morris grew up in New York City, then studied history at Harvard. That was in the days when the Red Line ended at Harvard Square — not *so* long ago, but long enough. She has lived in the Boston area, with a brief break to get New York out of her system, since 1981. Since 1997 she has written the *Frommer's Boston* travel guide and contributed to *Frommer's New England.* She has also been, among other things, a contributor to Worth Interactive's travel coverage, an assistant sports editor at the *Boston Herald,* and an editor at *Boston* magazine. Marie lives in the North End, not far from the Freedom Trail, and close enough to "Old Ironsides" to feel safe and secure.

Author's Acknowledgments

A book is like a movie — more people than you can possibly imagine feel responsible for it, and they never get enough recognition. I'd like to thank everyone with a proprietary interest in *Boston For Dummies*. Thanks also to Suzanne Jannetta, who trusted me with this assignment, and to the many friends and family members who talked me through it. Finally, and far most important, infinite thanks to the infinitely patient Lisa Torrance.

Publisher's Acknowledgments

We're proud of this book; please send us your comments through our Online Registration Form located at www.dummies.com.

Some of the people who helped bring this book to market include the following:

Editorial

Editors: Linda Brandon, Project Editor; Lisa Torrance, Development Editor

Copy Editor: Ellen Considine

Cartographer: John Decamillis

Editorial Manager: Christine Beck

Editorial Assistant: Jennifer Young

Senior Photo Editor: Richard Fox

Assistant Photo Editor: Michael Ross

Cover Photos: Viesti Collection, ©Walter Bibikow (front cover); The Image Bank, ©Steve Dunwell (back cover)

Production

Project Coordinator: Nancee Reeves

Layout and Graphics: LeAndra Johnson, Kristin Pickett, Kendra Span, Julie Trippetti

Proofreaders: Angel Perez, Nancy Price, York Production Services, Inc.

Indexer: York Production Services, Inc.

Special Help
Robert Annis

General and Administrative

Hungry Minds, Inc.: John Kilcullen, CEO; Bill Barry, President and COO; John Ball, Executive VP, Operations & Administration; John Harris, CFO

Hungry Minds Consumer Reference Group

Business: Kathleen A. Welton, Vice President and Publisher; Kevin Thornton, Acquisitions Manager

Cooking/Gardening: Jennifer Feldman, Associate Vice President and Publisher

Education/Reference: Diane Graves Steele, Vice President and Publisher; Greg Tubach, Publishing Director

Lifestyles: Kathleen Nebenhaus, Vice President and Publisher; Tracy Boggier, Managing Editor

Pets: Dominique De Vito, Associate Vice President and Publisher; Tracy Boggier, Managing Editor

Travel: Michael Spring, Vice President and Publisher; Suzanne Jannetta, Editorial Director; Brice Gosnell, Managing Editor

Hungry Minds Consumer Editorial Services: Kathleen Nebenhaus, Vice President and Publisher; Kristin A. Cocks, Editorial Director; Cindy Kitchel, Editorial Director

Hungry Minds Consumer Production: Debbie Stailey, Production Director

◆

The publisher would like to give special thanks to Patrick J. McGovern, without whom this book would not have been possible.

◆

Contents at a Glance

Cartoons at a Glance

By Rich Tennant

page 237

page 39

page 7

page 93

page 111

page 259

page 147

Cartoon Information:
Fax: 978-546-7747
E-Mail: richtennant@the5thwave.com
World Wide Web: www.the5thwave.com

Maps at a Glance

Table of Contents

Introduction

• •

Some residents of Boston think of their home as just another typical large American city. They complain about the traffic, the cost of living, the ceaseless construction, the students who return like locusts every September, and the tourists who flock like lemmings (or students) to the historic sights. Forced to think about why they live here, they admit that Boston has good points, too — "It's near my job," they say.

Sometimes it takes a visit from an out-of-towner to make the locals realize the obvious: If their city weren't so enjoyable, it wouldn't be so popular.

So, in a sense, you're lucky. Even if you visited Boston before, you can approach this city with a fresh eye and an unjaded attitude. Come for the seafood and stay for the history. Pause as you rush to a meeting and admire the sun-dappled harbor. Seek out some great shopping and stumble upon an impromptu concert. Finally, get into Harvard *and* Fenway Park.

In theory, Boston is just another large city. In practice, it offers a unique blend of elements that make this city a singularly enjoyable destination.

About This Book

Boston For Dummies takes the information you need and breaks it down into manageable pieces. I start with the basics, guiding you from the "I think it may be somewhere in New England" stage all the way through to "I know just what hot spots to hit!"

Treat the book as a reference, not a "travel narrative." Read it cover-to-cover or dip into the sections that particularly interest you. If you already know that you'll be staying on your friend's couch, for instance, you can skip the accommodations information without worrying that you're missing something crucial. If you're burning to do some serious shopping . . . well, you probably don't have your nose buried in the Introduction anyway.

In assembling the information, suggestions, and listings in this book, I took a "greatest hits" approach. I present discriminating choices rather than encyclopedic directories. The focus is on what you need to know, not on "in case you were wondering" observations. Throughout, I offer plenty of insider advice to make you feel as comfortable as possible.

In addition, although I can't physically protect you every step of your journey, your safety is important to me. I encourage you to stay alert and be aware of your surroundings. Keep a close eye on cameras, purses, and wallets — all favorite targets of thieves and pickpockets.

Conventions Used in This Book

Like any reference book, *Boston For Dummies* uses some shorthand phrases and abbreviations. The most obvious are "Boston" and "the Boston area." Throughout eastern Massachusetts, you'll find people born in Newton, raised in Wellesley, educated in Cambridge, and living in Quincy who say they're "from Boston" without thinking twice. Rather than subject you to "Boston, Cambridge, sometimes Brookline, occasionally Somerville, and maybe a few other nearby suburbs," I use the shorter terms. When you need specifics (as in addresses), you get them.

You'll see the following credit card abbreviations:

AE   American Express

CB   Carte Blanche

DC   Diner's Club

DISC   Discover

JCB   Japan Credit Bank

MC   MasterCard

V   Visa

The hotel and restaurant reviews in Chapters 8 and 14 employ a system of dollar signs to give you a sense of the price range for each establishment. For a double-occupancy hotel room (not including tax) or dinner for one (not including tax and tip), these ranges are as follows:

Cost	Hotel	Restaurant
$	less than $100	less than $20
$$	$100–$200	$20–$30
$$$	$200–$300	$30–$45
$$$$	$300 and up	$45 and up

Please be aware that travel information is subject to change at any time, and that this fact is especially true of prices. I suggest that you write or call ahead for confirmations when making your travel plans.

Foolish Assumptions

This book aims to be as handy for a time-pressed frequent flyer as it is for an inexperienced traveler. Which chapters turn out to be most useful depends on you. I assume that you have constraints on your time and your willingness to process boatloads of information, not on your *ability* to do so. (And if those assumptions sound foolish, I can live with that!)

Other assumptions:

- ✔ Maybe you just don't have time to wade through a conventional guidebook.

- ✔ Maybe you are an experienced traveler, but you don't have a lot of time to devote to trip planning or you don't have a lot of time to spend in Boston once you get there. You want expert advice on how to maximize your time and enjoy a hassle-free trip.

- ✔ Maybe you've visited Boston before, and you suspect (rightly) that there has to be more to this city than crowds from every-where in the world except New England.

- ✔ Maybe you've never even been on a plane, traveled by train, reserved a room at a B&B, or bought tickets for the symphony — and you want a clear explanation of what to expect.

Whatever you're looking for, I provide as much information as you need.

How This Book Is Organized

This book consists of seven parts that lead you through the process of arriving and navigating the city, finding a great place to stay, searching out the restaurants that cater to your tastes, discovering the worth-while attractions and shopping areas, and well, having a great time.

Part 1: Getting Started

In this section, I describe what you need to know before you go. You get an insider's view of what Boston is really like and the lowdown on the best times to visit. I also help you develop a budget. Here, too, you find information for families, seniors, travelers with disabilities, and gay and lesbian travelers.

Part II: Ironing Out the Details

Now you move from the theoretical to the specific. How will you get to Boston? Where will you stay? What else do you need to know before you leave home? I tell you everything you need to know.

Part III: Settling in to Boston

You don't truly arrive in Boston, until you check into your hotel. In this part, I outline that final leg of your journey, sketch the city's neighborhoods, and explain how to get around and between them. I also address the all-important question of where to get cash.

Part IV: Dining in Boston

This part is all about food. From fusion-cuisine hot spots to 275-year-old standbys, Boston is a treat. I tell you where the locals chow down, where foodies *dine,* and where to go to grab a quick bite.

Part V: Exploring Boston

Here I give you the scoop on the city's sights and attractions — from museums and historic buildings to tours and cruises. If those places sound too highfalutin, check out this part for my tips on sports and shopping. I also recommend some favorite itineraries and day trips.

Part VI: Living It Up after the Sun Goes Down: Boston Nightlife

Boston makes up for its somewhat anemic nightlife with enough cultural offerings to class up a wrestling match — and enough bars and pubs to make up for early closing hours. You can't dance till dawn, but you can still have a ball after dark. I set the scene in this section.

Part VII: The Part of Tens

Veteran . . .*For Dummies* readers know about the Part of Tens, and newcomers will recognize the contents of these chapters: Interesting stuff that doesn't seem to fit anywhere else. I submit facts, pointers, and observations that complement the rest of this book. Enjoy.

Part VIII: Appendix

Information that could clutter the other chapters migrates here and appears in handy list form. Turn here for "Facts at Your Fingertips," toll-free numbers, and Web sites for airlines and hotels, and other sources of information. You're welcome.

Also at the back of the book are yellow planning worksheets. These forms help you set a budget, outline itineraries, and keep track of attractions, hotels, and restaurants that appeal to you. These worksheets make it easy for you to keep all the information you gather in one place.

Icons Used in This Book

In the margins of this book, five icons guide you toward information of your particular interests:

Handy facts, hints, and my insider info. This bull's-eye flags advice about what to do and how to make the best use of your time.

Tourist traps, rip-offs, travel hazards, and activities that aren't worth the trouble. I steer you away from potential pitfalls with this symbol.

Activities, attractions, and establishments that particularly suit people traveling with children. Boston is an exceptionally family-friendly city; I indicate these places as the standouts with this symbol.

If you want to splurge on one activity, you probably need to cut back on another; seek out this icon for pointers on cutting corners (relatively) painlessly, so you can spend your bucks on what you like best.

History flavors nearly everything you see and do in Boston. I use this symbol to single out particularly tasty morsels of information about the city's past.

Where to Go from Here

For most of the past 20 years, I've called Boston home. Friends puzzle over my refusal to even consider relocating — until they hear me talk about my adopted hometown. I still can't get enough of Boston's sights and sounds, its history and geography, its walkability and its proximity to the full range of New England's natural resources. From the salty ocean smell that comes in on the east wind to the United Nations of visitors that comes in with the autumn foliage — it's a thrill. And I'm thrilled to be able to share it with you. Here we go!

Part I
Getting Started

In this part . . .

*T*hink of the early stages of planning your trip as a pyramid: It begins with a base of nearly infinite possibilities, narrows as you zero in on viable options, and peaks sometime after you scratch "Boston?" on the back of an envelope. Now that you see where your pyramid is pointing, how will you get there?

The four chapters in this part put you (figuratively and perhaps literally) on the road to Boston. What sights and sensations will you experience? When should you visit? How much will it cost? Where can travelers with special needs turn for information? Here, naturally.

Chapter 1

Discovering the Best of Boston

. . . .

. . . .

*P*eople from all over the world seem to feel a connection to Boston. Whether or not you've visited the city, you probably already know something about it.

Maybe your best friend went to college here, or your next-door neighbor worships the Red Sox, or your baby-sitter's favorite movie is *Good Will Hunting,* or your internist did her residency at Massachusetts General. You see *Cheers* reruns and the Boston Pops' Fourth of July concert on TV, Fidelity manages your retirement savings, and you remember something about a tea party. You find yourself thinking that Boston sounds like a fun place to visit. You're right.

The city's historic and cultural attractions, entertaining diversions, and manageable size make it a wildly popular business, convention, and tourist destination. In order to plan the most enjoyable trip, I let you know a little about what to expect.

The Hub of the Solar System

Oliver Wendell Holmes gave Boston perhaps its most popular nickname: The Hub of the Solar System (which survives partly because headline writers love short words like "Hub"!). The solar system may be a bit of an exaggeration, but eastern Massachusetts has become an important destination for education, high-tech companies, financial services, and health care organizations.

Don't be too quick to envision legions of pasty-faced techies glowing under fluorescent lights, though. Boston is downright beautiful.

Redbrick buildings and cobblestone streets contrast delightfully with modern glass towers (and concrete boxes that seemed like a good idea at the time). Countless millions of dollars went into cleaning up Boston Harbor and the result is worth every penny. The "Boston Miracle" — the local manifestation of the plunging national crime rate — means that the city feels safer than it has in many years.

The Athens of America

Boston has a lot of goofy nicknames (I'll get to "Beantown" shortly), but this one is most useful for my purposes. The Athens of America description came about because some pointy-headed 19th-century social critics considered ancient Athens a paragon of education and culture. Lending its name to the closest New World equivalent must have seemed perfectly natural, not to mention irresistibly alliterative.

Consider what that comparison means today: Where you find education, you find students. In the Boston area, that means thousands and thousands of college students. With students come noise, crowds, musical innovation, outlandish fashions, cheap diversions, and flat-out fun. Boston and Cambridge positively buzz with youthful energy.

As for culture, Boston is a major center for the performing arts. The city is home to some of the world's best and best-loved art, one of the finest symphony orchestras anywhere, and countless student efforts in every artistic field. Remember that where you find high culture, you find, well, less high culture (but not the borderline-scandalous kind, such as tattoo parlors and strip clubs). Boston is nearly as well known for bar bands, stand-up comedy, and street performance.

Full of Beans

"Beantown" is a nod to colonial Boston, when the Puritans' strict rules about working on the Sabbath meant no cooking on Sunday. A pot of beans could go into the oven in a brick kitchen fireplace on Saturday and cook in the retained heat, emerging for Sunday dinner at noon and giving the world "Boston baked beans."

Some traditional restaurants serve beans today, but nobody's coming to Boston for legumes. Folks come here to dine on fish and shellfish in every imaginable style, and they've come to the right place. From cutting-edge cuisine (for all those Internet gazillionaires) to down-home ethnic fare (for all those budget-conscious students) — nearly every menu includes succulent seafood.

Posterity and Prosperity

If you're like most visitors, you won't get out of Boston without at least a brief, painless history lesson. You can certainly immerse yourself in the past, visit innumerable colonial and Revolutionary landmarks, and stuff your head full of random facts. But you don't need to — merely walking around exposes you to the Boston of a bygone age.

Boston's original landmass was about one-third the size of the modern city. Landfill accounts for the growth, most famously in the Back Bay, the only central area laid out in a grid pattern. Widely circulated myth notwithstanding, the circuitous street patterns in older neighborhoods such as the North End and Beacon Hill don't owe their apparently random designs to cow paths. (They hark back to long-gone property lines and misguided efforts to replicate London's layout.) Every step downtown takes you over and through centuries' worth of history, with no exam at the end of the day.

For example, consider Faneuil Hall: Once accessible directly from the harbor, today it doesn't even enjoy a water view. The shops of Faneuil Hall Marketplace stand (on landfill) between the historic building and the shore. A few blocks away lies a monument to legendary Yankee thrift, the original Filene's Basement. Not far from there is the retail fantasyland known as Newbury Street. Between these extremes, Boston offers the full range of retail recreation.

This Is a Hard Hat Area

Peerless symbol of Bostonian ingenuity or unprecedented pain in the neck? The Central Artery/Third Harbor Tunnel project, better known as the "Big Dig," is both.

Interstate 93, the main north-south route through downtown Boston, currently runs on the elevated expressway that separates the waterfront from the rest of downtown. In 2004, when the Big Dig (assuming it's on schedule) is over, the expressway will be gone. Traffic will run through a tunnel and onto a gorgeous bridge over the Charles River. The techniques that are making this happen have construction engineers all over the world salivating — and Boston-area commuters foaming at the mouth.

On a brief visit, you'll probably find the Big Dig inconvenient but fascinating, and perhaps a source of fashion tips. Right around the time that many downtown businesses shifted from casual Fridays to casual weekdays, construction workers in the de facto Big Dig uniform (hard hat, orange T-shirt, jeans, boots) started turning up all over town. Coincidence? It's anyone's guess.

Chapter 2

Deciding When to Go

· ·

In This Chapter

▶ Figuring out the best time to visit

▶ Reviewing a month-by-month list of events

· ·

*E*very season is a good time to visit Boston. The climate is relatively temperate — with some exceptions, which I'll get to. Citywide events are generally entertaining but not overwhelming — with some exceptions, which I'll get to. The people are typically friendly and welcoming — with some exceptions, which you can (but hopefully won't) discover on your own.

The Secrets of the Seasons

After a kicky New Year's Eve celebration, Boston moves into the slowest travel season of the year. From January through March, many hotels offer great deals, especially on weekends. Conventions, when they happen, tend to be small, short, and local (which means they attract relatively few people who spend the night in town). If you can't take bitter cold and biting winds, plan to concentrate on indoor activities. Snow sometimes overwhelms the city during these months, and some suburban attractions close for the winter.

During the **February** school vacation week (starting with Presidents' Day), kid-oriented places and activities fill up fast. Second honeymooners and other child-free vacationers may want to steer clear.

In **April,** spring comes to the mid-Atlantic states, but only occasionally reaches New England. Snow can linger into the early part of the month, and reluctant outdoorspeople may want to note that this is the height of mud season. (Pack shoes that you don't care about ever wearing again.) The Boston Marathon, on the third Monday of the month, attracts unbelievable crowds — you'll need a hotel reservation (see Chapter 8) far in advance. The marathon falls on Patriots' Day, a state holiday that also marks the start of another school vacation week. This week is not a restful time to visit.

Between April and November, Boston experiences few slow periods. Conventions take place all year, clustering in the spring and fall. The Convention and Visitors Bureau (see the Appendix for contact information) can tip you off to especially large gatherings.

Full-blown spring usually doesn't arrive until early **May,** but that makes the first run of balmy weather all the more enjoyable. Regardless of the weather, this month marks the beginning of college graduation season. Hotels book up in apparently random patterns, and out-of-state drivers flood the city.

Graduation pandemonium lingers into **June,** when pleasant weather and the end of the younger kids' school year translate into a jump in occupancy rates at hotels and in crowds all around town.

In **July** and **August,** vacationing families flock to Boston, creating long lines and lots of opportunities to witness tantrums. For a week around July 4, Harborfest draws hordes of people with its extremely fun, extremely crowded activities. Toward the end of August, the flood of returning college students begins.

June, July, and August are about the only months when you may encounter consecutive days of 90-plus temperatures, usually accompanied by debilitating humidity. Be ready to concentrate on indoor activities or willing to take it slow outside.

In early **September,** college starts in earnest; watch out for moving vans, especially on September 1. The weather turns cooler and humidity drops. Foliage season begins in late September and runs to mid-November. Many "leaf-peepers" stay in the Boston area or pass through on the way to northern New England, creating tour-bus gridlock.

September and **October** are the months most likely to include a run of exhilarating weather, with comfortably warm days and cool to chilly nights. The Head of the Charles Regatta, on the third weekend of October, attracts hundreds of thousands of people; many are students who crash in friends' dorms, but you may experience trouble booking a room on short notice.

November, the end of the foliage season, is also when convention business grows slower. The weather may turn cold and raw, but snow is seldom a problem.

In **December,** the leaves are gone but the meetings linger. You may be able to nab a good deal on a weekend, especially if you find a hotel that offers holiday shopping specials. On New Year's Eve, rooms fill with suburbanites who don't want to deal with driving home after midnight; book far in advance.

A weather report, for better or verse

This poem is the second-best verse about Boston to know (after "Paul Revere's Ride"). The description applies to the short column of lights on top of the old John Hancock building in the Back Bay (right next to the 60-story glass Hancock Tower):

> Steady blue, clear view;
>
> flashing blue, clouds due;
>
> steady red, rain ahead;
>
> flashing red, snow instead.

During the summer, flashing red means bad weather has postponed the Red Sox.

Weather Alert

Lots of places claim to be the inspiration for the ancient weather cliché "If you don't like it, wait 10 minutes," but a few days in Boston will make you a believer that the New England climate inspired the expression. My advice: Think twice before letting the weather determine your plans.

You simply cannot escape New England weather. Steering clear of late winter, because you hate the cold, or avoiding midsummer, because you can't take humidity, seems to guarantee that you'll miss a spell of especially temperate conditions. (Actually, what trying to avoid bad weather guarantees is that you'll really, really notice when the national weather service exclaims over the nice weather in Boston, but that's an issue for the author of *Relativity For Dummies*.) Table 2-1 will at least give you an idea of the monthly temperatures you can expect.

Table 2-1   Boston's Average Temperatures and Rainfall

	Jan	Feb	Mar	Apr	May	June	July	Aug	Sept	Oct	Nov	Dec
Temp. (°F)	30	31	38	49	59	68	74	72	65	55	45	34
Temp. (°C)	-1.1	-0.5	3.3	9.4	15.0	20.0	23.3	22.2	18.3	12.8	7.2	1.1
Rainfall (in.)	4.0	3.7	4.1	3.7	3.5	2.9	2.7	3.7	3.4	3.4	4.2	4.9

It's a Date: Calendar of Events

Crowds flood Boston for many of these popular events. Expect full hotels, booked-up restaurants, and crowds galore. To avoid disappointment, always double-check before scheduling a trip to coincide with a particular event.

Spontaneous travelers and others who haven't planned ahead can pick up suggestions from the event hotline of the **Greater Boston Convention and Visitors Bureau** (☎ **800-SEE-BOSTON** or 617-536-4100; Internet: www.bostonusa.com), the "Calendar" section of the Thursday *Boston Globe* (Internet: www.boston.com/globe), and the "Scene" section of the Friday *Boston Herald* (Internet: www.bostonherald.com).

January

Events surrounding **Martin Luther King, Jr. Day** (the third Monday of the month) include gospel celebrations and other musical happenings, lectures, and panel discussions at various venues. Check special listings in the Thursday *Globe* "Calendar" section for specifics.

For **Chinese New Year,** the dragon parade draws a crowd to Chinatown no matter how cold it is, and the **Children's Museum** (☎ **617-426-8855**; Internet: www.bostonkids.org) puts on special programs. The date depends on the Chinese lunar calendar: In 2001, January 24; in 2002, February 12. Call the city **Office of Special Events and Tourism** (☎ **617- 635-3911**).

February

Special museum exhibits and children's programs highlight **Black History Month.** Many institutions schedule concerts, films, and other activities. **National Park Service** rangers (☎ **617-742-5415**; Internet: www.nps.gov/boaf) lead tours of the Black Heritage Trail.

During **School Vacation Week,** which starts with Presidents' Day, almost every school in the state closes. Special cultural activities include kid-oriented exhibitions, plays, concerts, and tours. Contact individual attractions for information on special offerings and extended hours.

March

The **New England Spring Flower Show,** in the middle of the month, is a perfect antidote to cabin fever. At the end of an especially snowy winter, expect especially huge crowds. The **Massachusetts Horticultural Society** (☎ **617-536-9280**; Internet: www.masshort.org) presents the show at the Bayside Expo Center in Dorchester.

April

The **Big Apple Circus** performs in a heated tent near the South Boston waterfront for about a month every spring (late March through early May). Proceeds support the Children's Museum. Visit the museum box office or contact **Ticketmaster** (☎ **617-931-ARTS;** Internet: www. ticketmaster.com).

On the third Monday of the month, **Patriots' Day** marks the unofficial end of winter. The state holiday commemorates the events of April 18 and 19, 1775, when the Revolutionary War began. Lanterns (as in "two if by sea") hang in the steeple of the **Old North Church** (☎ **617-523-6676**; Internet: www.oldnorth.com), and riders dressed as Paul Revere and William Dawes travel from Boston's North End to Lexington and Concord. "Minutemen" and "redcoats" re-enact the battles on the town green in Lexington and at the Old North Bridge in Concord. See Chapter 21 for information on visiting Lexington and Concord.

The legendary **Boston Marathon** starts at noon on Patriots' Day. The leaders cross the finish line on Boylston Street in front of the Boston Public Library, starting a little after 2 p.m. Good vantage points include Commonwealth Avenue and Kenmore Square. For information, call ☎ **617-236-1652** or visit www.bostonmarathon.org.

May

Usually on the third weekend of the month, **Lilac Sunday** is the only day of the year when the Arnold Arboretum permits picnicking. The gorgeous botanical garden, in Boston's Jamaica Plain neighborhood, boasts sensational spring flowers, including more than 400 varieties of lilacs. Call ☎ **617-524-1717** or visit www.arnold.harvard.edu.

At the end of the month, the **Street Performers Festival** takes over Faneuil Hall Marketplace. Musicians, magicians, jugglers, sword-swallowers, and artists strut their stuff. Call ☎ **617-338-2323** for more information.

June

International headliners and local stars play the **Boston Globe Jazz & Blues Festival,** held the third week of the month. Concerts are indoors and outdoors, at lunch, after work, in the evening, and on the weekend. Some performances require advance tickets; some are free. Call ☎ **617-267-4301** or visit www.boston.com/jazzfest for more details.

July

July 4 is the high point of the week-long **Boston Harborfest** and a guaranteed *blast.* Events include fireworks (twice!), concerts, guided tours, cruises, the Boston Chowderfest, and USS *Constitution*'s annual turnaround. Call ☎ **617-227-1528** or visit www.bostonharborfest.com for more information.

The centerpiece is the **Boston Pops Concert & Fireworks Display,** at the Hatch Shell amphitheater on the Esplanade. Live music begins in the evening, but this is an all-day affair — fans arrive at dawn to stake out pieces of the lawn in front of the stage. The program includes the "1812 Overture," with actual cannon fire, and amazing fireworks at about 10 p.m. (If you're not keen on roasting in the sun, wait until dark, ride the Red Line to Kendall/MIT and watch the pyrotechnics from the Cambridge side of the river.) Visit www.july4th.org for more details.

August

The North End is always fun to visit, and during the **Italian-American feasts** on summer weekends, it rocks. The street fairs begin in July, and the last two — the Fishermen's Feast (middle of the month) and the Feast of St. Anthony (end of the month) — are the biggest. All include food, carnival games, live and recorded music, and real live dancing in the streets. Call the city **Office of Special Events and Tourism** (☎ 617- 635-3911).

October

Thousands of rowers plus tens of thousands of spectators flood Boston and Cambridge for the **Head of the Charles Regatta,** on the third or fourth weekend of the month. A huge party (without alcohol) rages on the banks of the Charles River and its bridges on Saturday afternoon and all day Sunday. Call ☎ **617-864-8415** or visit www.hocr.org.

In the middle of the month, the **Ringling Brothers and Barnum & Bailey Circus** makes its annual 2-week visit to the **FleetCenter** (☎ 617- 624-1000; Internet: www.fleetcenter.com).

Just about all month, the Witch City observes its biggest holiday with **Salem Haunted Happenings.** Special offerings include parades, parties, fortune-telling, cruises, and tours. Visit www.salemhauntedhappenings.com for more scoop on the activities.

November

The spirit of the original **Thanksgiving Celebration** endures in Plymouth. The "stroll through the ages" showcases 17th- and 19th-century Thanksgiving preparations in historic homes. **Plimoth Plantation** (☎ **800-262-9356** or 508-746-1622; Internet: www.plimoth. org), which re-creates the colony's first years, offers a reservation-only Victorian Thanksgiving feast (trust me, you're not sorry to miss out on Pilgrim food). Call ☎ **800-USA-1620** or check out www.visit-plymouth.com.

December

Boston Ballet's *Nutcracker,* one of the country's biggest and best, starts its annual run the day after Thanksgiving. The spectacular sets help make the ballet an enticing way to introduce children to theater-going. Call **Tele-charge** (☎ **800-447-7400**) as soon as you plan your trip, ask whether your hotel offers a *Nutcracker* package, or check for returned tickets in person at the Wang Theatre box office, 270 Tremont St.

The year ends with **First Night,** a spectacular, arts-oriented New Year's Eve blowout all over town from early afternoon to midnight. The parade is in the late afternoon; ice sculptures and art exhibitions dot the city; theatrical performances and indoor and outdoor entertainment run all day. The midnight fireworks display explodes over the harbor. For most activities, you need a First Night button, available for about $15 at visitor centers and stores around the city. Call ☎ **617- 542-1399** or visit www.firstnight.org.

Chapter 3

Planning Your Budget

*B*oston possesses all the elements of an outrageously expensive destination, starting with a hotel shortage that shows no signs of abating. For those weighing in on the luxury end of the scale, the limited hotel space means your biggest problem is likely to be finding someone to take your money. For us regular folks, the hotel shortage doesn't mean "stay home"; it means "stay home until you have a workable budget."

Let's give thanks for the Boston area's ever-present students. They occupy a parallel universe where food is plentiful and reasonably priced, entertainment is cheap or free, and the whole point of shopping is getting the most out of your (and your parents') hard-earned money.

Of course, if you imitate them too slavishly, you can wind up sleeping in a stranger's bathtub and eating mystery meat. You get the idea, though: Know what's important to you and try not to overpay for it.

Adding Up the Elements

A well-constructed budget is like a tricky jigsaw puzzle and making it work can be as satisfying as dropping that 1,000th piece into place. Think hard (and make your companions do the same) about what's important to you.

For instance, corporate travelers rank Boston among the country's most expensive business destinations. If you seal that once-in-a-lifetime deal, though, the high price tag may feel like a bargain. Flexibility is important, but knowing when you can't be flexible is even more important when determining your budget. Turn to the end of this book for a budget worksheet to help you through this process. Here are some other guidelines.

What Things Cost

Taxi from airport to downtown or Back Bay	$18–$24
Water shuttle from airport to downtown	$10
Bus from airport to downtown or Back Bay	$6–$8
Subway token	$1
Local bus fare	75¢
Pay phone call	35¢
Double at Omni Parker House hotel	$189.00–$295.00
Double at Newbury Guest House	$100.00–$155.00
Double at Longwood Inn	$65.00–$109.00
Lunch for one at Ye Olde Union Oyster House	$10.00–$23.00
Lunch for one at Durgin-Park	$6.00–$20.00
Lunch for one at Bartley's Burger Cottage	$4.00–$10.50
Dinner for one, without wine, at Rialto	$23.00–$50.00
Dinner for one, without wine, at Legal Sea Foods	$14.00–$30.00
Dinner for one, without wine, at the Elephant Walk	$10.00–$23.00
Glass of beer	$2.50–$5
Can of soda	75¢–$1.25
Cup of coffee	$1 and up
Roll of ASA 100 Kodacolor film, 36 exposures	$6.75–$8
Adult admission to the Museum of Fine Arts	$12
Child (under 18) admission to the MFA	Free
Movie ticket	$5–$9
Theater ticket	$30–$90

Lodging

Boston's hotel shortage has one positive: Rooms are in such short supply that formerly borderline choices have upgraded to take advantage of the red-hot market. But as you might recall from freshman economics, low supply means high demand. The average price of a room is nearly $180.

If you can't book a relatively inexpensive B&B and don't like the idea of a hostel, expect to spend at least $110 a night, plus the 12.45 percent hotel tax. The price of a centrally located chain hotel might seem high (and, except in the dead of winter, probably will be closer to $180 than to $110). Just remember that the lower cost of many suburban establishments doesn't include the time and expense of commuting to the downtown attractions — or the psychic damage commuting to Boston inflicts.

Transportation

Before discussing anything else, I should point out that many popular destinations are easiest to reach on foot. (If you want to pro-rate the wear on your walking shoes, be my guest.)

I plan to harp on this until out-of-state drivers are as rare as mastodons: You do not need to rent a car to get around Boston and Cambridge. What you think you get — flexibility and convenience — are exactly the things you sacrifice. Boston in particular is as nightmarish for drivers as New York or San Francisco, and that's before you consider the heavy construction equipment in use on many downtown streets.

Driving can appear to be a budget-conscious option, if you resign yourself to parking the car when you arrive and not retrieving it until you leave. But before you shout "road trip," compare the cost of tolls, gas, parking, and incidentals to the best airfare you can find — you may find that driving isn't such a great deal after all.

Taxis are expensive and can be hard to find, but you'll track one down eventually. The car-rental money you save can pay for several days' worth of cab rides. (See Chapter 11 for information on taxis.)

Massachusetts Bay Transportation Authority (MBTA) provides cheap transportation ($1 for a subway token, 75 cents for the local bus) in and around the city. Visitor passports good for unlimited local rides, and sold for 1-, 3-, and 7-day periods (costing $6, $11, and $22, respectively), can make public transit an even better deal. Note that service shuts down by 1 a.m. and doesn't go everywhere — that means more cabs. (For the lowdown on public transit, see Chapter 11.)

Restaurants

Again, thank the students: You can find tasty, inexpensive food all over the place. But don't get carried away. If you've been waiting for years to try fresh lobster, this is not the time to cut corners.

Serious penny-pinchers can enjoy a decent breakfast for $5 or less, lunch for $6 or so, and a more-than-adequate dinner for as little as $15.

Making lunch the big meal of the day can be a good strategy if your budget or appetite (or both) is small. Or start with a bagel and coffee or juice ($2 to $3), lunch on a sandwich or salad ($5), and go wild at dinner.

Attractions

I would be remiss if I didn't tell you that plenty of people visit Boston just to shop, eat, and watch sports (namely the Red Sox, plus the Celtics, Bruins, and local colleges). If you can't return home without soaking up a little culture, turn to Part 5, make a list, and start adding up those admission costs. First, check out potential deals. The MBTA's visitor passports include discounts, the Arts/Boston coupon book and Boston CityPass offer good deals on attractions (see Chapter 16 for details), and many institutions, such as the Museum of Fine Arts, schedule hours when admission is by donation or free (see "Tips for Cutting Costs," later in this chapter).

Shopping

Maybe this activity should fall under "Attractions." (Shopping is an attraction for me!) Budget what you like, not forgetting souvenirs — and not forgetting that a great deal from Filene's Basement makes a better souvenir than a T-shirt or refrigerator magnet ever could. Shopping-wise, Boston is celebrated for high-end arts and crafts, merchandise from its dozens of colleges, and deals on clothing. That doesn't mean that prices are especially good, though (unless, of course, you're at Filene's Basement); it means the sales tax (5 percent) doesn't apply to clothing priced below $175. For more information on Boston's shopping scene, check out Chapter 19.

Nightlife

If culture is your main motivation, start with, say, the Boston Symphony Orchestra (known as the BSO), and build the rest of your visit around that. Good seats for the BSO, the Boston Pops, Boston Ballet, or a Broadway-bound show likely will set you back at least $50 a head. Less expensive but equally enjoyable options include numerous local performing-arts companies and two superb jazz clubs (see Part 6 for details).

Even if a splashy night out isn't your thing, consider reserving time, money, and energy for an after-dark excursion. Boston offers lots of relatively inexpensive cultural opportunities, such as half-price theater tickets and cheap or free student performances in every field. Or warm yourself at a congenial pub; a couple of hours and a couple of pints with the locals can tell you more about the city than an army of tour guides. (For information on the city's nightlife, again see Part 6.)

Wolves in cheap clothing: Bargains that aren't

Looking back on other trips you've taken, you tend to focus on obvious missteps. The hotel renovation special, the discount tour with a guide your uncle saw on *America's Most Wanted,* and the time you said, "If it were that terrible, would it be a special?" — dumb moves you know enough not to repeat.

The cost-cutting steps to worry about are the ones that sound so good that you may forget they could be mistakes. Here are two biggies:

✔ **Sacrificing convenience for price.** Sometimes the deal is so good that you can't ignore it. (I flew out of Providence instead of Boston to save $600, and I'd do it again.) Before you decide to save $50 by leaving at 6 a.m. and returning at 1 a.m. — a mere 7 hours before your workday starts — think hard about just how good a deal that is. Are the sacrifices worth the bucks?

✔ **Paying for things you don't need.** The 5-day transit pass saves tons of money, but only when you use it enough. If you don't eat breakfast, the room rate that includes this meal is subsidizing someone else's. The weekend special at the hotel with the great spa is no deal for someone who just wants a lap pool. A bargain is a bargain only if you get something you wanted anyway.

Keeping a Lid on Hidden Expenses

At home, your wallet seems to be made of solid leather (or nylon, or whatever). Your bucks are secure inside and don't leak out without careful consideration. Then you leave town and money starts gushing out of your wallet like water from a broken dam. Knowing what to watch out for can help you stem this spending tide. Let me offer some advice.

Taxes and fees

These expenses aren't usually paid in cash, so you may not take note of them as you should. When you arrange any commercial transaction — hotel rooms, car rentals, dining — be sure to ask for the total cost as well as the great-sounding price the business quotes you. For example:

✔ Boston and Cambridge impose 12.45 percent **lodging** taxes. (Boom! Your $159 hotel room costs $20 more.)

✔ **Car rentals** that originate in Boston carry $10 surcharges that go toward the construction of a new convention center, and you agreed to return the gas tank full. (Zip! That's another $20.)

> ✔ Many **restaurants** add a 15 to 18 percent gratuity to the bill if your party is larger than six or eight people; accidentally leave your own tip and you're out another chunk of change. (Bang! That's an extra $30 or more.)

In conclusion, let me remind you to double-check the total and what the bill includes before you fork over your hard-earned cash.

Gratuities

The average tip for most service providers, such as waiters and cab drivers, is 15 percent, rising to 20 percent for particularly good service. The state meal tax is 5 percent — in restaurants, triple (or quadruple) the tax to calculate the tip. A 10 to 15 percent tip is sufficient if you just drink at a bar. Bellhops get $1 or $2 a bag, hotel housekeepers should receive at least $1 per person per day, and valet parking and coat-check attendants expect $1 to $2 for their services.

Incidentals

This low-profile category of expenses is the most insidious. In a day of spending $1 here and $5 there — postcards, stamps, water, maps, snacks, and other random items — you can easily spend $20 or $30 and barely notice it. Budget for these extra expenditures and be a bit more aware of what you're frittering away — you'll save a bundle.

My top tip in this category concerns water. You can bring a bottle from home and fill it at your hotel or from water fountains at attractions and visitor centers. If that seems a bit maniacal, consider picking up a six-pack at a drugstore and keeping bottles handy in your room. This suggestion may sound silly, but buying individual bottles throughout the day can really add up.

Money: Will That Be Paper or Plastic?

ATMs usually are the easiest way to get cash on vacation. Most cities (including Boston) have plenty of 24-hour machines linked to a national network that probably includes your bank at home. Even if you use traveler's checks, you'll want to keep some cash handy for incidentals.

If you plan to rely on your ATM card, see what networks accept your bank's cards before leaving home. **Cirrus** (☎ 800-424-7787 or 800-4CIRRUS) and **Plus** (☎ 800-843-7587) are the most popular networks; these toll-free numbers give you specific locations of ATMs.

The largest banks in Massachusetts are Fleet and Citizens; smaller institutions and credit unions also operate ATMs. These handy little machines are everywhere, including some subway stations. In busy areas, you'll seldom go more than 2 blocks without seeing one.

Try not to hit the ATM every time you need 20 bucks, but try not to walk around with a fat roll of bills, either. ATM transactions usually carry service charges and the fees can add up. Especially costly are privately operated non-bank ATMs (most commonly found in convenience stores).

Many banks impose a fee every time you use a card from a "foreign" bank. By law, Massachusetts banks' ATMs must display a message warning you that you're about to be charged and offer you the chance to cancel the transaction. Even if the bank doesn't charge you, that doesn't stop your out-of-state bank from tacking on its own fee (for using another bank's ATM) of 50 cents to $3.

If your ATM card is also a debit card, consider carrying at least one conventional credit card. When using a debit card, you may forget that you're spending the equivalent of cash and depleting your checking account, instead of running up a credit-card balance. If you don't keep a large balance, be aware that some banks "freeze" part of the money in your account when you use a debit card for a transaction without a set amount (like a car rental, restaurant meal, or tank of gas).

All charged up

Credit cards are invaluable when traveling. They are a safe way to carry money and provide a convenient record of your expenses. Most establishments in the Boston area accept major credit cards.

In an emergency, you can get cash advances off your credit cards at any bank. (The fees can be hefty, and interest charges start accruing the moment you receive the cash.) At most banks, you don't need to go to a teller; you can get a cash advance at the ATM if you know your personal identification number (PIN). If you don't know your PIN, call the phone number on the back of your credit card *before you leave home* and ask the bank to send it. You should receive your PIN in 5 to 7 business days. (I offer more details regarding ATMs in Chapter 12.)

Check this out

Traveler's checks are a holdover from the pre-ATM days when out-of-towners could not be sure that they'd be able to cash personal checks. Because lost or stolen traveler's checks can be replaced, they are still a sound alternative to carrying a lot of cash. **American Express** (☎ 800-221-7282), **Visa** (☎ 800-227-6811), and **MasterCard** (☎ 800-223-9920) all issue traveler's checks. (See Chapter 9 for pointers on buying them.)

Tips for Cutting Costs

"Yankee thrift" is not an artifact, it's an art form. Even in this go-go economy, saving money is a highly respected pastime. Here are some tips to help you trim your travel costs like a true Yank.

✔ **Travel during the off-season.** If you can visit Boston during non-peak times (especially January through March), you'll find hotel prices that are as much as half the cost of what they run during peak months.

✔ **Fly on off-peak days of the week.** If you can travel on Tuesday, Wednesday, or Thursday, you may lock in a cheaper airfare. When you inquire about airfares, ask if flying on a different day reduces the rate. See Chapter 5 for more tips on getting the best airfare.

✔ **Reserve your flight well in advance.** A ticket purchased 14 to 21 days in advance can save you over $500 on a full fare. See Chapter 5 for details.

✔ **Or reserve your flight only a couple of days in advance.** Last-minute Internet fares (released Wednesday for the weekend that starts 2 days later) aren't a sure thing, since you never know what destinations will be included each Wednesday, but they sure are a bargain. Check out Chapter 5 for more information.

✔ **Don't fly into Boston.** You'll get to Boston eventually. Flying to Warwick, Rhode Island, or Manchester, New Hampshire can be *much* cheaper than flying to Boston's Logan International Airport. If you have more time than money, these alternate cities are worth checking out. See Chapter 5 for details.

✔ **Weigh that package.** An arrangement that includes airfare, lodging, airport transfers, and perhaps some extras (such as a trolley tour) can save both money and time. Turn to Chapter 5 for more details.

✔ **Bring only as much luggage as you can carry easily.** A pile of heavy bags weighs you down so much that jumping on the T isn't a reasonable option. So you'll wind up hailing a cab, which costs an awful lot more than that $1 subway token, and possibly tipping skycaps and bellmen. Plan to handle your own lightly packed luggage, and don't forget to leave room for souvenirs you might want to carry home.

✔ **Reserve a hotel room with a kitchen.** It may not feel like as much of a vacation if you do your own cooking and dishes, but eating in restaurants three times a day can be pricey. Even if you only make your own breakfast and take an occasional bag lunch, you'll still save. And you'll never be shocked by a hefty room service bill.

✔ **Don't be shy about asking for a discount.** All that money you pay to belong to the auto club, the AARP, a trade union, or another organization with group bargaining power can finally pay off — but only if you remember to ask about deals. When you book transportation and accommodations, have your membership cards handy.

✔ **Double up with the kids.** Rates typically are about the same whether you book one bed or two, and many hotels allow children to stay free with their parents. Plus, an extra bed is much cheaper than an extra room, especially on a long trip.

✔ **Don't rent a car while in Boston.** And I'm going to *keep* saying this. If you're planning an out-of-town day trip, go wild. Otherwise, save the expense of renting and parking.

✔ **Buy an MBTA Visitor Passport.** And use it. The passport can be a great deal, especially if you take advantage of the accompanying discounts on attractions, shopping, and dining (see Chapter 16 for details).

✔ **Buy an ArtsBoston coupon book or a Boston CityPass.** The coupon book's discounts include a wide selection of attractions and activities, such as museums, trolley tours, and sightseeing cruises. The CityPass covers just six attractions (including the Museum of Fine Arts) but represents a 50 percent discount if you visit all of them. See Chapter 16 for details.

✔ **Take advantage of cheap or free museum admission.** The Museum of Fine Arts is pay-what-you-wish ($5 suggested) Wednesday after 4 p.m; the Children's Museum costs $1 after 5 p.m. on Friday; the USS Constitution Museum is free; the Institute of Contemporary Art is free to all Wednesday after 5 p.m.; the Harvard art museums are free Saturday before noon and all day Wednesday; and the Harvard natural history museums are free on Sunday morning.

✔ **Try expensive restaurants at lunch instead of dinner.** Your lunch tab can be a fraction of the dinner bill at the same establishment, and the menu often includes many of the same specialties.

✔ **Pass on the souvenirs.** Your photographs and your memories should be the best mementos of your trip. If you're worried about money, you can do without the T-shirts and trinkets.

✔ **Let the kids do some planning.** You may be pleasantly surprised to learn that they consider a ride on a swan boat and a session of duck feeding at the Public Garden a full and fulfilling morning. (If your children have champagne taste and you're on a beer budget, forget I said anything.)

Chapter 4

Planning for Special Travel Needs

- -

In This Chapter

▶ Setting up a smooth family trip

▶ Traveling senior style

▶ Finding the best places for travelers with disabilities

▶ Getting tips for gay and lesbian travelers

- -

*O*ne-size-fits-all travel is a myth; all travelers, especially those with particular needs, want their plans custom tailored. This chapter offers pointers for people in four specific situations: families, senior citizens, travelers with disabilities, and gay and lesbian travelers.

Fun Family Travel: Not a Contradiction

Families from around the world flock to Boston (and the ones who prepare wisely return home still on speaking terms). Many, if not most, Boston-area activities appeal to children and nearly every hotel and restaurant caters to kids. Just getting around Boston becomes a family activity as you are bound to do a fair amount of hand-in-hand strolling — a plus if walking tires the kids enough to make for a peaceful, early bedtime, but a negative if it does the same to you.

The best advice I can offer to family travelers is so simple that it verges on insulting: Give your kids a voice in the trip-planning process. Children have so little control of their daily lives; on vacation, offering them a bit of power may go a long way.

Overall, try to keep your kids' needs in mind when considering the three stages of your trip: Before you leave home, while you're on the road, and, of course, when you're in Boston. Look for the Kid-Friendly icon throughout this book for family-oriented tips and activities.

Boston on the children's bookshelf

Your kids may know more about these tiny slices of Boston than you do (or at least, more than you remember). Literally hundreds of children's books about Boston are available; here are three of my favorites:

- *Make Way for Ducklings,* by Robert McCloskey. You've probably lost count of how many times you've read this one to your preschoolers. Adorable bronze renderings illustrate this delightful story of a duck family that occupies its own corner of the Public Garden.

- *The Trumpet of the Swan,* by E. B. White. He's not as famous as Charlotte the spider, but Louis the trumpeter swan has delightful adventures in Boston. Like the Mallard family, he winds up at the Public Garden.

- *Johnny Tremain,* by Esther Forbes. A boy's-eye view (with several strong female characters) of the events that took place in Boston before the Revolutionary War. Johnny's interesting escapades make this a painless introduction to the history of the period — and a cracking good story.

Doing your homework

Another borderline-obvious suggestion: Make sure everyone knows what to expect. (This is all too easy to forget even when you're traveling only with adults!) A huge part of Boston's appeal is that it's a working city, not a theme park. That's no consolation to a child who thinks that "vacation" always means roller coasters and cotton candy.

Children old enough to enjoy traveling can help with planning. (For a lesson in life skills, you may ask your kids to lend a hand with the vacation budgeting.) Give your children some time with this book and a not-too-overwhelming assortment of other planning materials. After everyone contributes suggestions, all of you will have a better sense of what the other family members have in mind for your Boston vacation.

Spare yourself some angst by including potentially unenthusiastic teenagers early in the planning process. A college tour, time out for mall hopping, or some other inducement may help counteract the totally uncool concept of the family vacation.

Booking a hotel

I want to take the stress out of finding hotel rooms that suit your family and your budget. Here are booking strategies you can follow to simplify the process:

✔ **Accommodate the kids' needs first.** If the only thing they care about is a swimming pool (and if they haven't traveled much, they may not know that not every hotel has one), start with confirming that amenity.

✔ **Choose a hotel that lets children stay free.** Most do; the cut-off age can be as young as 12 or as old as 19. A room with two double beds typically costs the same as a room with one queen- or king-size bed. Even if a crib or rollaway costs extra, it's still cheaper than taking two rooms.

✔ **Consider booking a second room or a suite.** Some hotels offer families a deal (usually half price) on the extra room, which is sometimes an adjoining unit connected by an interior door. Even then, a suite may be less expensive — not to mention, more luxurious.

✔ **A refrigerator or kitchenette can pay for itself.** Stock up on cereal and juice, make a bag lunch or two, and invest the savings (in money and good behavior) in a fancy dinner.

Don't put off thinking about child care. I strongly, strongly recommend that you book a sitter in advance — if possible, when you reserve your room. As in other areas of the country, demand for child care is high and the number of providers is limited. The good news is that most hotels in the Boston area can recommend reliable baby-sitters. If you choose to use a child-care referral service, keep in mind that referral fees are steep. If you're in town on business, ask your host company if it has a corporate membership in a child-care referral service. This membership may mean reduced rates for you.

The agency **Parents in a Pinch** (☎ **800-688-4697** or 617-739-KIDS; Internet: www.parentsinapinch.com) can line up a carefully screened child-care provider and offer references to parents who request them. The annual registration fee is $150; the per-day referral fee is $40 for evenings and weekends, $60 for weekdays. The sitter gets $9 per hour for one child, 50¢ an hour for each additional child, reimbursement for transportation (30¢ a mile), and other authorized expenses.

Keeping the peace on the road

Book a nonstop flight. If you can't, try to fly early in the day. If you can't do that, try not to book the last flight of the day. A canceled connecting flight may leave you stranded, especially in the winter, when weather delays plague the entire East Coast.

If you fly, remember to pack chewing gum to help with ear-pressure problems.

Flying or not, pack diverting materials and toys — crayons or markers, a deck of cards, a computer game, a personal stereo or portable radio with headphones, or a favorite book. Keep a surprise toy or two in reserve. These items are handy on the road and can buy weary parents some TV-free downtime in the middle of a busy day in Boston.

Bring more diapers than you think you could possibly need. For a small child, pack a change of clothes where you can reach it easily; for an older child, a clean shirt is always a good idea (let the youngster carry it).

Going out on the town

Be realistic. You may need to adjust your expectations to accommo-date your traveling companions' short legs and shorter attention spans. Three important reminders: Don't try to do too much, don't forget to schedule some playtime, and don't assume that more expen-sive is better.

Remember that children are creatures of habit, and travel is disruptive for everyone. In unfamiliar surroundings, something as simple as a favorite breakfast cereal or flavor of juice may make the difference between wary-but-willing and freaked out.

You probably have a sense of your sightseeing timetable from the groundwork you laid at home. If your schedule isn't set, try this: Ask each child for a short list of his or her top activity picks (no more than three, and no make-or-break activities). Then ask each child to choose one activity from someone else's list. This idea may sound a tad crafty, but it cuts down on the cries of "this wasn't my idea."

Larger groups may consider splitting up for a while and reuniting to swap notes over a family dinner. This idea works especially well if the children are far apart in age. For example, the teenagers can explore the New England Aquarium while the younger kids check out the Children's Museum. This strategy can help keep the peace and keep everyone satisfied.

Savings for Seniors

Many Boston-area businesses, including hotels, restaurants, museums, and movie theaters, offer discounts to seniors who present valid identi-fication. The cut-off age usually is 65 or (less often) 62. Some senior deals can be found through **AARP (American Association of Retired Persons)** and are available to any member age 50 or older. Membership in AARP (601 E St. NW, Washington, DC 20049; ☎ **800-424-3410** or 202-434-AARP; Internet: www.aarp.org) costs $10 a year and includes discounts on package tours, airfares, car rentals, and hotels — to men-tion only the travel-related discounts.

Get in the habit of asking whether a business offers a senior discount. Restaurants and theaters usually extend discounts only during off-peak hours, but museums and other attractions may charge reduced rates at all times. Carry your driver's license or other document that shows your date of birth.

Seniors 65 and over can buy passes that allow them to ride the MBTA (Massachusetts Bay Transportation Authority) subways for 25 cents (75 cents less than regular fare), and local buses for 15 cents (60 cents less than regular fare). On zoned and express buses and the commuter rail, the senior fare is half the regular fare. The Senior Pass is available for a nominal fee (currently, 50 cents) weekdays from 8:30 a.m. to 5 p.m. at the Office for Transportation Access, Back Bay Station, 105 Dartmouth St. Or write to the **Office for Transportation Access,** 145 Dartmouth St., Boston, MA 02116 (☎ **617-222-5438** or 617-222-5854 [TTY]; Internet: www.mbta.com). Enclose a 1-by-1-inch photo and a check or money order for 50 cents.

A Golden Age Passport from the National Park Service is one of the best deals around. For $10, it gives you free lifetime admission to all recreation areas run by the federal government, including parks and monuments. The passport can pay for itself in one visit to the Boston area. For example, it covers the Longfellow House in Cambridge and the Maritime National Historic Site in Salem, among many other destinations. It's available to citizens and permanent residents 62 and older at any Park Service site that charges admission.

In addition, most major domestic airlines, including American, United, Continental, US Airways, and TWA all offer discount programs for senior travelers; be sure to ask when you book your flight. If you experience mobility difficulties, see the following section for information about getting around Boston.

Traveling without Barriers

Boston is a generally accessible city, with some deviations. Rampant construction and uneven walking surfaces can keep you from getting around as quickly as you may like. I recommend that you allow plenty of time to reach your destinations, especially near the Big Dig, which dominates the area between North Station and South Station and can disrupt every mode of transportation in the downtown area (see Chapter 1 for more on the Big Dig).

The narrow streets, cobbled thoroughfares, and brick sidewalks that make older neighborhoods like Beacon Hill and the North End so picturesque can make navigation difficult. However, once you reach them, almost all attractions are accessible. Note that the upper levels of some historic buildings — for example, the second floor of the

Paul Revere House — can't accommodate wheelchairs. If you have severe mobility issues, contact attractions in advance for accessibility information.

Many North End and Beacon Hill streets don't allow buses and trolleys. Motor tours touch on the edges of these neighborhoods, but they don't get up close. If you want to experience these areas, you must disembark from public transit and venture into these vicinities on your own. (Beware of salespeople who try to tell you otherwise.) For example, the Paul Revere House is 4 blocks from the closest trolley stop.

An excellent source of information is **Very Special Arts Massachusetts,** 2 Boylston St., Boston, MA 02116 (☎ **617-350-7713**; TTY 617-350-6836; Internet: www.vsamass.org). Its comprehensive Web site includes a searchable database of general access information and specifics about more than 200 arts and entertainment facilities in the state.

Finding accommodating accommodations

Most Boston-area lodgings comply with the Americans with Disabilities Act (ADA), but the true level of accessibility can be harder to gauge without asking some pointed questions. Many hotels occupy antique buildings, and the updating process worked better on some than on others. Be explicit about your needs when you make your reservations. If you have a specific concern that a certain hotel can't address, the staff should be able to direct you to a more appropriate establishment.

Some older, smaller hotels and B&Bs comply with federal law only partly or not at all. Large national chain hotels are more likely to offer the full range of ADA-compliant accommodations, including roll-in showers, lower sinks, extra space for maneuvering wheelchairs, and so forth. The **Royal Sonesta Hotel** in Cambridge (☎ **800-SONESTA**) trains its staff in disability awareness; at the **Westin Copley Place Boston** (☎ **800-WESTIN-1**), 48 accessible rooms adjoin standard units.

Getting around

Under the ADA, all forms of public transit must provide special services to patrons with disabilities. Newer stations on the Red, Blue, and Orange lines are wheelchair accessible, and the MBTA is in the process of converting Green Line trolleys. Call ☎ **800-392-6100** (outside Massachusetts) or 617-222-3200 to see if the stations that you need are accessible.

Do not rely on system maps to tell you which subway stations are accessible; these maps tend to be sorely out-of-date.

All MBTA buses are equipped with lifts or kneelers; call ☎ **800-LIFT-BUS** for more information. Some bus routes are wheelchair accessible at all times, but you may need to make a reservation as much as a day in advance for others. One taxicab company with wheelchair-accessible vehicles is **Boston Cab** (☎ **617-536-5010**); advance notice is recommended. In addition, Airport Handicap Van (☎ **617-561-1769**) offers wheelchair-accessible service.

For discounted public transit fares, persons with disabilities can apply for a $3 Transportation Access Pass. The process takes 6 to 8 weeks and may not be worth the trouble for a short visit. Contact the **Office for Transportation Access,** 145 Dartmouth St., Boston, MA 02116; ☎ **617- 222-5438** or 617-222-5854 (TTY); Internet: www.mbta.com.

General information

Several national organizations provide disabled travelers with the information and tools they need to experience the world.

Access-Able Travel Source (www.access-able.com) is a comprehensive database of travel agents who specialize in travel for the disabled; it's also a clearinghouse for information about accessible destinations around the world.

Many major car rental companies now offer hand-controlled cars for disabled drivers. Avis can provide such a vehicle at any of its locations in the United States with 48-hour advance notice; Hertz requires between 24 and 72 hours of advance reservation at most of its locations. **Wheelchair Getaways** (☎ **800-536-5518** or 606-873-4973; Internet: www.wheelchair-getaways.com) rents specialized vans with wheelchair lifts and other features for the disabled in more than 35 states, including Massachusetts.

A World of Options, a 658-page book of resources for disabled travelers, covers everything from biking trips to scuba outfitters. The book costs $35 and is available from **Mobility International USA**, P.O. Box 10767, Eugene, OR 97440 (☎ **541-343-1284** [voice and TTY]; Internet: www.miusa.org). You may also want to consider joining a tour that caters specifically to folks with disabilities. One such company is **FEDCAP Rehabilitation Services,** 211 W. 14th St., New York, NY 10011 (☎ **212-727-4200;** Fax: 212-727-4373).

Vision-impaired travelers can get information on traveling with Seeing Eye dogs from the **American Foundation for the Blind,** 11 Penn Plaza, Suite 300, New York, NY 10001 (☎ **800-232-5463**).

Advice for Gay and Lesbian Travelers

Boston is one of the most gay- and lesbian-friendly year-round destinations in New England (Provincetown holds the seasonal title). The neighborhoods of South End, Jamaica Plain, and Cambridge's Porter Square are home to many gay men and lesbians. A number of nightclubs cater to a gay clientele on at least one night a week.

One of the area's best resources, the **Gay and Lesbian Helpline** (☎ 617- 267-9001), offers information Monday to Friday 6 to 11 p.m., weekends 5 to 10 p.m. The weekly newspaper **Bay Windows** (☎ 617-266-6670; Internet: www.baywindows.com) covers New England and offers extensive cultural listings. The arts-oriented weekly **Boston Phoenix** publishes a monthly supplement, "One in 10," and has a gay-interest area at its Web site: www.bostonphoenix.com.

The **Pink Pages,** 66 Charles St. #283, Boston, MA 02114 (☎ **800-338-6550**), is a guide to gay- and lesbian-owned and gay-friendly businesses. Check the wide-ranging Web site at www.pinkweb.com/boston.index.html. If you don't have Web access, you can order a copy of the annual directory for $11, including shipping.

Other information sources include the **Boston Alliance of Gay and Lesbian Youth** (☎ **800-42-BAGLY** or 617-227-4314; TTY 617-983-9845; Internet: www.bagly.org) and the **Bisexual Resource Center** (☎ **617- 424-9595**; Internet: www.biresource.org).

Part II
Ironing Out the Details

The 5th Wave   By Rich Tennant

"The closest hotel room I could get you to Copley Square for that amount of money is in Cleveland."

In this part . . .

*N*ow comes the component of planning that can feel like ditch digging and can pay off like gold mining. Here you learn something about travel agents, package tours, and airfare pricing. Then it's time to choose a hotel, look at lodging options, check out different neighborhoods, and discover ways of booking a room. Finally, we double-knot the loose ends and send you on your way.

Chapter 5

Getting to Boston

In This Chapter

▶ Using a travel agent — or not

▶ Discussing the pluses and minuses of package tours

▶ Flying to Boston — or not

▶ Getting to town by car or train

*I*f the details of trip planning start to bog you down, you may begin to suspect that the *longest* distance between two points is a straight line. You don't have to feel that way. This chapter outlines your options, from hands off to hands on, and explores choices for flying and riding to Boston.

The Travel Agent Question

A good travel agent is like a good mechanic or good plumber: Hard to find, but invaluable when you locate the right one. The best way to find a good travel agent is the same way you find a good plumber or mechanic or doctor — word-of-mouth.

To get the most out of your travel agent, do a little homework. Read up on your destination (you've already made a sound decision by buying this book) and pick out some accommodations and attractions that appeal to you. If you have access to the Internet, check prices on the Web yourself (see "Getting the Best Deals on Airfares" later in this chapter for ideas) to get a sense of ballpark figures. Then take your guidebook and Web information to your travel agent and ask him or her to make the arrangements for you. Because travel agents can access more resources than even the most complete travel Web site, they generally can get you better prices than you can get by yourself. And they can issue your tickets and vouchers right in the agency. In addition, your travel agent can recommend an alternative if he or she can't get you into the hotel of your choice.

Travel agents work on commissions. The good news is that *you* don't pay the commissions — the airlines, accommodations, and tour companies do. The bad news is that unscrupulous travel agents may try to persuade you to book the vacation that nabs them the most money in commissions. But over the past few years, some airlines and resorts have begun to limit or eliminate these commissions altogether. The immediate result has been that travel agents don't bother booking certain services unless the customer specifically requests them. Additionally, some travel agents have started charging customers for their services.

Handle with Care: All-in-One Packages

Say the words "escorted tour" or "package tour" and you may automatically feel as though you're being forced to choose: Your money or your lifestyle. Think again, my friends. Times — and tours — have changed.

An **escorted tour** does, in fact, involve an escort, but that doesn't mean it has to be dull — or even tame. Escorted tours range from cushy bus trips, where you sit back and let the driver worry about the traffic, to adventures that include walking the Freedom Trail. You do, however, travel with a group, which may be just the thing for you if you're single and want company. In general, your expenses are taken care of after you arrive at your destination, but you still need to cover your airfare.

Which brings us to **package tours.** Unlike escorted tours, these generally "package" costs rather than people. Some tour companies bundle every aspect of your trip, including tours to various sights. However, most tour companies deal just with selected aspects of your trip, allowing you to get good deals by combining airfare and hotel costs, for example. A package tends to leave you a lot of leeway, while saving you a lot of money.

How do you find these deals? Well, I suggest some strategies in the next two sections, but keep in mind that every city is different. The tour operators I mention may not offer deals convenient to your departure city. If that's the case, check with your local travel agent: They generally know the most options close to home and how best to put together things such as escorted tours and airline packages.

Joining an escorted tour

You may be one of the many people who love escorted tours. The tour company takes care of all the details and tells you what to expect at each leg of your journey. You know your costs upfront, and, in the case of the tamer ones, there aren't many surprises. Escorted tours can take you to the maximum number of sights in the minimum amount of time with the least amount of hassle.

If you decide to go with an escorted tour, I strongly recommend purchasing travel insurance, especially if the tour operator asks to you pay upfront. But don't buy insurance from the tour operator! If the tour operators don't fulfill their obligation to provide you with the vacation you paid for, there's no reason to think they'll fulfill their insurance obligations either. Get travel insurance through an independent agency. (I give you more about the ins and outs of travel insurance in Chapter 9.)

When choosing an escorted tour, along with finding out whether you need to put down a deposit and when final payment is due, ask a few simple questions before you buy:

- ✔ **What is the cancellation policy?** How late can you cancel if you are unable to go? Do you get a refund if you cancel? If they cancel?

- ✔ **How jam-packed is the schedule?** Does the tour schedule try to fit 25 hours into a 24-hour day, or does it give you ample time to relax by the pool or shop? If getting up at 7 a.m. every day and not returning to your hotel until 6 or 7 p.m. at night sounds like a grind, certain escorted tours may not be for you.

- ✔ **How big is the group?** The smaller the group, the less time you spend waiting for people to get on and off the bus. Tour operators may be evasive about this, because they may not know the exact size of the group until everybody has made their reservations. But they should be able to give you a rough estimate.

- ✔ **Does the tour require a minimum group size?** Some tour operators exact a minimum group size and may cancel the tour if they don't book enough people. If a quota exists, find out what it is and how close they are to reaching it. Again, tour operators may be evasive in their answers, but the information may help you select a tour that's sure to happen.

- ✔ **What exactly is included?** Don't assume anything. You may be required to get yourself to and from the airports at your own expense. A box lunch may be included in an excursion, but drinks may be extra. Beer may be included, but not wine. How much flexibility does the tour offer? Can you opt out of certain activities or does the bus leave once a day, with no exceptions? Are all your meals planned in advance? Can you choose your entree at dinner or does everybody get the same chicken cutlet?

Picking a peck of package tours

For many destinations, package tours can be a smart way to go. In many cases, packages that include airfare, hotel, and transportation to and from the airport cost less than if you book the individual elements yourself. That's because packages are sold in bulk to tour operators, who resell them to the public. The process is kind of like buying your vacation at a buy-in-bulk store — except the tour operator is the one who buys the 1,000-count box of garbage bags and resells them 10 at a time at a cost that undercuts the local supermarket.

The cost of package tours can vary. Ask a lot of questions when you book your trip. Prices vary according to departure city, hotel, and extras such as car rental and optional tours. Timing is as important as other options in determining price. Adjusting your travel dates by a week (or even a day) can yield substantial savings.

Tips for choosing a Boston package

Details of packages to Boston don't vary much, which makes comparison shopping relatively easy. Lodging options aren't extensive simply because there aren't that many hotels. The sightseeing component, if there is one, usually is a free or discounted one-day trolley tour rather than a customized offering.

Look into hotel packages that include tickets to a cultural event, such as a major museum show or a Boston Ballet extravaganza (notably *The Nutcracker*). Even if you don't get a discount, landing a hot ticket can be a great time-saver.

Don't automatically add a rental car to your package. If you use the car every day and have access to free parking, it can be a good deal. If it sits in the hotel garage racking up parking fees, you're wasting money.

On the other hand, an excursion to a suburban town can be a worthwhile addition to your vacation. If time is short and you just can't leave town without seeing Plymouth (or Gloucester or another day-trip destination), paying someone else to handle the logistics of renting a car may be worth the money.

Package specialists

If you decide to investigate these package options further, your next task is to find the package that fits your needs. Check the ads in national magazines like *Arthur Frommer's Budget Travel, Travel & Leisure,* and *Condé Nast Traveler.* The travel section of your Sunday newspaper is another place to check, but your best bets are the choices I describe here:

✔ One of the biggest packagers in the Northeast, **Liberty Travel** (☎ **888-271-1584**; Internet: www.libertytravel.com) makes up in volume discounts what it lacks in personalized service.

✔ A more local option is **Yankee Magazine Vacations** (☎ **877-481-5986**; Internet: www.newengland.com/vacations). Its menu of add-ons includes an impressive variety of excursions to other New England destinations.

A new leaf

Every fall, New England's colorful trees exert a magnetic pull over millions of people. Travelers sign up for bus tours that start and end in Boston and return home with the false impression that they've seen the city. I'm not telling you not to, but I will say this: Foliage season offers no guarantees. "Peak color" may not start or end when you think it will, and the traffic and weather may keep you from making the best of it. If you're lucky enough to get a flight to Boston in October, consider making it your base and scheduling a day trip or two (after you've seen the forecast) that includes some leaf-peeping.

✔ Airline packages can be a good alternative for some destinations, but Boston (a "spoke" rather than a "hub") isn't a hot option for most carriers. A happy exception is **American Airlines Vacations** (☎ **800-321-2121**; Internet: www.aavacations.com), which handles arrangements with and without airfare. Some of its deals even undercut Amtrak and involve a lot less travel time.

✔ If you live close enough to take advantage of it, **Amtrak Vacations** (☎ **800-654-5748**; Internet: www.amtrakvacations.com) can be a reasonable option. But don't book a train trip without at least checking your air options and don't assume that this is a more reliable choice during bad weather. Snow falls on train tracks, too.

To explore other airline possibilities, see the phone numbers and Web sites listed in the Appendix at the back of this book.

Getting the Best Deals on Airfares

Count the number of passengers in the cabin the next time you fly. You may just have counted the number of different fares, too. *Yield management* — making each flight as full and as profitable as possible — can be harsh, but it can also work to your advantage.

If you need flexibility, be ready to pay for it. The full fare usually applies to last-minute bookings, sudden itinerary changes, and round trips that get you home before the weekend. On most flights, even the shortest routes, a full fare can approach $1,000.

You'll pay far less than full fare if you book well in advance, can stay over Saturday night, or can travel on Tuesday, Wednesday, or Thursday. A ticket bought as little as 7 or 14 days in advance will cost only 20 to 30 percent of the full fare. If you can travel with just a couple days' notice, you may also get a deal (usually on a weekend fare that you book through an airline's Web site — see "Tips for weekend warriors," later in this chapter, for more on this).

Airlines periodically lower prices on their most popular routes. Restrictions abound, but the sales translate into savings. For instance, a cross-country flight may cost as little as $400 (in other words, less than the walk-up shuttle fare for the 218-mile trip from Boston to New York). You may also score a deal when an airline introduces a new route or increases service on an existing one.

Watch newspaper and television ads and airline Web sites (see the Appendix for Web addresses and phone numbers), and when you see a good price, grab it. These sales usually run during slow seasons — for Boston, January through March. Sales rarely coincide with peak travel times such as summer vacation and the winter holidays, when people must fly, regardless of price.

Attractive airport alternatives

If you have lots of time but not lots of money, booking a flight into Warwick, Rhode Island (outside Providence) or Manchester, New Hampshire can be a great deal. Southwest Airlines broke these markets open, and many other carriers now serve both cities. Getting to Boston can be a hassle, but saving hundreds of dollars to spend on other things makes up for a lot of hassles.

The problem with this approach can be timing, since you need extra time to drive from these airports to Boston. Plus, if you have to pay a lot for a rental car, there goes your great deal. However, for someone with lots of time who also finds a good deal on a rental car, or has a friend pick them up, this could be the way to go.

T. F. Green Airport (☎ 888-268-7222; Internet: www.pvd-ri.com; airport code PVD) is in Warwick, Rhode Island, about 60 miles south of Boston. **Bonanza** (☎ 800-556-3815) offers bus service between the airport and Boston's South Station.

Manchester International Airport (☎ 603-624-6556; Internet: www.flymanchester.com; airport code MHT) is about 51 miles north of Boston. **Vermont Transit** (☎ 800-552-8737) operates bus service to and from Boston; **Flight Line** (☎ 800-245-2525; Internet: www.flightlineinc.com) offers reservation-only van service.

Cutting ticket costs by using consolidators

Consolidators, also known as bucket shops, are good places to find low fares. Consolidators buy seats in bulk and resell them at prices that undercut the airlines' discounted rates. Be aware that tickets bought this way usually are nonrefundable or carry stiff (as much as 75 percent of the ticket price) cancellation penalties. Important: Before you pay, ask the consolidator for a confirmation number, and then call the airline to confirm your seat. Be prepared to book your ticket through a different consolidator if the airline can't confirm your reservation.

Consolidators' small ads usually appear in major newspapers' Sunday travel sections at the bottom of the page. **Council Travel** (☎ **800-226-8624;** Internet: www.counciltravel.com) and **STA Travel** (☎ **800-781-4040;** Internet: www.statravel.com) cater to young travelers, but offer bargain prices to people of all ages. **Travel Bargains** (☎ **800-247-3273**; Internet: www.1800airfare.com) offers deep discounts with a 4-day advance purchase. Other reliable consolidators include **1-800-FLY-CHEAP** (☎ **800-359-2432**; Internet: www.1800flycheap.com); **TFI Tours International** (☎ **800-745-8000** or 212-736-1140), which serves as a clearinghouse for unused seats; and "rebaters" such as **Travel Avenue** (☎ **800-333-3335** or 312-876-1116; Internet: www.travelavenue.com) and the **Smart Traveller** (☎ **800-448-3338** in the U.S. or 305-448-3338), which rebate part of their commissions to you.

How to snare a deal on the Web

Use the Internet to search for deals on airfare, hotels, and (if you insist) car rentals. Among the leading sites are **Arthur Frommer's Budget Travel Online** (www.frommers.com), **Travelocity** (www.travelocity.com), **Lowestfare** (www.lowestfare.com), **Microsoft Expedia** (www.expedia.com), **The Trip** (www.thetrip.com), **Smarter Living** (www.smarterliving.com), and **Yahoo!** (http://travel.yahoo.com).

Each site provides roughly the same service, with variations you may find useful or useless. Enter your travel dates and route, and the computer searches for the lowest fares. Several other features are standard, and periodic bell-and-whistle updates make occasional visits worthwhile. You can check flights at different times or on different dates in hopes of finding a lower price, sign up for e-mail alerts that tell you when the fare on a route you specify drops below a certain level, and gain access to databases that advertise cheap packages and fares for those who can get away at a moment's notice.

Remember that you don't have to book online; you can ask your flesh-and-blood travel agent to match or beat the best price you find.

Tips for weekend warriors

The airlines make great last-minute deals available through their Web sites once a week, usually on Wednesday. Flights generally leave on Friday or Saturday (that is, only 2 or 3 days later) and return the following Sunday, Monday, or Tuesday. Some carriers offer hotel and car bargains at the same time.

Avoiding cabin fever

Whether you think of flying as an adventure or an ordeal, you're probably not thrilled by the prospect of a bone-dry cabin and a ration of personal space that would make a sardine claustrophobic. (Imagine how I'd sound if I didn't love flying.) Here are some strategies that may make your trip more tolerable.

✔ **Bulkhead seats,** in the front row of each cabin, usually offer the most legroom. Don't storm forward just yet. Without a seat in front of you, you must fit your carry-on luggage into the overhead bin. The front row may not be the best place to see the in-flight movie and many airlines save these seats for full-fare frequent flyers.

✔ **Emergency-exit row seats** also offer extra legroom. Ask when you check in whether you can be seated in one of these rows; assignment is usually first come, first served. You must be at least 15 years old and able to open the emergency exit door and help direct traffic if necessary.

✔ **Wear comfortable clothes.** And dress in layers; the supposedly controlled cabin climate can leave you sweltering or shivering. You'll be glad to have a sweater or jacket that can help regulate your body temperature.

✔ **Drink a lot of water.** This won't make you any friends if you're in a window seat, but aisle-huggers won't be sorry. Not only does your body stay hydrated, but walking back and forth to the "lavatory" (only in airplane cabins — why, why?) helps keep your legs from cramping.

✔ **Bring some toiletries** on long flights. Take a travel-size bottle of moisturizer or lotion to refresh your face and hands at the end of the flight. On an overnight flight (also known as the red-eye), always pack a toothbrush. You'll probably also want some petroleum jelly to keep your lips from cracking while you sleep in the dry cabin. If you wear contact lenses, take them out before you board, or at least bring eye drops.

✔ **Order a special meal** if you have special dietary needs. Most airlines can accommodate dietary restrictions, and nobody has to know that your restriction is that you're a picky eater. The airlines make special meals (vegetarian, kosher, and so forth) to order, unlike the mass-produced chow they feed the other passengers.

✔ **If you're flying with kids,** pack chewing gum to help with ear-pressure problems. Don't forget diapers, toys, and a brand-new distraction (however small) — if a meltdown's looming, you want the element of surprise on your side. See Chapter 4 for other suggestions.

You can sign up for e-mail alerts through individual Web sites or all at once through **Smarter Living** (www.smarterliving.com). And if you already know what airline you want to fly, consider staying up late on Tuesday and checking the site until the bargains for the coming weekend appears. Book right away and avoid losing out on the limited number of seats.

Other Ways to Reach Boston

Sometimes flying just won't do. Maybe you have mobility issues, you're on a big road-trip vacation, or every flight is booked. Maybe you can't fly, and driving into construction purgatory holds no appeal. Here's the scoop on traveling by car and train.

Driving: A necessary evil

The roads into Boston look perfectly manageable — on paper. If only that map could be three-dimensional. You'd see little construction workers and equipment all over downtown, making the already-dire traffic even worse. I-93, the main north-south highway through town, continues to carry vehicles while its replacement, a tunnel beneath the current road, takes shape. The scheduled completion date for the $14 billion (and counting) "Big Dig" is 2004. How big is it? It has its own Web site, www.bigdig.com. Highway access *to* the Boston area is good. If it's not rush hour and you don't need to venture all the way into town, your trip probably won't be too awful.

The Massachusetts Turnpike (I-90), or Mass. Pike, is a toll road that runs from the New York border to downtown Boston. The next-to-last exit serves Cambridge. The main north-south route through Boston is I-93, which extends north into New Hampshire. The main north-south route on the East Coast is I-95, which detours around Boston as a sort of beltway about 11 miles from downtown, where it's better known as state Route 128.

 Try not to approach downtown Boston on weekdays from 7 to 9 a.m. and 3:30 to 6:30 p.m. Friday afternoon is especially problematic — make sure the car has plenty of gas and antifreeze. Here are some basic directions for driving into Boston from other parts of New England:

- **From New York City, points south, and southwestern Connecticut,** you have several options. My favorite is to take the Hutchinson River Parkway into Connecticut, where it becomes the Merritt/Wilbur Cross Parkway. About 20 miles south of Hartford, follow signs to I-91 north, and take it to I-84 east. At Sturbridge, Massachusetts, pick up the Mass. Pike. (I-95 from New York, a busy truck route, is sometimes a bit faster.)

- **From Vermont and western New Hampshire,** take I-89 to Concord, New Hampshire, and then I-93 south.

- **From Maine and southeastern New Hampshire,** take I-95 south to Route 1 or I-93 south.

- **From Rhode Island and eastern Connecticut,** you're stuck with I-95. Where it intersects with I-93/Mass. 128, follow signs to Braintree, which outnumber signs for Boston.

Arriving by train

Amtrak (☎ **800-USA-RAIL** or 617-482-3660; Internet: www.amtrak.com) runs to Back Bay Station and South Station from the south. Use Back Bay Station, on Dartmouth Street across from the Copley Place mall, if you're staying in the Back Bay or South End. Back Bay is also an Orange Line stop. Go to South Station, on Atlantic Avenue near the waterfront, if you're staying downtown or in Cambridge (South Station is also a Red Line subway stop).

Airline-style booking strategies increasingly apply to train travel. Booking far ahead usually will land you a discounted excursion fare. Discounts don't apply during high-volume times such as Friday afternoon, Sunday afternoon, and periods around holidays.

In 2000, Amtrak introduced Acela, a high-speed rail on its Northeast Corridor, Washington-to-Boston route. Acela trains run as fast as 150 MPH on their own tracks, making them (in theory) less susceptible to delays than the old cars. The new service replaced Metroliners between Washington and New York, cutting the trip time on the Washington-Boston route to just under 6 hours. Call Amtrak or check its Web site (www.acela.com) for more details, schedules, and fares on the new routes.

Chapter 6

Finding the Hotel that's Right for You

• •

• •

*T*aking the time to find the right hotel room is like taking the time to eat breakfast. Skip the most important meal of the day and you probably won't notice until lunchtime, when you're light-headed and crabby. Book the wrong accommodations and they can haunt you hours later, when noise and lumpy beds keep you awake, or weeks later, when you open your credit-card bill and can't *believe* you paid so much.

The Boston area is in the midst of both a hotel-room shortage and an economic boom. Prices are up, amenities and service are improving, and just about every property is in excellent shape. The options that suit your wishes and wallet are out there. The next three chapters help you find them.

Choosing the Type of Hotel for You

The Boston area offers a full range of accommodations, but not in the same abundant numbers as other destinations. At busy times, "take it or leave it" is more of a daily affirmation than an idle threat. Here's a look at what to expect.

The Goldilocks factor: What property feels right?

Put some thought into this one, but be ready to compromise, especially if you're traveling during a busy season. Sometimes the best thing about a room is simply that nobody else is in it.

Giant chain hotels tend to be well appointed, centrally located, and somewhat boring. But don't reflexively dismiss them — the benefits of size include a larger supply of rooms and a wider range of prices. The listings in Chapter 8 include some agreeable choices, and the suburbs boast plenty of reliable options as well. (See the Appendix for a list of the major chains' toll-free numbers and Web sites.)

Independent hotels tend to compare favorably with the mega-chains, with less of a cookie-cutter feel and more personal service. These smaller establishments can't compete with chains in every area, though, so know which features are most important to you. (If you *must* swim a mile every morning, even remarkable service won't make a pool materialize.)

Chapter 8 also lists some motels, inns, and guest houses. These smaller properties tend to be less conveniently located, less luxurious, and less expensive than larger establishments. If you just want a comfy place to rest your head, they can be just right.

The ABCs of B&Bs

Travelers priced out of hotels or tired of generic lodgings are driving a boom in the bed-and-breakfast market. In the Boston area, B&Bs offer everything from simple spare rooms to opulent suites. Most rent only a few units, so unless you have unlimited time to call around until you find a vacancy, you'll want to use an agency that specializes in B&Bs. Here are some reliable agencies to help you with your reservations:

- ✔ **Bed and Breakfast Agency of Boston,** 47 Commercial Wharf #3, Boston, MA 02110 (☎ **800-248-9262** or 617-720-3540; ☎ 0800-89-5128 from the U.K.; Internet: www.boston-bnbagency.com).

- ✔ **Bed and Breakfast Associates Bay Colony Ltd.,** P.O. Box 57166, Babson Park Branch, Boston, MA 02457 (☎ **888-486-6018** or 781-449-5302; Internet: www.bnbboston.com).

- ✔ **Bed & Breakfast Reservations North Shore/Greater Boston/Cape Cod,** 11A Beach Rd., Gloucester, MA 01930 (☎ **800-832-2632** outside MA, 617-964-1606 or 978-281-9505; Fax 978-281-9426; Internet: www.bbreserve.com).

The demand for lodgings mean you may want to consider the following tips before booking your B&B:

- ✔ **Book as early as possible, especially during busy seasons.** This tip is particularly important if money is tight, because greater demand means higher prices.

- ✔ **Know what you want and what you don't.** Another reason to use an agency — the staff should know enough about each property to keep a guest who starts the day with a muffin over the fax machine away from a host who serves cooing honeymooners eggs Benedict.

> ✔ **Know your budget.** Expect to pay at least $65 a night, and some-times much more, for a double. Prices soar during high seasons and during special events. Most places require a 2-night minimum stay, and many offer winter discounts.

Finding the Perfect Location

Considering Boston's well-founded reputation as a city of neighbor-hoods, the question of location is surprisingly easy to answer. The central city is so tiny, and its neighborhoods so small, that the most popular parts of Boston break neatly into two main sections. Spread out a map and find Boston Common. For your purposes, north and east of it is downtown, and west and south is the Back Bay.

The other two major options are Cambridge and slightly less central areas such as Brookline, which I describe as "in the vicinity." See Chapter 10 for more neighborhood descriptions.

Deciding where to stay: Downtown

Between Charles Street and the harbor you find the oldest and newest (that is, still under construction) areas of the city. Downtown is con-gested but safe, and notably picturesque. The area encompasses Beacon Hill, the bustling Financial District and Faneuil Hall Marketplace, the North End, Downtown Crossing, Government Center, the gorgeous Waterfront, and the ungorgeous Big Dig. Prices tend to be high, but you're paying for convenience: Most of the Freedom Trail is here, and you can walk everywhere.

Advantages to staying downtown include

> ✔ Easy access to many popular attractions and business destinations.
>
> ✔ Convenient public transportation.
>
> ✔ The lively atmosphere, especially during the day and around Faneuil Hall Marketplace.

Drawbacks include

> ✔ The Big Dig. The ever-changing construction site is frantic and noisy. The Big Dig is most problematic if you stay close by, but it influences traffic for miles around.
>
> ✔ Distance from the Back Bay and Cambridge. Factor in the time and cost of getting back and forth.
>
> ✔ The less-than-lively atmosphere at night, particularly in areas that aren't near Faneuil Hall.

Finding a place to stay in the Back Bay

What I call the Back Bay stretches from Charles Street to the Brookline border. Other neighborhoods I include in this area (both south of the Back Bay proper) are the Theater District and the South End. With the exception of the parks and a small part of the Theater District, where you should be cautious at night, this is a safe area. Prices tend to be high, but the sheer number of hotel rooms means that the spread is broader. One of New England's prime shopping destinations, this area has a posh air but also abounds with budget-conscious students. Here you find the Public Garden, the Prudential Center, Copley Place, the Hynes Convention Center, and Kenmore Square.

The perks of staying in this area include

- The abundance of hotel rooms.
- Decent public transportation. The creaky Green Line is no prize, but the Orange Line is reasonably close. The bus to Cambridge runs along Massachusetts Avenue, better known as Mass. Ave.
- Everything you need to shop till you drop.

Drawbacks include

- You need to commute to the downtown attractions.
- Cambridge isn't all that convenient (the bus can be slow).
- Everything you need to shop till you drop.

Determining where to stay in the vicinity

If busier, more centrally located areas aren't for you, consider staying a little farther out. The large town of Brookline begins just past Kenmore Square, and past it is the Allston/Brighton section of Boston. Prices are generally lower, life is less rushed, and most of the popular attractions are less convenient. Without a car, you'll essentially be a commuter, usually on the ancient Green Line. (One hotel in this area, the Doubletree Guest Suites, isn't on a public transit line.) Again, check a map — only spoiled Bostonians would seriously think of this area as out of the way, but it can feel inconvenient, especially at night and when you're spending a lot of time in Cambridge.

Good reasons to stay in the vicinity include

- Generally lower prices.
- A more residential, less frantic atmosphere.
- Easy access to the Back Bay and Fenway Park.

Getting out of town: The suburban motel question

By now, you probably have some idea of what you can expect to pay for a stay in Boston. When that cost just won't do, the notion of a moderately priced suburban chain hotel tends to arise. After all, staying outside the city is considered an excellent option in many parts of the U.S. Whether this option works for you depends on your answers to the following questions:

✓ **What season is it?** You may not have a choice about this. During the foliage and graduation seasons, just being in Massachusetts can feel like a triumph.

✓ **Do you mind commuting?** You'll likely drive or take the commuter rail (or both) to downtown Boston. Before you reserve your room, nail down the specifics of the journey, including whether the hotel operates a shuttle and how late the train runs. If it sounds like a hassle, try another place.

✓ **How long will you be in the Boston area?** A few extra days of vacation may mean that you don't mind spending some time commuting. In addition, not being stuck downtown can make day-tripping easier.

✓ **Are you behind the wheel?** If you must drive, you may welcome the combination of a chain hotel's free parking (if offered) and access to the city via your auto.

✓ **Are the kids with you?** Their expectations may be entirely different from yours. (A swimming pool, vending machines, and a game room were usually enough to satisfy me and my siblings.) Talk to your kids before booking an expensive hotel with business features they don't care about and easy access to activities they don't want to do anyway.

✓ **How deep are your pockets?** An out-of-the-way location doesn't necessarily mean a deal. Account for hidden costs before you book a room. For example, if you need to drive to Boston, parking fees can easily add $25 a day to your travel expenses. If the "bargain" room rate saves $30 a day, that's no deal.

If you opt for a suburban motel, check with your travel agent, pick one from a guide-book (AAA is my favorite for this sort of thing), or call your favorite chain and ask for a room in the Boston area. (You can find contact information for hotels in the Appendix.) Be sure you understand the definition of "Boston area" before you hang up the phone — Rhode Island and New Hampshire aren't in it, but you'd never know that to judge from some motels' names.

Drawbacks include

   ✓ The distance from most of the top attractions.

   ✓ The necessity to rely on the Green Line.

   ✓ Cambridge is inconvenient, unless you rent a car.

Figuring out where to stay in Cambridge

The listings in this section concentrate on Harvard Square, which offers a good mix of transit access, sightseeing, and shopping. It's not a typical bohemian college town, but a generally expensive area that centers on the Harvard T stop, at John F. Kennedy and Brattle Streets and Mass. Ave. Moving away from the train station, things grow quieter; the peaceful Charles River is nearby. Downtown Boston is a 15- to 20-minute subway ride away, and the Back Bay is approximately 30 minutes away on the Mass. Ave. bus.

Pluses of staying in Cambridge include

- ✔ The energetic, student-oriented atmosphere.
- ✔ Public transportation is good.
- ✔ Shopping and sightseeing options are excellent.

Drawbacks include

- ✔ The prices of lodging.
- ✔ Crowds of students, shoppers, and sightseers.
- ✔ The commute to Boston attractions.

Choosing a Hotel That's Right on the Money

Each listing in the following section (and in Chapter 8) includes a $ symbol to help you compare prices. The $ symbols correspond to *rack rates* (nondiscounted standard rates), and they usually reflect the average of hotels' low to high rates. Prices do not include taxes. And remember that off-season rates and package deals can knock the price down a category or two. (Review the off-season travel periods in Chapter 2.)

Unfortunately, room prices can (and often do) change without notice, so the rates in this book may be different by the time you call the hotel for reservations. Don't be surprised if the rate the hotel offers is lower than the rack rates in this book. Likewise, don't be alarmed if the price has jumped a little.

$ (less than $100): These hotels offer basic accommodations — essentially, comfortable spots to crash after a day of sightseeing. These places don't offer lots of extras, such as room service or a health club, and some may have shared bathrooms. These establishments tend to be small and not all that convenient, but they're clean, safe, and well kept.

$$ ($100–$200): In this category, you find slightly larger rooms with private bathrooms, TVs, and air-conditioning. No room service is generally offered, but the room rate may include a continental breakfast. These places are more centrally located, and some offer access to pools or fitness rooms (ask if an extra charge applies). In a less competitive market, most would be inns and family-run motels. In Boston, many are part of moderately priced chains.

$$$ ($200–$300): Now things get confusing. In this range, the repeat business customer is the gold standard, and these hotels cater to that market. Rooms tend to be decent sized and well appointed, with abundant business amenities. Each hotel offers a range of perks and facilities, but every property defines "essential" slightly differently. For instance, some hotels don't provide minibars or swimming pools, but some do. Ask a lot of questions, and keep asking until you find the place that feels right — or comes closest.

$$$$ ($300 and up): Here you find tycoons, Texans, and trysting couples. Expect everything you'd get at a $$$ hotel, delivered to your huge room by an employee who can't do enough for you, plus such extras as courtesy cars and personal office equipment. You may reasonably expect your every need to be met.

Remember, there's a room shortage in Boston. A hotel that doesn't offer every imaginable perk can still get away with charging unimaginable prices and fall into the $$$$ category. The feature that's most likely to be missing in a less-than-optimal hotel in this high-price range is an on-premises health club with a pool. If a certain amenity is crucial to you, be sure to ask about it.

Chapter 7

Booking Your Room

In This Chapter

▶ Getting a good deal on your hotel room

▶ Shopping for a hotel on the Internet

▶ Heading to Boston without a reservation

Some people book a room by calling a hotel, asking for a reservation, and paying whatever price the clerk quotes. These people also pay sticker price for their cars. That won't be you, though, because after reading this chapter, you'll know how to find the best hotel rates.

The Truth about Rack Rates

The rack rate is the standard amount that a hotel charges for a room. If you walked in off the street and asked for a room for the night, you'd pay the rack rate. You sometimes see this rate printed on the emergency-exit diagrams on the back of your hotel room door.

You don't have to pay the rack rate. Hardly anybody does. Perhaps the best way to avoid paying it is surprisingly simple: Ask for a cheaper or discounted rate.

In all but the smallest accommodations, room rates depend on many factors, not the least of which is how you make your reservation. For example, a travel agent may be able to negotiate a better deal with certain hotels than you could get by yourself. (That's because hotels sometimes give agents discounts in exchange for steering business their way.)

Prices also fluctuate with the seasons and the occupancy rate. If a hotel is nearly full, it's less likely to offer you a discount. If it's nearly empty, the reservations staff may be willing to negotiate. These circumstances can change from day to day, so if you're willing to be flexible, say so. Business hotels often offer special weekend rates and packages. Lodgings in vacation areas may extend midweek discounts, especially during the off-season.

Boston's unpredictable weather makes January through March the only slow season. This season is especially slow if conditions have been particularly cold and snowy. (A mild winter can be surprisingly busy.) The hospitality industry aims its "Boston Overnight! Just for the Fun of It" campaign at suburban weekenders, but travelers from farther away can take good advantage of the discounts, too.

Room prices can change without notice, so the rates in this book may differ from the rate you receive when you make your reservation.

Throughout this book, you'll see $ symbols for an at-a-glance price comparison of the various hotels. (See the Introduction for an explanation of the $ rates.) Boston is expensive — the average room rate is nearly $180 — but packages and other deals may pleasantly surprise you.

Getting the Best Rate for the Best Room

Finding the best rate may require some digging. For example, reserving through the hotel's toll-free number may result in a lower rate than if you call the reservations desk directly. On the other hand, the central reservations number may not know about discounts at specific locations. For example, local franchises may offer a special group rate for a wedding or family reunion, but may neglect to tell the central booking line. Your best bet is to call both the local number and the central number and see which one offers you a better deal.

Be sure to mention your membership in AAA, AARP, frequent flyer programs, and any other corporate rewards program you belong to when you make your reservation. You never know when a membership may be worth a few dollars off your room rate.

Boston and Cambridge levy a 12.45 percent room tax, which includes the 5.7 percent state tax and 2.75 percent that goes toward a new convention center. When you make your reservation, be sure to ask whether the quoted rate includes taxes. Package rates generally do, but it never hurts to be sure. Brookline doesn't charge the convention center tax, but don't choose a hotel based on that — the savings is negligible and probably won't even offset the extra subway fares.

Once you know where you're staying, asking a few more questions can help you land the best possible room. Ask for a corner room. They're usually larger, quieter, and brighter, and may cost a bit more. Request a room on a high floor. Upper floors may contain "club" or "concierge" level rooms; if you don't want to pay for extra features, ask for the highest standard floor. Ask if the hotel is renovating; if it is, request a room away from the renovation work, and ask again when you check in. Inquire about the location of restaurants, bars, and meeting facilities, which can be noisy. And if you aren't happy with your room when you arrive, return to the front desk right away. If another room is available, the staff should be able to accommodate you, within reason.

If you need a room where you can smoke, be sure to request one when you reserve. If you can't bear the lingering smell of smoke, tell everyone who handles your reservation that you need a smoke-free room.

Surfing the Web for Hotel Deals

Many Web sites allow you to gather information about Boston-area hotels. The Internet is an invaluable resource, allowing you to compare various properties' features and to see hotels before you book. Reserving online can save not just time but also money — Internet-only deals can represent substantial savings.

Subpar travel arrangements can cost you time and money. Choosing the wrong hotel based on incomplete information can drag down your whole trip. If you are not satisfied with the information you gather via the Internet, pick up the phone and call the hotel directly. The extra time you spend on a single phone call may help you confirm that the hotel meets your expectations.

You may want to start at a general travel site (see Chapter 5 for more details); at the site of a hotel chain you know and trust (see the Appendix for a list of major chains' toll-free numbers and Web sites); or at a locally oriented site.

The Web sites of the **Greater Boston Convention & Visitors Bureau** (www.bostonusa.com) and the **Massachusetts Office of Travel and Tourism** (www.mass-vacation.com) offer searchable databases and secure online reservations. Don't book through either site until you do enough comparison shopping to know when you find a competitive price.

Reservation bureaus can be a good option if you're not up for negotiating on your own. These bureaus reserve blocks of rooms, a practice that allows them to offer rooms in sold-out hotels. Do remember that the deep discounts they tout generally calculate savings off the rack rate — which you probably wouldn't pay anyway.

Reputable operators include **Citywide Reservation Services** (☎ 800-HOTEL-93; Internet: www.cityres.com); **Hotel Conxions** (☎ 800-522-9991; Internet: www.hotelconxions.com); **Accommodations Express** (☎ 800-906-4685; Internet: www.accommodationsxpress.com); and hoteldiscount!com, also known as **Hotel Reservations Network** (☎ 800-964-6835; Internet: www.180096hotel.com).

Use the Web to do some sleuthing. Suppose a hotel description says "overlooking the water" (or the park, or some other desirable neighbor), but its photos don't show the building in relation to the water. Download a map from another source that shows the eight-lane highway between the hotel and the beach.

Arriving without a Reservation

During foliage or graduation season, hang your head. Let it droop all the way down to the floor of the airport terminal, because that may be where you spend the night. Or stand up straight and try one or more of the following:

✔ **Call the Hotel Hot Line** (☎ **800-777-6001**), a service of the Greater Boston Convention & Visitors Bureau. The hotline can help you make reservations even during the busiest times. Actual people, rather than recordings, handle calls weekdays until 8 p.m., weekends until 4 p.m.

✔ If you're at the airport, head to the **Visitor Service Center in Terminal C.** Staff members with concierge training can lend a hand.

✔ **Phone hotels from the airport or train station.** Ask *everyone* you reach who doesn't have a room available to suggest another property.

✔ If you drive from the west, stop at the **Massachusetts Turnpike's Natick rest area** and try the reservation service at the visitor information center.

✔ **Call a B&B referral agency** and ask if any of its properties have cancellations. (See Chapter 6 for more details.)

✔ **Call a reservation bureau.** As I explain earlier in this chapter, these bureaus can save you time by checking the availabilities at several lodgings (see "Surfing the Web for Hotel Deals," earlier in this chapter).

✔ **Rent a car and head for the suburbs.** Although not being downtown is inconvenient, many lodgings lie within commuting distance. If you have a favorite chain, call its toll-free reservations number for information about Boston-area locations and tips for reaching them from the airport. For the full story, see Chapter 6.

Chapter 8

Boston's Best Hotels

. . . .

In This Chapter

▶ At-a-glance lists arranged by location and price

▶ A look at Boston's best hotels

▶ More options in case your top picks are full

. . . .

*A*lthough I complain about Boston's limited lodging choices, keeping this list to a manageable size is difficult. These hotels are my favorites, the ones I suggest when friends call to ask for recommendations. Although I list my top picks, by no means are these lodgings the only acceptable choices. Near the end of this chapter, I also include options that can be helpful if you find your top choices booked.

Each listing in this chapter includes a $ symbol that indicates the price range of the hotel's rack rates. (Remember: You should never pay the rack rate — always ask about discounts.) Prices are for a standard double room for one night, not including taxes. The $ signs correspond with the following ranges (for more information about these symbols and ranges, see Chapter 6):

$	less than $100
$$	$100–$200
$$$	$200–$300
$$$$	more than $300

Also remember that the $ symbols are guidelines. A great off-season rate or package deal can knock a hotel down a category or two, and a huge citywide event can drive up prices even at modest establishments. (See Chapter 7 for pointers on getting the best rates.)

This icon indicates hotels that are especially family friendly. Most of these accommodations have swimming pools, some offer family packages (usually on weekends), and all offer their all-ages clientele plenty of patience and good advice. Bear in mind that every hotel in town accommodates children's needs; a listing without this symbol does not mean "kid unfriendly." Most properties allow kids to stay free with their parents, but the cut-off age varies. Always ask when you're booking.

Boston Hotels

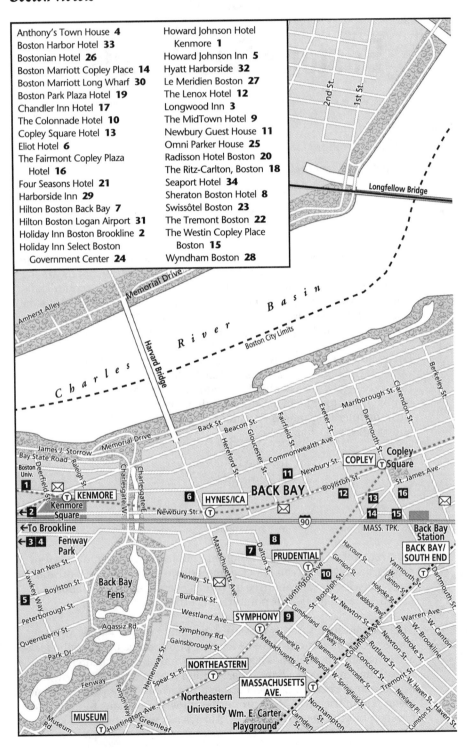

Anthony's Town House **4**
Boston Harbor Hotel **33**
Bostonian Hotel **26**
Boston Marriott Copley Place **14**
Boston Marriott Long Wharf **30**
Boston Park Plaza Hotel **19**
Chandler Inn Hotel **17**
The Colonnade Hotel **10**
Copley Square Hotel **13**
Eliot Hotel **6**
The Fairmont Copley Plaza
   Hotel **16**
Four Seasons Hotel **21**
Harborside Inn **29**
Hilton Boston Back Bay **7**
Hilton Boston Logan Airport **31**
Holiday Inn Boston Brookline **2**
Holiday Inn Select Boston
   Government Center **24**

Howard Johnson Hotel
   Kenmore **1**
Howard Johnson Inn **5**
Hyatt Harborside **32**
Le Meridien Boston **27**
The Lenox Hotel **12**
Longwood Inn **3**
The MidTown Hotel **9**
Newbury Guest House **11**
Omni Parker House **25**
Radisson Hotel Boston **20**
The Ritz-Carlton, Boston **18**
Seaport Hotel **34**
Sheraton Boston Hotel **8**
Swissôtel Boston **23**
The Tremont Boston **22**
The Westin Copley Place
   Boston **15**
Wyndham Boston **28**

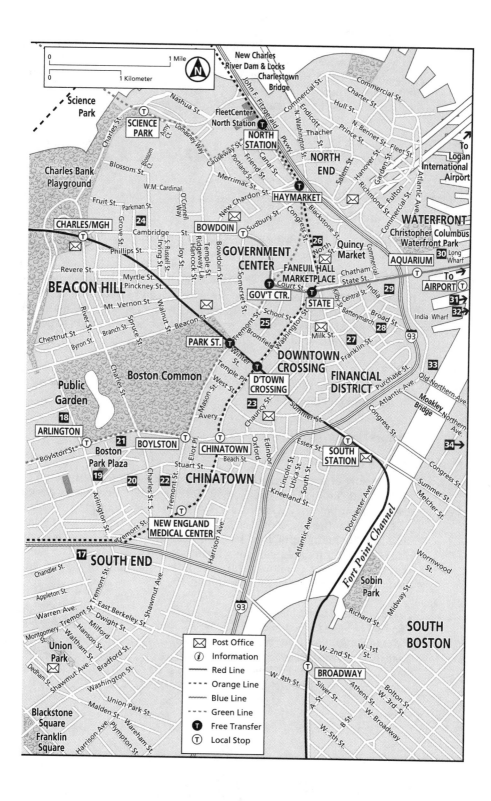

Every hotel in this chapter is clean and safe. As I said, I'd send a friend to any one of them — but I wouldn't send every friend to every one of them. These hotels all offer TVs and air-conditioning; almost all include phones and private bathrooms. With the exception of the Doubletree Guest Suites, they're all within walking distance of the subway, known in Boston as the T. That's where my blanket statements end. For a general discussion of hotel features and amenities, see Chapter 6.

The Lowdown on Boston-Area Hotels

Anthony's Town House

$ In the Vicinity (Brookline)

The Green Line runs past Anthony's Town House, embodying the pluses and minuses of this well-kept, old-fashioned brownstone. The trolley is handy, but the street is busy and can be noisy. The price is great, but you don't get your own bathroom or phone. Each floor holds one bathroom and three good-sized, high-ceilinged rooms with TVs and air-conditioning; units that face the street are larger but less quiet. The agreeable residential neighborhood lies about a mile from Boston's Kenmore Square and 15 to 20 minutes from downtown.

1085 Beacon St. (near Hawes St.). ☎ *617-566-3972. Fax: 617-232-1085. 12 units. T: Hawes St. (Green Line C). Parking: Free. Rack rates: $65–$95. Ask about winter discounts. No credit cards.*

Boston Harbor Hotel

$$$$ Downtown (Waterfront)

The finest hotel downtown is this luxurious edifice overlooking the harbor and the Big Dig. The Boston Harbor Hotel offers every perk or appointment you may want or need — from easy access to the airport (the water shuttle docks out back) to top-of-the-line business and fitness facilities, including a 60-foot lap pool. Guest rooms are spacious and plush, with traditional mahogany furniture and great views. The Rowes Wharf Restaurant is among the best in the city and the lobby café, Intrigue, offers seasonal outdoor dining.

70 Rowes Wharf (entrance on Atlantic Ave. at High St., off Northern Ave.). ☎ *800-752-7077 or 617-439-7000. Fax: 617-330-9450. Internet:* www.bhh.com. *230 units. T: South Station (Red Line); walk 2½ blocks north. Or Aquarium (Blue Line), if it's open; walk 2½ blocks south. If closed, State (Blue Line); then take shuttle bus to Aquarium. Parking: Valet $28 per day, self $24 per day; weekend discounts. Rack rates: $255–$510 and up. Ask about weekend packages. AE, CB, DC, DISC, MC, V.*

Chandler Inn Hotel

$$ Back Bay (South End)

You can't beat this location at this price. The newly renovated rooms and bathrooms are comfortable but small — a real-estate ad might say "cozy," and for once it'd be accurate. The contemporary-style rooms contain queen or double beds or two twin beds, hair dryers, and climate controls. Rates include continental breakfast, and the staff is accommodating and friendly. This property is the largest gay-owned hotel in town, and it's popular with bargain hunters of all persuasions. Fritz, the bar off the lobby, is a lively neighborhood hangout.

26 Chandler St. (at Berkeley St.). ☎ ***800-842-3450*** *or 617-482-3450. Fax: 617-542-3428. Internet:* www.chandlerinn.com. *56 units. T: Back Bay (Orange Line); cross Columbus Ave., turn left onto Chandler St., and walk 2 blocks. Parking: Nearby public garages and lots. Rack rates: $145–$155. Ask about winter discounts. AE, CB, DC, DISC, MC, V.*

The Charles Hotel

$$$$ Cambridge   199ᵒ + tax   13327

The most prestigious short-term address in Cambridge, the Charles represents an appealing contrast of sleek, contemporary style and luxurious appointments. In a great location off Harvard Square, it offers large rooms with Shaker-style furnishings and indulgent extras such as a Bose Wave radio in every room and a TV in each bathroom. Guests enjoy complimentary access to the pool and facilities at the adjacent WellBridge Health and Fitness Center. The pool sets aside time each afternoon for children under 16. The hotel complex also includes an excellent day spa, Le Pli. Rialto, off the lobby, is the best restaurant in the Boston area (see Chapter 14 for a review). Henrietta's Table serves contemporary American cuisine, and the Regattabar is one of the best jazz clubs in the area.

300

1 Bennett St. (off Eliot St., near Mt. Auburn St.). ☎ ***800-882-1818*** *outside MA, or 617-864-1200. Fax: 617-864-5715. Internet:* www.charleshotel.com. *293 units. T: Harvard (Red Line); follow Brattle St. 2 blocks, bear left onto Eliot St., and go 2 blocks. Parking: Valet or self $18 per day. Rack rates: $349–$429 and up. Ask about weekend, spa, and other packages. AE, CB, DC, JCB, MC, V.*

Doubletree Guest Suites

$$$ In the Vicinity (Allston)

The less-than-central location is no bonus, but everything else about this all-suite hotel makes it one of the best deals around. Doubletree is popular with business travelers and families alike. Each of the large units contains a living room with a full-size sofa bed, a coffeemaker, and a good-sized refrigerator. Suites on higher floors offer splendid views. The hotel has an indoor pool, fitness facilities, and a laundry room. Doubletree sits across the street from the Charles River and the jogging path that runs along its banks. The hotel offers complimentary van service to and from attractions and business areas in Boston and Cambridge. The celebrated Scullers Jazz Club schedules two shows nightly.

400 Soldiers Field Rd. (at Mass. Turnpike Allston/Cambridge exit). ☎ *800-222-TREE or 617-783-0090. Fax: 617-783-0897. Internet:* www.doubletreehotels.com. *308 units. Parking: $15–$18. Rack rates: $139–$259. Ask about weekend packages, AAA and AARP discounts. AE, CB, DC, DISC, JCB, MC, V.*

The Fairmont Copley Plaza Hotel

$$$$ Back Bay

The Copley Plaza is one of Boston's two stately, old-fashioned luxury hotels; just saying their names evokes an era of grand accommodations, excellent service, and ornate architecture. (The Ritz-Carlton is the other.) The Edwardian elegance of this 1912 building belies the up-to-date features of the large, recently restored guest rooms. They contain every perk you can think of (and then some), including VCRs and oversized towels. The hotel has two restaurants, two bars, a business center, and a fitness center. The Copley Plaza doesn't have an on-premises pool; guests are given access to the nearby, coed YWCA.

138 St. James Ave. (at Dartmouth St., facing Copley Square). ☎ *800-527-4727 or 617-267-5300. Fax: 617-247-6681. Internet:* www.fairmont.com. *379 units. T: Copley (Green Line); cross Copley Square. Or Back Bay (Orange Line); walk 1½ blocks on Dartmouth St. with Copley Place on your left. Parking: Valet $30. Rack rates: $249 and up. Ask about weekend packages. AE, CB, DC, JCB, MC, V.*

Four Seasons Hotel

$$$$ Back Bay

This hotel is the best in New England. You may stay here at the same time as a movie star, a CEO, a rock legend, or a head of state, and (here's the key) the staff makes you feel as important as any of them. Great service doesn't replace a lack of services, but that's not a problem here: The accommodations, amenities, business center, health club, and restaurants are all top of the line. The bill is, too. The second-floor restaurant, Aujourd'hui, is one of Boston's best, and the Bristol Lounge serves a celebrated afternoon tea (as well as lunch and dinner).

200 Boylston St. (at Arlington St.). ☎ *800-332-3442 or 617-338-4400. Fax: 617-423-0154. Internet:* www.fourseasons.com. *288 units. T: Arlington (Green Line); walk 1 block on Boylston St. opposite the Public Garden. Parking: Valet $27. Rack rates: $465–$695 and up. Ask about weekend packages. AE, CB, DC, DISC, JCB, MC, V.*

Harborside Inn

$$ Downtown (Faneuil Hall Marketplace)

The central location is the main selling point of this renovated 1858 warehouse, which also represents good value for the neighborhood. The Harborside Inn features can't compete with those of the city's business-oriented pleasure domes — but neither can its price. The location, across the street from Faneuil Hall Marketplace, is an easy stroll from most downtown destinations. Each guest room contains a queen bed, hardwood floors, and Oriental rugs. The ceilings are lower in the rooms on the top floor, but the views are better; units that face the atrium are quieter than those that face the street. All local phone calls and voice mail are free, and room service is available until 10 p.m. The inn, under the same ownership as the Newbury Guest House (see later in this section), has a restaurant and a small exercise room.

185 State St. (between India St. and I-93). ☎ *617-723-7500. Fax: 617-670-2010. Internet:* www.hagopianhotels.com. *54 units. T: State (Blue or Orange Line) or, if it's open, Aquarium (Blue Line). Parking: Nearby public garages. Rack rates: $170–$210 and up. Ask about winter discounts. AE, DC, DISC, MC, V.*

Harvard Square Hotel

$$ Cambridge

Comfortable and unpretentious, this newly renovated hotel occupies a great location that makes up for its lack of bells and whistles. In the heart of Harvard Square, it simply is what it is: a good place to retreat after a day of running around (whether sightseeing, visiting a student, or on business). Rooms aren't large, but they have new furnishings, dataports, and voice mail. This hotel is not the place for coddled business travelers, but the low-key atmosphere makes it a good alternative to pricier competitors in the area.

110 Mount Auburn St. (at Eliot St.). ☎ *800-458-5886 or 617-864-5200. Fax: 617-864-2409. Internet:* www.doubletreehotels.com. *73 units. T: Harvard (Red Line); follow Brattle St. 2 blocks, bear left onto Eliot St., and go 1 block. Parking: $20. Rack rates: $129–$209. Ask about corporate, AAA, and AARP discounts. AE, DC, DISC, MC, V.*

Hilton Boston Back Bay

$$$ Back Bay

A business hotel with terrific weekend packages, the Hilton offers a full range of chain amenities in a handy location across the street from the Prudential Center complex. The hotel is near the Back Bay action but not right at the center of it — which isn't necessarily a bad thing. The large, contemporary accommodations include 44 executive rooms added in 1998; units on higher floors offer excellent views. The hotel has a swimming pool and 24-hour health club, a restaurant, a bar, and a nightclub.

Cambridge Hotels

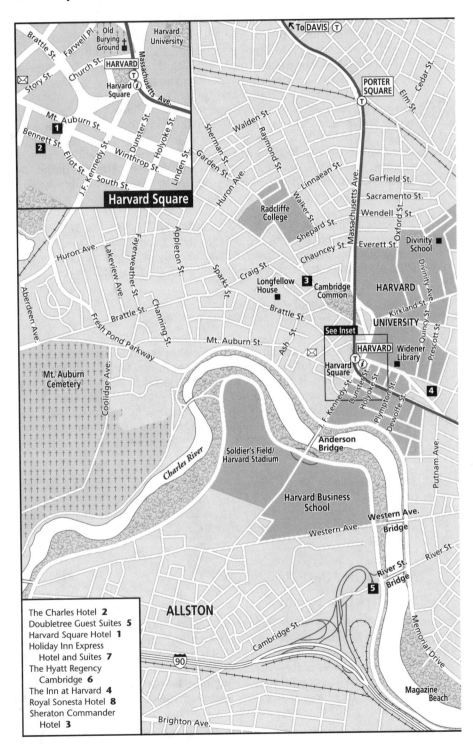

Harvard Square (inset map)

Locations referenced on the map:

Brattle St. • Farwell Pl. • Old Burying Ground • Harvard University • Church St. • HARVARD • Harvard Square • Massachusetts Ave. • Story St. • Mt. Auburn St. • Dunster St. • Holyoke St. • **1** • Bennett St. • Ellot St. • Kennedy St. • Winthrop St. • J.F. Kennedy South St. • Linden St. • **2**

To DAVIS • PORTER SQUARE • Cedar St. • Elm St. • Walden St. • Raymond St. • Sherman St. • Garden Ave. • Huron Ave. • Linnaean St. • Garfield St. • Sacramento St. • Wendell St. • Oxford St. • Radcliffe College • Shepard St. • Walker St. • Chauncey St. • Everett St. • Divinity School • Divinity Ave. • Huron Ave. • Fayerweather St. • Appleton St. • Sparks St. • Craig St. • Longfellow House • **3** • Cambridge Common • HARVARD • Kirkland St. • Lakeview Ave. • Channing St. • Brattle St. • Brattle St. • Mt. Auburn St. • Ash St. • UNIVERSITY • Quincy St. • Prescott St. • Aberdeen Ave. • Fresh Pond Parkway • See Inset • HARVARD • Widener Library • **4** • Harvard Square • J.F. Kennedy St. • Dunster St. • Holyoke St. • Plympton St. • DeWolfe St. • Mt. Auburn Cemetery • Coolidge Ave. • Charles River • Anderson Bridge • Soldier's Field/ Harvard Stadium • Putnam Ave. • Harvard Business School • Western Ave. • Western Ave. • Bridge • River St. • River St. • **5** • Bridge • ALLSTON • Cambridge St. • Memorial Drive • 90 • Magazine Beach • Brighton Ave.

The Charles Hotel **2**
Doubletree Guest Suites **5**
Harvard Square Hotel **1**
Holiday Inn Express
   Hotel and Suites **7**
The Hyatt Regency
   Cambridge **6**
The Inn at Harvard **4**
Royal Sonesta Hotel **8**
Sheraton Commander
   Hotel **3**

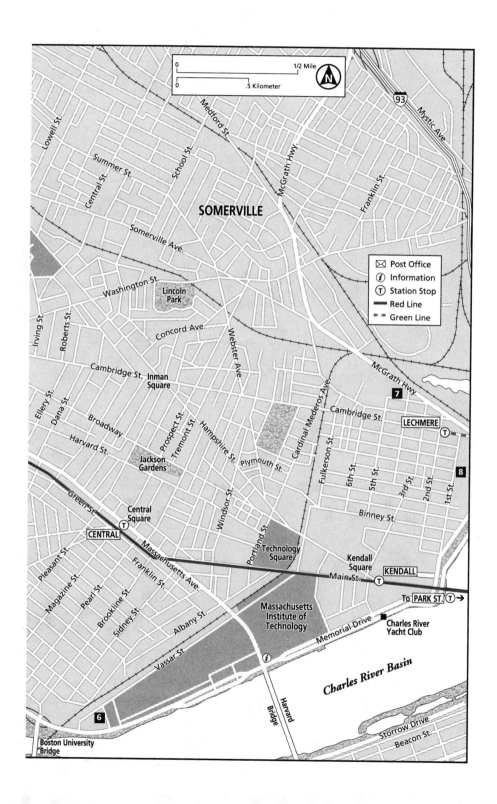

0   1/2 Mile

0   .5 Kilometer

N

93

Mystic Ave.

Lowell St.

Summer St.

Central St.

School St.

Medford St.

McGrath Hwy.

Franklin St.

SOMERVILLE

Somerville Ave.

✉ Post Office
ⓘ Information
Ⓣ Station Stop
━━━ Red Line
▪ ▪ Green Line

Washington St.

Lincoln
Park

Irving St.

Roberts St.

Concord Ave.

Webster Ave.

McGrath Hwy.

Cambridge St. Inman
Square

7

Cardinal Medeiros Ave.

Cambridge St.

LECHMERE Ⓣ

Ellery St.

Dana St.

Broadway

Prospect St.

Tremont St.

Hampshire St.

Plymouth St.

Fulkerson St.

6th St.

5th St.

3rd St.

2nd St.

1st St.

8

Harvard St.

Jackson
Gardens

Windsor St.

Binney St.

Green St.

Central
Square Ⓣ

CENTRAL

Massachusetts Ave.

Portland St.

Technology
Square

Kendall
Square

KENDALL Ⓣ

Main St.

To **PARK ST.** Ⓣ →

Pleasant St.

Franklin St.

Magazine St.

Pearl St.

Brookline St.

Sidney St.

Albany St.

**Massachusetts
Institute of
Technology**

Memorial Drive

■ **Charles River
Yacht Club**

Vassar St.

ⓘ

Charles River Basin

6

Harvard
Bridge

Storrow Drive

Beacon St.

**Boston University
Bridge**

40 Dalton St. (off Boylston St. at Belvidere St., opposite the Hynes Convention Center). ☎ 800-874-0663, 800-HILTONS, or 617-236-1100. Fax: 617-867-6104. Internet: www.hilton.com. 385 units. T: Hynes/ICA (Green Line B, C, or D); walk past rear of trolley and use Boylston St. exit, turn left, take first right onto Dalton St., and walk 2 blocks. Parking: Valet $24, self $17. Rack rates: $179–$295 and up. Ask about packages and AAA discounts. AE, CB, DC, DISC, MC, V.

Hilton Boston Logan Airport

$$$ Logan Airport

An airport hotel that courts a business clientele may not seem a logical choice for sightseers. However, the airport Hilton, with its proximity to downtown, good access to public transit, and fine weekend packages is a sensible option for both types of travelers. The newly constructed building (unusual in a market where renovations dominate) opened in 1999. The spacious, quiet guest rooms contain plentiful perks, including wireless Internet access through the TV. Off the lobby is a health club with a lap pool; the hotel has a restaurant, a pub that serves lunch and dinner, and a coffee bar. The 24-hour shuttle bus serves all airport destinations, including car-rental offices and the ferry dock.

85 Terminal Rd., Logan International Airport (between Terminal A [a short walk] and Terminal E [a long walk]). ☎ 800-HILTONS or 617-568-6700. Fax: 617-568-6800. Internet: www.hilton.com. 599 units. T: Airport (Blue Line); and then take shuttle bus. Parking: Valet $25, self $18. Rack rates: $149–$259 and up. Ask about weekend and other packages. AE, CB, DC, DISC, MC, V.

Holiday Inn Boston Brookline

$$ In the Vicinity (Brookline)

A pleasant residential setting and good access to downtown make this Holiday Inn a reasonable alternative to hotels that are more convenient but more expensive. The large, well-maintained guest rooms offer no surprises (pleasant or unpleasant) — basically, this is an agreeable chain hotel. The hotel has a small indoor pool, whirlpool, and exercise room. The Green Line stops in front of the hotel; downtown Boston is about 15 minutes away. Coolidge Corner, an un-generic shopping destination, is a 10-minute walk away.

1200 Beacon St. (at St. Paul St.). ☎ 800-HOLIDAY or 617-277-1200. Fax: 617-734-6991. Internet: www.holiday-inn.com. 225 units. T: St. Paul (Green Line C). Parking: $10. Rack rates: $139–$199 and up. Ask about AAA and AARP discounts. AE, DC, DISC, JCB, MC, V.

Holiday Inn Select Boston Government Center

$$$ Downtown (Beacon Hill)

Holiday Inn launched its business brand with this hotel, which lies within easy walking distance of many downtown and Back Bay addresses and the Red Line to Cambridge. Renovation work may be under way by the time you read this; be sure to ask for a room away from the construction. The decent-sized rooms include good business features, such as fax machines. Units on higher floors enjoy picture-window views of the city or the State House. The hotel has a business center, an outdoor heated pool, and a small exercise room.

5 Blossom St. (at Cambridge St.). ☎ *800-HOLIDAY or 617-742-7630. Fax: 617-742-4192. Internet:* www.bristolhotels.com. *303 units. T: Charles/MGH (Red Line); walk 3 blocks on Cambridge St. Parking: $25. Rack rates: $200 and up. Ask about weekend and corporate packages, AARP discounts. AE, DC, DISC, JCB, MC, V.*

Howard Johnson Hotel Kenmore

$$ Back Bay

The Boston University campus surrounds this standard-issue Howard Johnson's, which makes up for its lack of individuality with free parking, good access to downtown, and a swimming pool. The Green Line is out front, and Fenway Park is nearby. Rooms are comfortable and well maintained; most are reasonable in size, but some are small. The indoor swimming pool on the roof is open year-round 11 a.m. to 9 p.m.

575 Commonwealth Ave. (at Sherborn St., 2 blocks from Kenmore Square). ☎ *800-654-2000 or 617-267-3100. Fax: 617-424-1045. Internet:* www.hojo.com. *179 units. T: Blandford St. (Green Line B). Parking: Free. Rack rates: $125–$225 and up. Ask about senior and AAA discounts. AE, CB, DC, DISC, JCB, MC, V.*

Howard Johnson Inn

$$ Back Bay

Proximity to Fenway Park and free parking distinguish this motel, which sits on a busy street in a commercial-residential neighborhood. T access is somewhat inconvenient, but the Back Bay colleges, the Museum of Fine Arts, and the Isabella Stewart Gardner Museum are nearby. Rooms are basic, decent-sized Howard Johnson's accommodations. The outdoor pool is open 9 a.m. to 7 p.m. in the summer.

1271 Boylston St. (at Jersey St.). ☎ *800-654-2000 or 617-267-8300. Fax: 617-267-2763. Internet:* www.hojo.com. *94 units. T: Fenway (Green Line D); follow Brookline Ave. ½ block, turn left (walking around the ballpark) follow Yawkey Way 2 blocks, and turn left. Or Kenmore (Green Line B, C, or D); go left at turnstiles, right at stairs, at first intersection (½ block up), turn left onto Brookline Ave., cross bridge, pass ballpark, turn left onto Yawkey Way, and take second right onto Boylston St. (Whew!) Total walking time: about 10 minutes. Parking: Free. Rack rates: $115–$185 double. Ask about family packages, senior and AAA discounts. AE, CB, DC, DISC, JCB, MC, V.*

Longwood Inn

$ In the Vicinity (Brookline)

This Victorian guest house in a quiet residential area projects a homey feel to go with its affordable rates. Seventeen units include private bathrooms, and all rooms have air-conditioning and phones. Guests may use the fully equipped kitchen and common dining room, coin laundry, and TV lounge. An apartment, which sleeps four, has a private kitchen and balcony. The tennis courts, running track, and playground at the school next door are open to the public.

123 Longwood Ave. ☎ *617-566-8615. Fax: 617-738-1070. Internet:* go.boston. com/longwoodinn. *22 units. T: Longwood (Green Line D); turn left, walk ½ block to Longwood Ave., turn right, and walk 2½ blocks. Or Coolidge Corner (Green Line C); walk 1 block south on Harvard St. (past Trader Joe's), turn left, and go 2 blocks on Longwood Ave. Parking: Free. Rack rates: $79–$109 ($89–$119 for 1-bedroom apartment). Ask about winter discounts. No credit cards.*

The MidTown Hotel

$$ Back Bay

The most centrally located Boston hotel with free parking is this two-story establishment near the Prudential Center. The recently renovated rooms are large and attractively outfitted in contemporary style, but bathrooms are small. Business travelers can request rooms with two-line phones; families can ask for adjoining rooms with connecting doors. Potential drawbacks are the hotel's popularity with tour groups and convention-goers and the busy street — rooms on the Huntington Avenue side of the low-rise building can be a little noisy. The heated outdoor pool is open from Memorial Day through Labor Day.

220 Huntington Ave. (at Cumberland St., near Mass. Ave.). ☎ *800-343-1177 or 617-262-1000. Fax: 617-262-8739. Internet:* www.midtownhotel.com. *T: Symphony (Green Line E); from the corner diagonally across from Symphony Hall, walk 1 block on Huntington Ave. Or Massachusetts Ave. (Orange Line); turn left, walk 2 blocks, turn right, and go 1 block on Huntington Ave. Parking: Free. Rack rates: $149–$249. Ask about winter, AARP, and government employee discounts. AE, DC, DISC, MC, V.*

Newbury Guest House

$$ Back Bay

The Newbury Guest House isn't the bargain it was when it opened (in 1991), but with room rates soaring all over town, it's still a deal. In a pair of renovated 19th-century town houses, it has a comfortable atmosphere and helpful staff. Rooms are modest in size but thoughtfully appointed and mercifully quiet. Rates include a buffet breakfast served in the ground-level dining room, which adjoins a brick patio. This B&B operates near capacity all year; reserve early.

261 Newbury St. (between Fairfield and Gloucester sts.). ☎ *617-437-7666. Fax: 617-262-4243. Internet:* www.hagopianhotels.com. *T: Copley (Green Line); follow Dartmouth St. 1 block away from Copley Square, turn left on Newbury St., and go 2½ blocks. Or Hynes/ICA (Green Line B, C, or D); exit onto Newbury St. and walk away from Mass. Ave. for 2½ blocks. Parking: $15 (reservation required). Rack rates: $140–$190. Minimum 2 nights on weekends. Ask about winter discounts. AE, CB, DC, DISC, MC, V.*

Omni Parker House

$$$ Downtown (Government Center)

The Parker House combines historic atmosphere and modern appointments to surprisingly good effect. This establishment is the oldest continuously operating hotel in the country (since 1855). People and rooms were smaller then, but several rounds of renovations since Omni Hotels took over in the early 1990s left the hotel in good shape. Guest rooms aren't large, but well-proportioned furnishings and tons of amenities make the rooms feel cozy, not cramped. The hotel has a business center, exercise facility, restaurant, and two bars. And in case you're wondering, yes, this is the birthplace of Parker House rolls.

60 School St. (at Tremont St.). ☎ *800-THE-OMNI or 617-227-8600. Fax: 617-742-5729. Internet:* www.omnihotels.com. *552 units. T: Government Center (Green or Blue Line); face away from City Hall, turn left, and follow Tremont St. 1 long block. Or Park Street (Red or Green Line); follow Tremont St. away from Boston Common 2 blocks. Parking: Valet $27, self $20. Rack rates: $189–$295 and up. Ask about weekend packages. AE, CB, DC, DISC, MC, V.*

Radisson Hotel Boston

$$$ Back Bay (Theater District)

This Radisson's central location, business features, and relatively reasonable rates make this hotel popular with both business and leisure travelers. The well-maintained guest rooms are among the largest in the city; each opens onto a private balcony, with terrific views from the higher floors. The hotel has an indoor pool, sun deck, and exercise room. On the premises are a restaurant, a café, and the Stuart Street Playhouse, a professional theater that usually presents one-person and cabaret-style shows.

200 Stuart St. (at Charles St. South). ☎ *800-333-3333 or 617-482-1800. Fax: 617-451-2750. Internet:* www.radisson.com. *356 units. T: Boylston (Green Line); follow Tremont St. away from Boston Common 1 block, turn right onto Stuart St., and go 2 blocks. Or New England Medical Center (Orange Line); turn left, walk ½ block, turn left, and go 3 blocks. Parking: $19. Rack rates: $160–$359. Ask about weekend and theater packages. AE, DC, DISC, DC, JCB, MC, V.*

The Ritz-Carlton, Boston

$$$$ Back Bay

Wherever Boston tradition prevails, this is *the* name to drop. This sumptuous hotel can't compete with the more expensive Four Seasons in some areas (the johnny-come-lately across the Public Garden boasts an on-premises pool and business center), but it generally dominates in the battle for prestige. The Ritz-Carlton comes well armed: Guest rooms are lavishly appointed, and the renowned service is unfailingly correct. The Dining Room and Bar at the Ritz are legendary, and the lounge serves the city's best afternoon tea. The hotel has a well-equipped fitness center, and guests have access to the pool at the nearby Candela of Boston spa.

15 Arlington St. (at Newbury St.). ☎ *800-241-3333 or 617-536-5700. Fax: 617-536-1335. Intetnet:* www.ritzcarlton.com. *278 units. T: Arlington (Green Line); follow Arlington St. opposite the Public Garden 1 block. Parking: Valet $26. Rack rates: $330–$495 and up. Ask about weekend packages. AE, CB, DC, DISC, JCB, MC, V.*

Sheraton Boston Hotel

199

$$$ Back Bay

Although I'm usually not high on huge hotels, this Sheraton is an exception (the Westin, below, is another). Direct access to the Prudential Center complex appeals to travelers of all stripes, and this hotel plays up to all of them. The Sheraton courts three major markets by, essentially, blending three parallel dimensions in one hotel: scads of meeting space and features for convention-goers, well outfitted rooms for business travelers, and a gigantic indoor/outdoor pool with a retractable dome for vacationers. Rooms are fairly large and freshly refurbished, with pillow-top beds; bathrooms are medium-sized but (unless you have a magazine named after you) better appointed than your bathrooms at home. Units on upper floors afford excellent views. The hotel has a large, well-equipped health club, restaurant, lounge, and cigar bar.

39 Dalton St. (at Belvidere St., between Huntington Ave. and Boylston St.). ☎ *800-325-3535 or 617-236-2000. Fax: 617-236-1702. Internet:* www.sheraton.com. *1,181 units. T: Prudential (Green Line E); facing tower, bear left onto Belvidere St. and walk 1 block. Or Hynes/ICA (Green Line B, C, or D); walk past rear of trolley and use Boylston St. exit, turn left, take first right onto Dalton St., and walk 2 blocks. Parking: Valet or self $28. Rack rates: $149–$369 and up. Ask about weekend packages and student, faculty, and senior discounts. AE, CB, DC, DISC, JCB, MC, V.*

Sheraton Commander Hotel

$$$ Cambridge

The traditional accommodations and close proximity to the Harvard campus are good; the free parking is great. The Sheraton Commander's low-key atmosphere appeals to guests who find the Charles too trendy (and too pricey). The hotel's well-kept guest rooms are moderate in size and traditional in décor. The hotel has a restaurant and café, small fitness center, sun deck, and laundry room. And did I mention that free parking?

16 Garden St. (at Waterhouse St., opposite Cambridge Common). ☎ *800-325-3535 or 617-547-4800. Fax: 617-868-8322. Internet:* www.sheratoncommander.com. *T: Harvard (Red Line); with Harvard Yard on your right, follow Mass. Ave. north 1 or 2 blocks to Garden St., turn left, and walk 4 blocks. Parking: Free valet. Rack rates: $195–$345 and up. Ask about weekend packages, AAA and AARP discounts. AE, CB, DC, DISC, JCB, MC, V.*

Swissôtel Boston

$$$$ Downtown Crossing

Weekend travelers, keep reading: This posh hotel, a busy business destination during the week, offers some of the most appealing weekend packages in town. The fanny-pack set creates an interesting contrast with the hotel's European style and lavish business amenities. The spacious guest rooms contain fax machines and everything else you may need to cut a blockbuster deal. The hotel has a restaurant, lounge, 52-foot indoor pool, sun terrace, and fitness center.

1 Avenue de Lafayette (off Washington St.). ☎ *888-73-SWISS or 617-451-2600. Fax: 617-451-0054. Internet:* www.swissotel.com. *501 units. T: Downtown Crossing (Red or Orange Line); walk 1 long block on Washington St. past Macy's and turn left onto Ave. de Lafayette. Or, during daylight hours, Boylston (Green Line); follow Boylston St. away from Boston Common 1 block, turn left onto Washington St., walk 2 blocks, and turn right onto Ave. de Lafayette. Parking: Valet $30, self $26. Rack rates: $329–$379 and up. Ask about weekend packages. AE, CB, DC, DISC, JCB, MC, V.*

The Westin Copley Place Boston

$$$$ Back Bay

A giant chain hotel that doesn't feel generic is a real find, and this Westin is one (the Sheraton Boston, previously mentioned, is another). This hotel starts with a great location adjoining the Copley Place–Prudential Center complex, adds the full range of business amenities, and throws in an excellent health club with a pool. Guest rooms are large and well appointed, and the views (rooms are all above the seventh floor) are amazing. Two first-class restaurants, the Palm and Turner Fisheries, face the street at ground level; there's a lounge off the second-floor lobby.

10 Huntington Ave. (at Dartmouth St., accessible through Copley Place). ☎ *800-WESTIN-1 or 617-262-9600. Fax: 617-424-7483. Internet:* www.westin.com. *800 units. T: Copley (Green Line); walk 1 block on Dartmouth St. past the Boston Public Library. Or Back Bay (Orange Line); walk 1½ blocks on Dartmouth St. past Copley Place. Parking: Valet $28. Rack rates: $229–$499 and up. Ask about weekend packages. AE, CB, DC, DISC, JCB, MC, V.*

Wyndham Boston

$$$$ **Downtown (Financial District)**

Three blocks from Faneuil Hall Marketplace and two blocks from the harbor, the Wyndham offers business and leisure travelers a handy location and excellent accommodations. The large, quiet guest rooms abound with amenities, including high-speed Internet access and high ceilings that make them feel even larger. The only potential minuses are the lack of a swimming pool and the (long, by spoiled-Bostonian standards) walk to the T. The hotel has a restaurant off the lobby and a 24-hour fitness center.

89 Broad St. (at Franklin St.). ☎ 800-WYNDHAM or 617-556-0006. Fax: 617-556-0053. Internet: www.wyndham.com. *362 units. T: State (Blue or Orange Line); follow State St. downhill 2 blocks, turn right, and go 3½ blocks on Broad St. Parking: Valet $30 weekdays, $16 weekends. Rack rates: $295–$535 and up. Ask about weekend, holiday, and other packages. AE, CB, DC, DISC, JCB, MC, V.*

No Room at the Inn?

Even after all that, you waited till the last minute, and your top choices are full. And, even your second choices are full. (Is it foliage season already?)

Now what? First, resign yourself to staying wherever you can and paying more than you had planned to. Then, if it's before 8 p.m. on a weekday or 4 p.m. on a weekend, call the **Greater Boston Convention & Visitors Bureau's Hotel Hot Line** (☎ 800-777-6001).

Call one of the bed-and-breakfast reservation services from Chapter 6 and ask about last-minute cancellations that may have freed up rooms. Try **Bed and Breakfast Agency of Boston** (☎ 800-248-9262 or 617-720-3540), **Bed and Breakfast Associates Bay Colony** (☎ 888-486-6018 or 781-449-5302), or **Bed & Breakfast Reservations** (☎ 800-832-2632 outside MA, 617-964-1606, or 978-281-9505).

Call your favorite chain's toll-free number and ask about vacancies in the Boston area. Be aware that this option may entail renting a car or tangling with public transportation to reach a nearby suburb. (See Chapter 6 for more information on staying in the 'burbs; for general suggestions on what to do if you arrive without a reservation, check out Chapter 7.)

Runner-up Accommodations

Here are some specific suggestions if your top choices are booked:

Bostonian Hotel

$$$$ Downtown   Nonstop luxury with important extras: The location attracts business travelers and shoppers; romance-minded vacationers revel in the atmosphere of the renovated 19th-century warehouses. *40 North St. (opposite Faneuil Hall Marketplace).* ☎ *800-343-0922 or 617-523-3600.*

Boston Marriott Copley Place

$$$ Back Bay   A huge convention hotel with the usual huge-convention-hotel features, including a pool and health club. *110 Huntington Ave., at Harcourt St. (accessible through Copley Place).* ☎ *800-228-9290 or 617-236-5800.*

Boston Marriott Long Wharf

$$$$ Downtown   The great location, within shouting distance of the New England Aquarium and the Financial District, makes up for the generic atmosphere. *296 State St., at Atlantic Ave.* ☎ *800-228-9290 or 617-227-0800.*

Boston Park Plaza Hotel

$$$ Back Bay   A temple of ornate Old Boston style (the building went up in 1927), with a function and convention clientele that leaves its sleek modern competitors in the dust. *64 Arlington St. (1 block from the Public Garden).* ☎ *800-225-2008 or 617-426-2000.*

The Colonnade Hotel

$$$$ Back Bay   Sleek and elegant, with large guest rooms and a seasonal rooftop pool that add to the Euro-chic atmosphere. *120 Huntington Ave., at W. Newton St. (opposite the Prudential Center).* ☎ *800-962-3030 or 617-424-7000.*

Copley Square Hotel

$$$ Back Bay   A small hotel that puts service and atmosphere ahead of nonstop business perks; you're paying for the location, but it's quite a location. *47 Huntington Ave., at Exeter St.* ☎ *800-225-7062 or 617-536-9000.*

Eliot Hotel

$$$$ Back Bay   A luxurious, romantic all-suite hotel, with superb business amenities; the residential feel and handy location add to the Eliot's considerable appeal. *370 Commonwealth Ave., at Massachusetts Ave.* ☎ *800-44-ELIOT or 617-267-1607.*

Holiday Inn Express Hotel and Suites

$$ Cambridge (East Cambridge)   It's not exactly peaceful or plush, but the convenient location and reasonable prices make this hotel popular with business and leisure travelers. *250 Msgr. O'Brien Hwy. (3 blocks from the Green Line Lechmere stop).* ☎ *888-887-7690 or 617-577-7600.*

Hyatt Harborside

$$$ At the Airport   The out-of-the-way location isn't great for thrifty sightseers, but the hotel courts business travelers with plenty of amenities and easy access to the Financial District, a 7-minute water-shuttle ride away. *101 Harborside Dr. (at Logan Airport ferry dock, East Boston).* ☎ *800-233-1234 or 617-568-1234.*

The Hyatt Regency Cambridge

$$$ Cambridge (Central Cambridge)   Business travelers enjoy tons of perks and proximity to MIT and its high-tech neighbors; fantastic weekend packages help vacationers overlook the scarcity of convenient public transit. *575 Memorial Dr. (near the Boston University Bridge).* ☎ *800-233-1234 or 617-492-1234.*

The Inn at Harvard

$$$ Cambridge (Harvard Square)   Elegant and traditional, with good business features and easy access (by crossing the street) to the university. *1201 Massachusetts Ave. (at Quincy St.).* ☎ *800-458-5886 or 617-491-2222.*

Le Meridien Boston

$$$$ Downtown   One of the city's best business hotels, with top-notch weekend packages; the T is a bit of a hike, but downtown and waterfront destinations are nearby. *250 Franklin St. (at Post Office Sq.).* ☎ *800-543-4300 or 617-451-1900.*

The Lenox Hotel

$$$$ Back Bay   A boutique hotel in everything but size, with outstanding business amenities in the posh, high-ceilinged guest rooms. *710 Boylston St. (at Exeter St.).* ☎ *800-225-7676 or 617-536-5300.*

Royal Sonesta Hotel

$$$ Cambridge (East Cambridge)   Luxurious and contemporary, the Royal Sonesta draws high-tech businesspeople during the week and families (who love the large indoor-outdoor pool) on weekends. *5 Cambridge Pkwy. (around the corner from the Museum of Science).* ☎ *800-SONESTA or 617-806-4200.*

Seaport Hotel

$$$ South Boston Waterfront (Seaport District)   Perfect if you need to be near the World Trade Center, with great business perks that offset the inconvenient location if you don't; the airport is 10 minutes away via the Ted Williams Tunnel. *1 Seaport Ln., off Northern Ave.* ☎ *877-SEAPORT or 617-385-4000.*

The Tremont Boston

$$$$ Back Bay A Wyndham Grand Heritage hotel, the Tremont is a major force in the Theater District's improvement from dicey to decent; check ahead to see if the planned business center and exercise room have opened. *275 Tremont St., near Stuart St.* ☎ *800-331-9998 or 617-426-1400.*

Index of Accommodations by Neighborhood

Back Bay

Chandler Inn Hotel ($$)
The Fairmont Copley Plaza Hotel ($$$$)
Four Seasons Hotel ($$$$)
Hilton Boston Back Bay ($$$)
Howard Johnson Hotel–Kenmore ($$)
Howard Johnson Inn ($$)
The MidTown Hotel ($$)
Newbury Guest House ($$)
Radisson Hotel Boston ($$$)
The Ritz-Carlton ($$$$)
Sheraton Boston Hotel ($$$)
The Westin Copley Place Boston ($$$$)

Cambridge

The Charles Hotel ($$$$)
Harvard Square Hotel ($$)
Sheraton Commander Hotel ($$$)

Downtown

Boston Harbor Hotel ($$$$)
Harborside Inn ($$)
Holiday Inn Select Boston Government Center ($$$)
Omni Parker House ($$$)
Swissôtel Boston ($$$$)
Wyndham Boston ($$$$)

In the Vicinity

Anthony's Town House ($)
Doubletree Guest Suites ($$$)
Hilton Boston Logan Airport ($$$)
Holiday Inn Boston Brookline ($$)
Longwood Inn ($)

Index of Accommodations by Price

$

Anthony's Town House (In the Vicinity)
Longwood Inn (In the Vicinity)

$$

Chandler Inn Hotel (Back Bay)
Harborside Inn (Downtown)
Harvard Square Hotel (Cambridge)
Holiday Inn Boston Brookline (In the Vicinity)
Howard Johnson Hotel–Kenmore (Back Bay)
Howard Johnson Inn (Back Bay)
The MidTown Hotel (Back Bay)
Newbury Guest House (Back Bay)

$$$

Doubletree Guest Suites (In the Vicinity)
Hilton Boston Back Bay (Back Bay)
Hilton Boston Logan Airport (Logan Airport)
Holiday Inn Select Boston Government Center (Downtown)
Omni Parker House (Downtown)
Radisson Hotel Boston (Back Bay)
Sheraton Boston Hotel (Back Bay)
Sheraton Commander Hotel (Cambridge)

$$$$

Boston Harbor Hotel (Downtown)
The Charles Hotel (Cambridge)
The Fairmont Copley Plaza Hotel (Back Bay)
Four Seasons Hotel (Back Bay)
The Ritz-Carlton (Back Bay)
Swissôtel Boston (Downtown)
The Westin Copley Place Boston (Back Bay)
Wyndham Boston (Downtown)

Chapter 9

Tying Up the Loose Ends: Last-Minute Details to Keep in Mind

● ●

In This Chapter

▶ Buying travel and medical insurance

▶ Dealing with illness away from home

▶ Renting a car (and why you don't need to)

▶ Making reservations and getting tickets in advance

▶ Packing tips

● ●

*W*hat's worse than the nagging feeling that you forgot something, but you don't know what it is? I'd nominate the sensation of remembering it just as your plane leaves the ground.

This chapter attempts to relieve that sense of impending doom (or at least inconvenience) with a roundup of topics that can simplify your final trip planning. Do you need insurance? What if you get sick? What's the story with rental cars? How far ahead can you schedule a fancy dinner and a night at the theater? Perhaps most important, what should you pack?

For more information about money, budgeting, and cost cutting, turn to Chapter 3. For information on laying your hands on some cash and what to do if someone steals it, see Chapter 12.

Buying Travel and Medical Insurance

Buying insurance is kind of like carrying around an umbrella; if you carry it, you won't need it. But insurance can be expensive. So, should you or shouldn't you?

Of the three primary kinds of travel insurance — **trip cancellation, medical,** and **lost luggage** — the only one I recommend is trip cancellation insurance in the event that you pay a large portion of your vacation expenses up front. Medical and lost luggage insurance don't make sense for most travelers. Your existing health insurance should cover you if you get sick while on vacation (though if you belong to an HMO, check to see whether you are fully covered when away from home). Homeowner's insurance policies cover stolen luggage if they include off-premises theft. Check your existing policies before you buy any additional coverage. The airlines are responsible for $2,500 on domestic flights (and $9.07 per pound, up to $640, on international flights) if they lose your luggage; if you plan to carry anything more valuable than that, keep it in your carry-on bag.

Some credit cards (American Express and certain gold and platinum Visas and MasterCards, for example) offer automatic flight insurance against death or dismemberment in case of an airplane crash. If you feel you need still more insurance, contact one of the companies listed, but don't pay for more insurance than you need. For example, if you only need trip cancellation insurance, don't buy coverage for lost or stolen property. Trip cancellation insurance costs approximately 6 to 8 percent of the total value of your vacation. Among the reputable issuers of all three kinds of travel insurance are the following:

- ✔ **Access America,** 6600 W. Broad St., Richmond, VA 23230 (☎ **800-284-8300;** Fax: 800-346-9265; Internet: www.accessamerica.com)

- ✔ **Travelex Insurance Services,** 11717 Burt St., Ste. 202, Omaha, NE 68154 (☎ **800-228-9792;** Internet: www.travelex-insurance.com)

- ✔ **Travel Guard International,** 1145 Clark St., Stevens Point, WI 54481 (☎ **800-826-1300;** Internet: www.travel-guard.com)

- ✔ **Travel Insured International, Inc.,** P.O. Box 280568, 52-S Oakland Ave., East Hartford, CT 06128-0568 (☎ **800-243-3174;** Internet: www.travelinsured.com)

Staying in the Pink on the Road

Medical issues that arise when you're out of town can be tough to resolve. Boston being a health-care mecca, a lot of reliable choices are available to you, if you should (heaven forbid) fall ill. Here are some things to keep in mind:

- ✔ If you are covered by health insurance, be sure to carry your identification card in your wallet. Note the emergency number you need to call if your provider requires pretreatment authorization. If you don't think your existing policy is sufficient, consider buying medical travel insurance.

- ✔ Don't forget to pack your medications (in your carry-on, never in checked luggage), as well as a prescription for each one if you think you may run out.

- ✔ Pack an extra pair of contact lenses or glasses in case you lose them.

✔ Remember over-the-counter remedies for common travelers' ailments like upset stomach and diarrhea.

✔ If you suffer from a chronic illness, discuss your trip with your doctor. For conditions such as epilepsy, diabetes, severe allergies, or heart ailments, wear a MedicAlert identification tag. This tag immediately alerts doctors to your condition and gives them access to your medical records through a 24-hour hotline. Membership costs $35, plus a $15 annual fee. Contact the **MedicAlert Foundation,** 2323 Colorado Ave., Turlock, CA 95382 (☎ **800-ID-ALERT;** Internet: www.medicalert.org).

If you need a doctor, ask your hotel's concierge or front desk. Most large hotels can recommend someone at any hour. If the situation is less than dire, try one of the area's many reliable physician referral services. Options include **Massachusetts General Hospital** (☎ **800-711-4MGH**) and **Brigham and Women's Hospital** (☎ **800-294-9999**).

If you can't get a doctor to help you right away, try a walk-in clinic. You may not get immediate attention, but you won't pay the high price of an emergency room visit. An affiliate of Massachusetts General Hospital, the **Boston Evening Medical Center,** 388 Commonwealth Ave. (☎ **617-267-7171**), honors most insurance plans and accepts credit cards.

If you need a dentist, the **Massachusetts Dental Society** (☎ **800-342-8747** or 508-651-7511; Internet: www.massdental.org) can recommend one.

See the Appendix for listings of local hospitals.

Detailing the Car Question

You may know someone who claims to have driven all over Boston without a moment's trouble. People handle poisonous snakes every day, too.

Are you sure I don't need to rent a car?

If you visit Boston and Cambridge, you won't have any trouble getting around, you really won't. Public transportation and your own feet are reliable, safe, and cheap. Parking is scarce and expensive — in both categories, among the worst *in the country.* Traffic is dreadful, and it grows worse the closer you get to downtown, where a traffic jam can spring up at any hour of the day or night. Boston drivers in particular are hostile and unpredictable, and the Big Dig isn't helping anyone's disposition.

If you drive to the Boston area, park the car at the hotel and save it for day trips.

Do I need to rent a car for a day trip?

You can, but you don't need to. Public transportation connects Boston with many popular day-trip destinations (see Chapter 21 for details). If time is short and you don't want to worry about a train or bus schedule, or you'd rather not join a tour group, a rental car can be a good investment.

Don't automatically rent a car for the duration of your trip if you won't use it every day (an easy mistake if you're booking a package). Wait until you know you need it and save money — not just on the rental, but also on parking. The major agencies operate offices throughout the Boston area. Some companies, including **Enterprise** (☎ **800-736-8222**), offer pickup and drop-off service.

The $10 surcharge on car rentals in Boston goes toward construction of a new convention center. Get around it by renting in Cambridge, Brookline, or another suburb.

How do I get the best deal?

Car rental rates vary even more than airline fares. The price depends on the size of the car, the length of time you keep it, where and when you pick it up and drop it off, where you take it, and a host of other factors. The following is a list of things to keep in mind to get the best deal:

- ✔ **Weekend rates may be lower than weekday rates.** If you keep the car 5 or more days, a weekly rate may be cheaper than the daily rate. Ask if the rate is the same for pickup Friday morning as it is for Thursday night.

- ✔ **Some companies may assess a drop-off charge.** This charge may occur if you don't return the car to the same location where you picked it up. National is one of the few companies that does not charge this fee.

- ✔ **Find out whether age is an issue.** Many car rental companies add on a fee for drivers under 25 — or don't rent to them at all.

- ✔ **If you see an advertised price in your local newspaper, be sure to ask for that specific rate.** If not, you may be charged the standard (higher) rate. Don't forget to mention membership in AAA, AARP, and trade unions. These memberships usually entitle you to discounts ranging from 5 to 30 percent.

✔ **Check your frequent flyer accounts.** Not only are your favorite (or at least most-used) airlines likely to send you discount coupons, but most car rentals add at least 500 miles to your account.

✔ **Use the Internet to comparison shop for a car rental.** All the major booking sites — **Travelocity** (www.travelocity.com), **Expedia** (www.expedia.com), **Yahoo! Travel** (www.travel.yahoo.com), and **Cheap Tickets** (www.cheaptickets.com), as examples — utilize search engines that can dig up discounted car-rental rates. Just enter the size of the car you want, the pickup and return dates and location, and the server returns a price. You can even make the reservation through any of these sites.

What are the additional charges?

In addition to the standard rental prices, other optional charges apply to most car rentals (and some not-so-optional charges, such as taxes). The **Collision Damage Waiver (CDW),** which requires you to pay for damage to the car in a collision, is covered by many credit card companies. Check with your credit card company before you go so you can avoid paying this hefty fee (as much as $15 a day).

The car rental companies also offer additional **liability insurance** (if you harm others in an accident), **personal accident insurance** (if you harm yourself or your passengers), and **personal effects insurance** (if your luggage is stolen from your car). Your insurance policy on your car at home probably covers most of these unlikely occurrences. However, if your own insurance doesn't cover you for rentals or if you don't have auto insurance, definitely consider the additional coverage (the car rental companies are liable for certain base amounts, depending on the state). Unless you're toting around the Hope diamond — and you don't want to leave that in your car trunk, anyway — you can probably skip the personal effects insurance. However, driving around without liability or personal accident coverage is never a good idea; even if you're a good driver, other people may not be, and liability claims can be complicated.

Some companies also offer **refueling packages,** in which you pay for your initial full tank of gas up front and return the car with an empty gas tank. The prices can be competitive with local gas prices, but you don't get credit for any gas remaining in the tank. If you reject this option, you pay only for the gas you use, but you need to return your rental car with a full tank or face charges of $3 to $4 a gallon for any shortfall. In my experience, gas prices in the refueling packages are at the high end. So, I usually forego the refueling package and allow plenty of time for refueling en route to the car rental return. However, if you usually run late and a refueling stop may make you miss your plane, you're a perfect candidate for the fuel-purchase option.

Making Reservations and Getting Tickets Ahead of Time

Boston is one of the best places I know for a fun, spontaneous afternoon or evening. Finding something to do when you get to town is no trouble. But spontaneity will only get you pitying smiles if your impromptu plans include a symphony performance, a high-profile museum exhibition, dinner at a hot restaurant, a Red Sox–Yankees game, or a show on a pre-Broadway run.

Reserving a ticket and getting event information

If you already know what you want to do, you're golden. If you need suggestions, surf ahead and browse around.

- ✔ Call ahead or visit the Web site of the museum, performing arts company, or sports team that interests you; most sell tickets online or redirect you to an outlet that does.

- ✔ Tourist information offices (see the Appendix for phone numbers and Web site addresses) often know about big museum and stage shows many months in advance.

- ✔ If you have a hotel in mind, see whether it's offering packages that include event or show tickets during the time you're thinking of traveling.

- ✔ Visit www.boston.com to check out the daily and weekly *Globe* and monthly *Boston* magazine listings.

- ✔ The weekly *Boston Phoenix* not only posts its content on www.bostonphoenix.com but also archives its back issues. A season preview (the fall preview is the largest) contains listings of selected events for the next several months.

- ✔ The major ticket agencies often make information available even before tickets go on sale. The ones that serve Boston are **Next Ticketing** (☎ 617-423-NEXT; Internet: www.nextticketing.com), **Tele-charge** (☎ 800-447-7400; Internet: www.telecharge.com, click on "across the USA"), and **Ticketmaster** (☎ 617-931-2000; Internet: www.ticketmaster.com).

The concierge or desk staff at your hotel may be your best source for tickets and information about what's going on around town. A good concierge can land you a restaurant reservation, too. And if you loiter in the lobby at a not-too-busy time, ask the bell staff for suggestions.

Reserving a table

If you make your own restaurant reservations, bear in mind that other people also read *Gourmet*. A prominent mention in any national publication, including the *New York Times*, guarantees long waits on the phone and in person. And unless you already made a reservation, don't expect to get near the subject of the weekly *Globe* review, which appears in the Thursday "Calendar" section, during the next couple of weekends.

 Friday and Saturday are the most popular nights for dining out. Early in the week (especially Sunday or Monday), most restaurants are calmer and less crowded than they are over the weekend. If you book a table for a slow night at a restaurant with a big-name chef, call a few days ahead to make sure he or she plans to be in the kitchen on the night you'll be there.

At every restaurant that takes reservations, make them for dinner. Small parties usually don't need lunch reservations. For special-occasion favorites (such as Aujourd'hui, L'Espalier, and Rialto) and the latest hotspots (such as the Federalist, Radius, and Zita), book as far ahead as possible. A month is not too far in advance, and sometimes not far enough in advance, especially around the holidays.

The go-go economy has turned restaurant name-dropping into an excruciatingly popular pastime. If you can't get a table at the bistro of the moment, don't despair. You may score one at the bistro of 10 minutes ago — and just the fact that it's still in business is an indication that it might actually be worth a trip.

Getting Traveler's Checks

If you feel you need the security of traveler's checks and don't mind the hassle of showing identification every time you want to cash one, you can get them at almost any bank. **American Express** offers checks in denominations of $10, $20, $50, $100, $500, and $1,000. You pay a service charge ranging from 1 to 4 percent, although AAA members can obtain checks without a fee at most AAA offices. You can also get American Express traveler's checks over the phone by calling ☎ 800-221-7282; American Express gold and platinum cardholders who call this number are exempt from the 1 percent fee.

Citibank offers **Citibank Visa** traveler's checks at Citibank locations across the country and at several other banks. To find the Citibank closest to you, call ☎ 800-541-8882. The service charge ranges between 1 and 2.5 percent; checks come in denominations of $20, $50, $100, $500, and $1,000. For information on non-Citibank **Visa** traveler's checks, call ☎ 800-732-1322. **MasterCard** also offers traveler's checks. Call ☎ 800-223-9920 for a location near you.

Packing It All In

Start by assembling enough clothing and accessories to get you through the trip and piling it all onto the bed. Now put half of it into your suitcase and return the other half to your dresser.

Pack light, not because you can't take everything you want on the plane — you can, with some limits — but because spraining your back in an attempt to lift your whole summer wardrobe is no way to start a vacation.

What not to bring

You don't need fancy clothes to visit Boston unless your plans include something fancy, and in certain places "fancy" is one tiny step past "khaki." (In some places, "fancy" *equals* "khaki.") Students and tourists roam the streets in jeans and loose-fitting logo-covered clothing, lowering the fashion bar for everyone. During the day, especially in the summer, just being neat and clean is usually enough.

What to bring

Most airlines allow each passenger two pieces of carry-on luggage, some just one (see the box regarding carry-on luggage later in this chapter). Airlines enforce the limit strictly, especially on crowded flights. The exact dimensions vary, so be sure you know what your carrier allows. In a carry-on bag that you know will get through, pack valuables, prescription drugs, vital documents, return tickets, and other irreplaceable items. Add a book or magazine, anything breakable, and a snack. Leave room for the sweater or light jacket you pull off after a few minutes of hauling bags through the overheated terminal.

Here are some packing specifics:

✔ Start with comfortable, broken-in walking shoes. This item is perhaps the only one you can't replace on the road, so triple-check it.

Note that in downtown Boston, sandals are not walking shoes; they're little magnets for every piece of grit, grime, and gravel the Big Dig generates. Sandals are not a good choice even if you wear them with socks (which will get you in trouble with the fashion police anyway).

✔ Second most important: Dress in layers. Indoors or out, the temperature can plummet or soar at a moment's notice, especially in spring and fall. Several thin layers (think T-shirt, fleece pullover, and nylon shell) are more versatile and easier to pack than one thick one (such as a sweatshirt).

✔ Remember your sun hat and sunscreen. All year. Really.

✔ Winter travelers need a warm jacket or coat, a hat, gloves or mittens, and sturdy boots. In an especially snowy year, boots are as acceptable as shoes in nearly every setting. (I've worn mine to some of the city's finest restaurants — the tablecloth hides them when you sit down.)

✔ If your plans include an elegant dinner or an evening of theater, classical music, or ballet, you won't feel overdressed in a coat and tie or a dressy outfit (pantsuits are okay everywhere).

✔ Most restaurants don't have dress codes, though a few require jackets for men. So yes, you probably can get away with just about anything, but have a heart — if you find yourself seated next to a couple celebrating their 50th anniversary, do you really want to be wearing that T-shirt from the most disgusting bar in Key West?

Learn the limits of carry-on luggage

Because the reports of lost luggage are at an all-time high, consumers are trying to divert disaster by bringing their possessions onboard. In addition, planes are more crowded with passengers than ever, and overhead compartment space is at a premium. Because of these factors, some domestic airlines have begun to crack down, imposing size restrictions to the bags you bring onboard and sometimes limiting you to a single carry-on when the flight is crowded. The dimensions vary, but the strictest airlines say carry-ons must measure no more than 22 x 14 x 9 inches, including wheels and handles, and weigh no more than 40 pounds. Many airports are already furnished with X-ray machines that literally block any carry-ons bigger than the posted size restrictions.

These measures may sound drastic, but they are important to follow to avoid overcrowding the cabin. Look on the bright side. For example, you may only carry on a small bag with your essentials, but your fellow traveler may try to carry on a bag big enough to hold a piano. Without the carry-on restrictions, the Liberace-wannabe may take up all the space in the overhead bin, leaving you to check your wee bag or allow it to be flattened like a pancake.

Keep in mind that many of these regulations are enforced only at the discretion of the gate attendants. If you plan to bring more than one bag aboard a crowded flight, be sure your medications, documents, and valuables are consolidated in one bag in case you are forced to check the second one.

Part III
Settling in to Boston

The 5th Wave   By Rich Tennant

"Where's the North End? Well, that depends. Where's the Big Dig today?"

In this part . . .

*B*oston can be a confusing city to navigate, but it
doesn't have to be. (Everyone who lives here has
gotten lost at least once.) This section helps clear things
up with a look at the airport, the neighborhoods, and the
public-transit system; get these particulars out of the
way and you can move on to the fun part of your trip —
spending your money. To that end, I cover the all-important
topic of accessing your bucks while in Boston as well.

Chapter 10

Orienting Yourself in Boston

. . . .

In This Chapter

▶ Getting to your destination from the airport

▶ Getting to know Boston's neighborhoods

▶ Finding information

. . . .

The streets of Boston appear to have minds of their own. The roads head off in random directions, change names at the drop of a Red Sox cap, and even seem bashful — an awful lot of them aren't wearing signs. How can you ever find your way around? Cast aside your reluctance to ask for directions, for one thing. This chapter begins by extricating you from the airport, and then briefs you on what to expect once you're in town.

The most important thing to remember: You can't get *that* lost.

Arriving in Boston

This orientation to Boston begins at your arrival point. Here I tell you what you need to know if you arrive by plane, train, or car and how to get to your next destination — your hotel.

By plane

Logan International Airport suffers from both insufficient capacity and ongoing construction (which will relieve the space crunch, someday). Good administration means that neither of these situations typically cause much trouble, but be mentally ready for air and ground delays all the same.

Logan consists of five relatively small terminals — A through E. Good signage and lack of space make getting lost difficult, except in construction areas (where employees usually can point the way). In terminals A through D, which serve domestic carriers, gates are on the upper level, baggage claim and ground transportation are on the first. Terminals A and C house children's play spaces. Each terminal is equipped with an

ATM, Internet kiosks, fax machine, and information booth (near baggage claim). The booth in Terminal C is a Visitor Service Center, where staffers with concierge training can help arrange hotel and restaurant reservations, theater and sports tickets, and tours.

The airport is located in East Boston, 3 miles across the harbor from downtown. Signs in the terminals indicate the curbside stops for each mode of transportation (shuttle bus, taxi, and so forth). Nearby tunnels connect "Eastie" to downtown. Sound simple? At the downtown end of the Callahan and Sumner tunnels, like a bad penny, is the Big Dig.

When traffic is heavy — rush hours, Sunday evening, any holiday period — or the weather is bad, public transportation is by far the fastest way to reach downtown. If your destination is not downtown, crossing the harbor by boat or train and grabbing a cab can still be faster than driving.

The **Massachusetts Port Authority** (☎ 800-23-LOGAN; Internet: www. massport.com/logan) coordinates airport transportation. The toll-free line provides information about getting to the city and to many nearby suburbs. The line is available 24 hours a day, with live operators weekdays 8 a.m. to 7 p.m.

Taking public transportation to your hotel

Free airport shuttle buses cover four routes in a continuous loop from 5:30 a.m. to 1 a.m. every day, year-round. Number 11 runs from terminal to terminal; the other three (numbers 66, 22, and 33) connect to public transit.

The quickest way to downtown is by water. Take the number 66 shuttle bus to the ferry terminal, buy a $10 ticket if the kiosk is open (if not open, buy your ticket on board), and cross the harbor in 7 minutes flat. The **Airport Water Shuttle** (☎ 617-330-8680) runs to Rowes Wharf, off Atlantic Avenue behind the Boston Harbor Hotel. **Harbor Express** (☎ 617-376-8417) serves Long Wharf, off Atlantic Avenue near the New England Aquarium.

The subway is almost as fast and can be more convenient. The numbers 22 and 33 shuttle buses run to Blue Line's Airport station, which is aboveground. At the station, buy a $1 token or a visitor passport (see Chapter 11 for information). The line can be long but moves quickly.

Construction may close the Aquarium station, the first Blue Line stop on the downtown side of the harbor, by the time you visit. The next stop, State, is four construction-choked blocks away; a planned shuttle-bus loop should connect State and Aquarium for the duration of the closing.

Transfer points from the Blue Line are State (for the Orange Line) and Government Center (for the Green Line). Transfers are free. The trip to Government Center takes about 10 minutes. To reach Cambridge, switch to the Green Line at Government Center, take it one stop, and transfer at Park Street to the Red Line.

A somewhat easier way to reach the Red Line is the $5 bus that connects every terminal with Gate 25 at South Station, on Atlantic Avenue near the waterfront. You can save time by taking the Ted Williams Tunnel, but you still must haul your bags a considerable distance from the bus station to the subway. The Ted Williams Tunnel is perfect if you're taking the commuter rail to or from South Station.

Taking private transportation to your hotel

Taxis queue up at every terminal. The trip takes 10 to 45 minutes, depending on traffic and the time of day. The fare to downtown or the Back Bay should be about $18 to $24, including the $3 toll and $1.50 airport fee, which the passenger pays. (See Chapter 11 for more information on taxis.)

The Ted Williams Tunnel runs from the airport to South Boston. On a map, it looks like a pricey detour. Because of restrictions on use of the tunnel and its access roads, though, it's often the fastest route to the Back Bay and Cambridge. During serious congestion, the tunnel is the best way to parts of downtown, too.

To arrange limousine service, you must call ahead — drivers can't cruise for fares. Ask if your hotel recommends a company, or try **Carey Limousine Boston** (☎ **800-336-4646** or 617-623-8700) or **Commonwealth Limousine Service** (☎ **800-558-LIMO** outside Massachusetts, or 617-787-5575).

If you don't need a rental car right away, spare yourself the hassle of navigating the airport and pick it up later.

The major rental companies all operate shuttle vans. If you must pick up a car immediately, ask the staff to map a route that incorporates the latest traffic patterns and construction sites. Make sure you obtain directions for returning the car, too; don't worry if you go astray — the main airport road is a loop.

By train

South Station is a train terminal, bus station, and subway stop at Atlantic Avenue and Summer Street. You must leave the train and bus station to reach the Red Line subway entrance, about five steps from the main exit. Cabs line up on Atlantic Avenue. The neighborhood is a major center of Big Dig activity, so be careful (and patient, if you take a cab).

Back Bay Station is on Dartmouth Street between Huntington and Columbus Avenues. This station is the next-to-last Amtrak stop, and serves the Orange Line and commuter rail. Cabs line up on Dartmouth Street.

By car

If you're staying downtown, call your hotel the day before you plan to arrive. Ask for directions and the latest changes in the traffic patterns. For Back Bay hotels, take the Mass. Pike to the Copley exit. For Cambridge hotels, take the Mass. Pike to the Allston/Cambridge exit and follow Storrow Drive to the Harvard Square exit.

Boston by Neighborhood

These neighborhoods contain the city's main attractions. Most of these neighborhoods are small and walkable, with loose boundaries and (except in the Back Bay) confusing street patterns. Do yourself a favor and wander around a little. (For a map of Boston's neighborhoods, see the inside front cover of this book.)

Downtown

What I define as "downtown" consists of these neighborhoods: The Waterfront, the North End, Faneuil Hall Marketplace, Government Center, Beacon Hill, Downtown Crossing, and the Financial District. Here's a description of each section of downtown:

- ✔ **The Waterfront:** Located along Commercial Street and Atlantic Avenue, it faces the Inner Harbor. Here you find the New England Aquarium and the wharves that handle tour boats and ferries.

- ✔ **North End:** The Freedom Trail runs through the North End, which lies east of I-93 and north of the Waterfront. The longtime immigrant enclave maintains its reputation as the city's Italian neighborhood (but it's *never* called "Little Italy") through commerce rather than population — newcomers outnumber Italian-American residents. The Paul Revere House and the Old North Church are here.

- ✔ **Faneuil Hall Marketplace:** Where the North End meets the Waterfront neighborhood, cross I-93 to find Faneuil Hall Marketplace (also called Quincy Market, the formal name of the central building). This tourist magnet with no equal abounds with shops, restaurants, and bars.

- ✔ **Government Center:** Across Congress Street from Faneuil Hall is this cluster of ugly city, state, and federal office buildings, which surrounds the even uglier City Hall Plaza.

- ✔ **Beacon Hill:** Rest your eyes with a stroll around Beacon Hill, the architectural treasure among the Government Center, Boston Common, and river. When you conjure up a mental picture of Boston, it probably includes Beacon Hill's Federal-style homes and redbrick sidewalks.

✔ **Downtown Crossing:** This shopping and business district is across Boston Common from Beacon Hill. Most of the Freedom Trail is in this area.

✔ **Financial District:** East of Downtown Crossing and west of I-93 lies the Financial District. The area's giant office towers loom over the landmark Custom House and its colorful clock tower.

✔ **Charlestown:** I include this neighborhood near downtown because it's home to the last two stops on the Freedom Trail. Charlestown is across the Inner Harbor from the North End.

The Back Bay

Confession: "The Back Bay" covers hotels in the centrally located neighborhoods outside downtown, including the Back Bay proper. The other neighborhoods I lump in with it are (working east to west) Chinatown, the Theater District, the South End, and Kenmore Square. Incidentally, Boston has no "midtown" or "uptown."

The neighborhood Bostonians know as the Back Bay starts at the Public Garden and the river and extends, approximately, to Massachusetts Avenue (or "Mass. Ave.") and Huntington Avenue. Boston's finest shopping is along Newbury and Boylston Streets; also in this area are Trinity Church, the Boston Public Library, the Hancock Tower, Copley Place, the Prudential Center, and the Hynes Convention Center.

Remember "two if by sea"? Incredibly, the Back Bay was the "sea." (In the Longfellow poem, Paul Revere watched the steeple of the Old North Church for a signal telling him whether to alert the Minutemen to watch for British troops approaching over land — one lantern — or by water.) This neighborhood was a marshy body of water until 1835, when development began pushing west from downtown. The Back Bay attained its current contours by 1882. In 1775, when British troops set out for Lexington and Concord, present-day Charles Street (between Boston Common and the Public Garden) was the shoreline.

Chinatown is a congested area where you'll find an enormous assortment of Asian restaurants and shops. This neighborhood lies south of Downtown Crossing and west of I-93. The **Theater District,** a small area around the intersection of Tremont and Stuart streets, holds the largest professional Boston theaters.

Victorian brownstones distinguish the **South End,** which lies south of the Back Bay proper. The landmark district underwent extensive gentrification beginning in the 1970s. The South End has a large gay community and some of the best restaurants in the city.

At Beacon Street and Commonwealth Avenue, **Kenmore Square** spread out below an enormous white-and-red Citgo sign, one of the city skyline's most famous features. Fenway Park lies 3 blocks away.

Cambridge

The Red Line of the subway cuts through the city that bills itself as "Boston's Left Bank." The most popular destination is **Harvard Square,** where you'll find upscale shops, historic landmarks, and, oh yeah, a big university. The city's other world-famous institution is Massachusetts Institute of Technology (MIT), in and around Kendall Square. Between the two is **Central Square,** a run-down but improving area that abounds with ethnic restaurants and clubs. One stop past Harvard (or an enjoyable stroll on Mass. Ave.) is **Porter Square,** where you'll find quirky shops like those that once characterized Harvard Square.

Where to Get Information in Person

Make your first stop the concierge or front-desk staff at your hotel. Many hotels have racks full of brochures and other information.

The **Boston National Historic Park Visitor Center,** 15 State St. (☎ 617-242-5642), across the street from the Old State House and the State Street T station, is another good resource. Open daily 9 a.m. to 5 p.m. except January 1, Thanksgiving Day, and December 25.

The Freedom Trail begins at the Boston Common Information Center, 146 Tremont St., on the Common. Open Monday to Saturday 8:30 a.m. to 5 p.m., Sunday 9 a.m. to 5 p.m. The Prudential Information Center, on the main level of the Prudential Center, is open Monday through Saturday 9 a.m. to 8 p.m., Sunday 11 a.m. to 6 p.m. The **Greater Boston Convention & Visitors Bureau** (☎ 888-SEE-BOSTON or 617-536-4100) operates both centers.

A small information booth is at Faneuil Hall Marketplace, between Quincy Market and the South Market Building. The outdoor booth is staffed in the spring, summer, and fall from 10 a.m. to 6 p.m. Monday through Saturday, noon to 6 p.m. Sunday.

In Cambridge, an information kiosk (☎ 617-497-1630) in the heart of Harvard Square (near the T entrance on Mass. Ave.) is open Monday to Saturday 9 a.m. to 5 p.m., Sunday 1 to 5 p.m.

Chapter 11

Getting around Boston

• •

In This Chapter

▶ Exploring on foot

▶ Navigating the T (subway, bus, and boat)

▶ Getting around on wheels (taxi or car)

• •

Some people consider an African safari an adventure. Others say that whitewater rafting in the Rockies is a daring experience. Still others, perhaps overdramatic but no less serious, may call the navigation of Boston's downtown streets a courageous undertaking.

Congestion, construction, unmarked streets — Boston has it all. My goal here is to scare you into walking everywhere. (How'm I doing so far?) But sometimes you can't — it's too far, it's too late, or you're too tired. This chapter contains pointers for getting from place to place by foot and, because you may need to take another means of transportation, by subway, bus, boat, taxi, and car — all without steering you into adventure territory.

Should you find yourself in a sightseeing mood in the early morning or late afternoon, no matter what your mode of transportation, remember that you're essentially a commuter. If you're on the move between 7 and 9 a.m. or 4 and 7 p.m., be patient while you're in transit. And don't stop in the middle of a busy sidewalk to check your map while you're not.

Hitting the Bricks: Foot Traffic

You packed your good walking shoes, right? The compact size and baffling layout of the central city make it a pedestrian's pleasure. Everywhere you turn, something picturesque catches your attention, and not being in a speeding vehicle means you can check it out for as long as you like.

Some trekking tips:

✔ The only steep areas are Beacon Hill and Copp's Hill, in the North End behind the Old North Church. All over town, brick and cobblestone sidewalks ripple gently, just waiting to trip you and mess up the heels of your good shoes. Step carefully.

✔ The Back Bay is the only neighborhood laid out in a grid. The cross streets begin at the Public Garden with Arlington and proceed alphabetically until Mass. Ave. jumps in after Hereford Street.

✔ At many downtown intersections, the timing mechanism that controls the traffic light allows pedestrians just 7 seconds to walk (sprint, really) across. Ignore the locals and stay put until the light changes. Always look both ways before crossing — careless drivers, bikers, and skaters don't worry about "one way" signs.

Hot T: Public Transit

The full name of the "T" is the **Massachusetts Bay Transportation Authority,** or MBTA (☎ **800-392-6100** outside Mass., or 617-222-3200; Internet: www.mbta.com). The system operates subway lines, surface transit, and trains to the suburbs. Call the main information number for round-the-clock automated information, and assistance from live operators Monday to Friday from 6:30 a.m. to 8 p.m., Saturday and Sunday from 7:30 a.m. to 6 p.m. Visit the Web site to view maps and schedules, and to buy passes online (subject to a service charge).

You'll hear subway stops called "T stops," "T stations," and just "T," as in "I'll meet you near the Government Center T." If someone gives you directions that include a subway ride, be sure you know which exit to use (most stations have more than one).

On subways and buses, kids under age 5 accompanied by an adult ride free, and those ages 5 to 11 get a 50 percent discount. The commuter rail family fare (equal to twice the adult fare) also applies to one adult traveling with as many as four kids under 18.

The **MBTA visitor pass** (☎ **877-927-7277** or 617-222-5218) covers the subway, local buses, commuter rail zones 1A and 1B, and two ferries. Passes are available over the phone or on the Web (a shipping charge applies), and in person at the Airport, Government Center, and Harvard T stops, South Station, Back Bay Station, and North Station. The Boston Common, Prudential Center, and Faneuil Hall Marketplace information centers and some hotels sell passes, too. The price is $6, $11, or $22 for 1 day, 3 consecutive days, or 7 consecutive days.

The subway and trolley systems

Red, Orange, and Blue line subways and **Green Line trolleys,** which cover most areas you're likely to want to visit, are the quickest non-pedestrian way to get around. The T is generally dependable and safe, with a couple of caveats: The Green Line is sometimes unreliable, and you should take the precautions (such as watching out for pick-pockets) that you would on any big-city transit system.

The local fare is $1, and transfers are free. You need a token or visitor pass to enter subway stations; if you're boarding a Green Line trolley aboveground (as you leave the Museum of Fine Arts, for instance), pay at the front of the first car. Tokens are for sale at booths in every station and machines at many stops. Buy an extra for your return trip.

The T does not run all night. The T operates from about 5:15 a.m. until at least 12:30, but no later than 1 a.m. On New Year's Eve, service shuts down at 2 a.m. and is free after 8 p.m.

The antiquated Green Line, which serves many areas of interest to visitors, is the most complicated. When riding the Green Line, make sure you know which branch (B, C, D, or E) you need. Each starts and ends at a different station; all four serve every stop between Government Center and Copley. If you take the wrong westbound train, you may need to backtrack and switch lines; ask the conductor to leave you at the right stop.

System maps, available on request from most token-booth clerks, display the subway lines (in the designated colors) and commuter rail (in purple). The maps in this book also show subway stops. To get route and fare information before your visit, check the Web site.

Renovations to make the Green Line wheelchair accessible are under way. Updated system maps show accessible stations on other lines, bu not all stations display up-to-date maps (check the date, if you can find it). To learn more, call the main information number or contact the **Office for Transportation Access, ☎ 617-222-5438** or 617-222-5854 (TTY); Internet: www.mbta.com. Also see Chapter 4 for more information.

Check a map that shows T stations superimposed on a street map before automatically hopping on the subway to get around downtown. South Station to Aquarium, for example, is a three-train trip but an easy 10-minute walk.

The bus system

T buses and "trackless trolleys" (electricity-powered buses) serve Boston, Cambridge, and other nearby suburbs. The local fare is 75¢. Fare boxes accept tokens but don't make change. Express bus fares start at $1.50. Buses with wheelchair lifts cover many routes; call ☎ **800-LIFT-BUS** for information.

Boston Transit

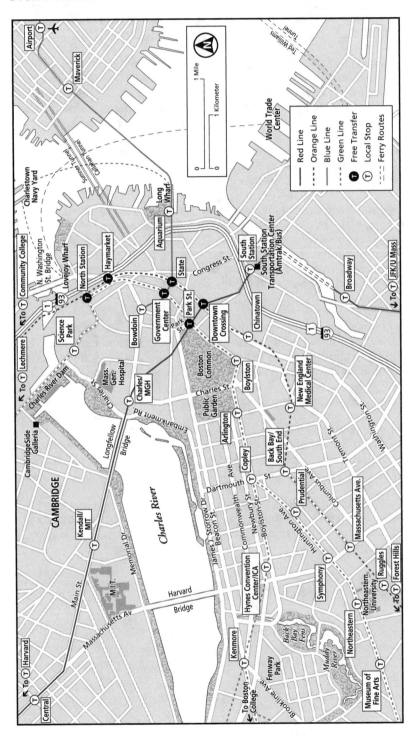

Local routes you may find useful:

- ✔ **Number 1,** along Mass. Ave. from Dudley station in Roxbury through the Back Bay and Cambridge to Harvard Square. During off-peak hours, this route is usually faster than the subway.

- ✔ **Numbers 92 and 93,** between Haymarket and Charlestown. Freedom Trail walkers may be too tired for anything except the bus, but the ferry (see later in this chapter) is more fun.

- ✔ **Number 77,** along Mass. Ave. north of Harvard Square to Porter Square, North Cambridge, and Arlington.

The ferry system

Water-transportation options change periodically, according to demand and other factors. Two popular routes on the Inner Harbor have a stop in common: Lovejoy Wharf, near North Station, and the FleetCenter off Causeway Street. The first connects Long Wharf, on State Street near Atlantic Avenue, with the Charlestown Navy Yard; it makes a good break from the Freedom Trail. The second runs to the World Trade Center, on Northern Avenue. The fare is $1.25; you can use your visitor pass on both routes. Call ☎ 617-227-4321 for more information.

Cab Session: Taxis

Taxis are pricey and can be tough to hail. At busy times such as rush hours and early morning (when bars and clubs are closing), you shouldn't have much trouble — the drivers go where the business is. Otherwise, find a cab stand or call a dispatcher.

Cabs line up near hotels and at designated stands. You'll find them queuing at Faneuil Hall Marketplace (on North Street), South Station, Back Bay Station, and at two stretches of Mass. Ave. in Harvard Square, near Brattle Street and near Dunster Street.

If the hour is late and you're desperate, look in front of a 24-hour business such as Dunkin' Donuts.

To call ahead for a cab, try the **Independent Taxi Operators Association** (☎ 617-426-8700), **Boston Cab** (☎ 617-536-5010), or **Town Taxi** (☎ 617-536-5000). In Cambridge, call **Ambassador Brattle** (☎ 617-492-1100) or **Yellow Cab** (☎ 617-547-3000). Boston Cab can dispatch a wheelchair-accessible vehicle; advance notice of an hour or so is recommended.

The "drop rate" (for the first ¼ mile) is $1.50. After that, the fare adds up at 25¢ per ⅛ mile. "Wait time" is extra, and the passenger pays all tolls as well as the $1.50 airport fee (on trips leaving Logan only). The law forbids charging a flat rate within Boston. If you need a cab to a suburb, the driver will charge you the price on the Police Department's list of flat rates (and show it to you if you ask).

Cabs licensed in Boston are white, and strenuously enforced regulations call for acceptable maintenance of both vehicle and driver.

Always, always ask for a receipt, which should state the name of the company. If you lose something or want to report a problem, call the **Police Department** (☎ **617-536-8294**).

Engine Block: Driving in Boston

Driving is not a good idea, but sometimes you have no choice. Start by buckling up, even if you never do. No kidding.

When you reach Boston or Cambridge, park the car, then walk or use public transportation. Do all you can to stay away during rush hours and weekend afternoons. Make sure you have a map and, if possible, a cool-headed navigator. Most streets are one-way, and your out-of-state plates make you more of a moving target than object of sympathy.

Be alert — no snacks, no phone calls. (Those bumper stickers that say "hang up and drive" come from Cambridge.) Watch out for cars that change lanes or leave the curb without signaling. Look both ways at intersections, even on one-way streets. Also keep an eye out for wrong-way bicyclists.

Enough! Where can I leave the car?

Not on the street, unless you're very lucky. Meters regulate most spaces, where nonresidents may park for no more than 2 hours (sometimes much less), and only between 8 a.m. and 6 p.m. The penalty is a $25 ticket, and parking-enforcement officers work long hours every day except Sunday. Most Boston and Cambridge meters take quarters only. In busy areas, that quarter only buys you 15 minutes — start hoarding now.

To see if your "missing" car is in the city tow lot, call ahead (☎ **617-635-3900**). Then take a taxi to 200 Frontage Rd., South Boston, or ride the Red Line to Andrew and flag a cab.

A parking lot or garage is easier but still no prize. The daily rate downtown, reputedly tops in the country, can be as much as $30; hourly rates are outrageous, too. Weekends and evenings usually are cheaper. Many establishments discount their weekday rates if you enter and exit before certain times. Some restaurants have deals with nearby garages; ask when you make your reservation.

The city operates a reasonably priced garage under Boston Common (☎ 617-954-2096). The entrance is on Charles Street between Boylston and Beacon streets. The Prudential Center garage (☎ 617-267-1002) offers a discount if you make a purchase at the Shops at Prudential Center and have your ticket validated. Enter from Boylston Street, Huntington Avenue, Exeter Street, or Dalton Street (at the Sheraton Boston Hotel). The Copley Place garage (☎ 617-375-4488) extends a discount to shoppers, too. It's off Huntington Avenue near Exeter Street. Many Faneuil Hall Marketplace shops and restaurants validate parking at the 75 State St. Garage (☎ 617-742-7275).

Other good-sized garages can be found at Government Center off Congress Street (☎ 617-227-0385), Sudbury Street off Congress Street (☎ 617-973-6954), the New England Aquarium (☎ 617-723-1731), Zero Post Office Square (☎ 617-423-1430), and near the Hynes Convention Center on Dalton Street (☎ 617-247-8006).

Harvard Square is even less hospitable to motorists than downtown Boston. It's a congested area with a few costly garages and parking lots, and many tow-away zones disguised as tempting university spaces. Be patient and have a backup plan and budget in case you don't find a metered space (maximum stay, 30 minutes to 2 hours).

Parking is free on North Harvard Street and Western Avenue, on the Boston side of the Charles River near Harvard Business School. Harvard Square is some distance away (use the bridge at Memorial Drive and John F. Kennedy Street), but it's not a bad walk, and the price is right.

Rules of the road

You may turn right at a red light after stopping when traffic permits, unless a sign says otherwise. Seat belts are mandatory for adults and children, children under 12 must ride in the back seat, and infants and children under 5 must be strapped into car seats.

Under state law, pedestrians in the crosswalk have the right of way, and vehicles already in a rotary (traffic circle or roundabout) have the right of way. Most suburbs post and enforce the crosswalk law; signs state the right-of-way law in every rotary, with little discernible effect.

Chapter 12

Money Matters

*Y*ou may hear that Boston is a great bargain because it's a college town. Well, a typical college kid isn't buying meals, snacks, tour tickets, and souvenirs for a family of four. If you are, you'll probably need some cash. This chapter discusses where to get money and where to turn for help if someone else makes off with yours. In addition, you can check out Chapter 3 for more money-management strategies.

Where to Get Cash in Boston

The largest banks in Massachusetts are **Fleet** (☎ **800-841-4000**) and **Citizens** (☎ **800-922-9999**); their ATMs accept most networks' cards and both impose fees for these services. This issue is a contentious one, but consumer advocates don't seem to be making much headway in their quest to eliminate surcharges. State law dictates only that the bank must warn you before imposing a fee for using a "foreign" bank card and offer you the chance to cancel the transaction.

You'll find ATMs everywhere, including grocery and convenience stores, most department stores, and some subway stations. Most are in safe, well-lit areas. If you don't feel secure, for whatever reason, keep walking; you'll pass another machine before long.

 When using the ATM, exercise the same caution you would at home (for example, protect your password). Don't be complacent, just because you're in a busy foot-traffic area — that makes running off with your money easier, not harder.

The largest national networks are **Cirrus** (☎ **800-424-7787** or 800-4CIRRUS) and **Plus** (☎ **800-843-7587**). Another widespread system, which operates primarily in the eastern U.S., is the **NYCE** network (Internet: www.nycenet.com). Check before leaving home (the logo should be on the back of your ATM card) to see which network accepts your bank's cards.

A consortium of smaller banks and credit unions, the **SUM** network (Internet: `www.sum-atm.com`) allows customers of member institutions free access to other members' ATMs. The network and its ATMs are mostly in New England. Check to see whether your bank belongs to the SUM network or has another arrangement that can help you avoid fees.

Even if the Massachusetts bank doesn't charge you, your out-of-state bank may impose a fee for using another bank's ATM. Weigh the cumulative cost against the potential risk of carrying around a wad of cash and adjust your withdrawal patterns accordingly.

Knowing What to Do if Your Money Gets Stolen

Most credit card companies operate emergency toll-free numbers to call if your wallet or purse is stolen. Your card issuer may be able to wire you a cash advance; in many places, it can provide an emergency replacement card in a day or two.

Check the back of your credit card for the issuing bank's name and toll-free number before you leave home. Keep it separate from your wallet. If you forget the number, call toll-free directory assistance (☎ 800-555-1212) to find out your bank's number.

Visa and MasterCard also operate global service numbers: For **Visa,** ☎ 800-847-2911; for **MasterCard,** ☎ 800-307-7309. (Both suggest that you contact your card issuer directly, though.) **American Express** cardholders and traveler's check holders should call ☎ 800-221-7282 for all money emergencies.

If you carry traveler's checks, keep a record of their serial numbers so you can handle just such an emergency. Keeping a similar record of your credit card numbers and the companies' emergency numbers is not a bad idea, either.

Always notify the police if your wallet is stolen, even though they probably won't be able to recover it. You may need a copy of the police report for your insurance or credit card company. And *somebody* has to be the lucky one in those heartwarming stories about the overflowing wallet returned intact by the last honest person in Western civilization — maybe you'll be the one.

Part IV
Dining in Boston

The 5th Wave   By Rich Tennant

"How you doin', sir? Why don't you let me show you an old New England way of getting meat out of a lobster?"

In this part . . .

One of the liveliest restaurant markets in the country, Boston offers choices to suit every budget, taste, and style. Volatility coexists with stability — you can enjoy back-to-back meals at a place that opened 18 days ago and a place that opened in the 1800s. This part explores your options, describes my favorite restaurants, and sets you on your path to dining well.

Your table is ready.

Chapter 13

The Scoop on the Boston Dining Scene

● ●

In This Chapter

▶ Enjoying the hot spots and local favorites

▶ Paying the check without getting heartburn

▶ Figuring out reservations, dress codes, and other considerations

● ●

*O*ut-of-towners ask the same question everywhere: Where do people who live in Boston (or Paris or Seattle or Harrisburg) go to eat? This chapter offers an overview of the local dining scene, plus pointers about the mechanics of getting strangers to bring you food. Turn to Chapter 14 for specifics about my favorites and to Chapter 15 if you're just grabbing a quick bite. For the locations of restaurants mentioned in this chapter, see the "Boston Dining" or "Cambridge Dining" maps in Chapter 14.

Finding Out What's Hot Now

New England cuisine abounds with seafood and local produce, but there's no particular "Boston style." Thanks to constant turnover, though, every chef in town seems to have supervised or worked for nearly every other chef. Many kitchens show signs of similar influences, particularly in the mingling of ethnic elements and ingredients, a practice that has become increasingly apparent on menus across the country.

Boston has shaken its reputation for stodgy food and stodgier restaurants, even among hard-core snobs and wannabe New Yorkers. Pockets of Gotham-esque see-and-be-seen action have sprung up in some improbable neighborhoods. The hottest places as I write (they could be different as you read) are **The Federalist,** in the XV Beacon hotel, 15 Beacon St., Beacon Hill (☎ **617-670-2515**); **Mistral,** 221 Columbus Ave.,

South End (☎ **617-867-9300**); and **Radius,** 8 High St., Financial District (☎ **617-426-1234**).

Although not open at press time, by the time you visit, the name to drop will definitely be **Zita.** The story is irresistible: A young bartender at The Federalist, Gwen Butler, impresses a customer with the cut of her jib (and *only* her jib — by all accounts, he's happily married). So he bankrolls her dream of opening her own restaurant. It's at 33 Stanhope St., on the edge of the Back Bay and South End (☎ **617-421-4455**).

You'll find smoked food at a ton of establishments, but smoking people are less welcome. The law is tough: Most restaurants ban smoking in dining areas, and smaller places don't permit it at all. If you must light up, say so when you make your reservation, and expect to wind up in or near the bar.

Hot on the trail of celebrity chefs

So you've seen a certain Boston-area chef on TV, in a national magazine, or at a culinary expo. The thrill of dropping a big name may not compare with being the first to "discover" an emerging talent, but the big name usually is a reliable indicator of excellent dining. In cooking, unlike a lot of other reputation-driven fields, fame generally does correlate with talent.

Important note: Celebrity is time-consuming; if you're planning a special trip to bask in its glow, call ahead to make sure the chef whose name you want to drop plans to be behind the stove.

Here's a selection of noted chefs and the restaurants they own or run (most do both):

- Todd English: **Olives,** 10 City Sq., Charlestown (☎ **617-242-1999**), and **Kingfish Hall,** 1 Faneuil Hall Marketplace (☎ **617-523-8862**); reservations only for six or more.

- Stan Frankenthaler: **Salamander,** Trinity Place, 25 Huntington Ave., Back Bay (☎ **617-451-2150**).

- Gordon Hamersley: **Hamersley's Bistro,** 553 Tremont St., South End (☎ **617-423-2700**).

- Ken Oringer: **Clio,** in the Eliot Hotel, 370 Commonwealth Ave., Back Bay (☎ **617-536-7200**).

- Lydia Shire and Susan Regis: **Biba,** 272 Boylston St. (☎ **617-426-7878**), Back Bay, and **Pignoli,** 79 Park Plaza, Back Bay (☎ **617-338-7500**).

- Jasper White: **Summer Shack,** 149 Alewife Brook Parkway, Cambridge (☎ **617-520-9500**); reservations not accepted.

Locating Where the Locals Eat

First, let me assure you that you're not going to get scurvy from eating *only* New England clam chowder, baked beans, and Boston cream pie. The menus here offer a lot more than stereotypical New England food, though; in fact, the renowned chowder, beans, and pie went out with disco and platform shoes — the first time around. The locals eat tons of seafood, appreciate chefs' increasing interest in local and organic produce, and demonstrate a willingness to try just about anything once.

Remember, many locals are students. They come from all over the world with lots of ambition and tuition, and often not much else. When collegians go out to eat, they're willing to experiment, but not to overpay. Seek out a busy place near a college campus when you're looking for generous portions and reasonable prices.

As in any city of neighborhoods, the local standby occupies an honored place. Depending on the neighborhood, this dependable eating establishment may be a pocket-sized bistro, an ethnic counter, a diner, or just about anything else. I'll suggest a few in Chapter 14, but never dismiss a restaurant just because you can't find it in a guidebook. Your friends who can't shut up about the great place around the corner may be ahead of the curve.

Tasting Boston's Ethnic Eats

Head to the North End — which would be Boston's Little Italy if anyone ever used that term — for good Italian food in every price range. Hanover and Salem Streets are the main drags, with some good spots on the streets nearby. In Chinatown, you'll find excellent and affordable Chinese, Japanese, Korean, Vietnamese, and Malaysian food. Start at Beach Street and wander the streets that intersect it.

Ethnic restaurants thrive all over Cambridge. Along Mass. Ave. in Central Square, you'll find a particularly appealing, eclectic mix.

Dressing to Dine

Boston is a college town with a down-to-earth attitude. A few lonely restaurants still ask that men wear jackets at dinner, but most have no dress code. At casual restaurants near campuses and in tourist areas, just about anything goes, particularly at lunch. That includes shorts in the summer and jeans and sneakers all year.

The key phrase above was "at casual restaurants." At more upscale places, if you take the time to look presentable, you should fit in better,

and the staff may even take you more seriously. Save your breath —
I've heard all the arguments. In theory, yes, you should get the same
treatment whether you're in footie pajamas or a tux. Get over it.

Unmoved? I'll appeal to your conscience. Even if you're not footing
the bill, consider the people who chose that expensive restaurant for
its "wow" factor, and try not to look as if you're about to come in off
the bench.

Trimming the Fat from Your Budget

Boston dining is terrific, but this city isn't New Orleans or San
Francisco — you're not here just to eat. You'll probably want
some cash left over for other activities.

The best cost-cutting move is to eat your big meal at lunch. Many
restaurants serve dinner only, but the ones that open at midday
(or even for breakfast) offer great values at lunch.

Other strategies: Split an appetizer or dessert. Skip the alcohol. Skip
beverages altogether — those $2 Diet Cokes can really add up. Plan a
picnic for lunch (see Chapter 15 for suggestions) and run up the bill at
dinner.

A server who rattles off daily specials without prices may be busy or
forgetful — or may be counting on your reluctance to look cheap in
front of your friends or family. Always ask, and no $23 plate of noodles
(true story) will ever sneak up on you.

A final thought: A fancy dinner every night is no vacation for anyone
but a hard-core foodie. Give yourself a break, dip into the less expensive categories, and chow down. You just may like the experience.

Tackling Tipping and Taxes

The Massachusetts meal tax (which also applies to take-out food) is
5 percent. Tip three or four times the tax, and you're set. Don't leave
less than 15 percent unless the service was awful, and round up, not
down — that extra dollar means more to your server than it does to
you.

If you're with a large group (six, eight, or more, depending on the
restaurant), the check may include a service charge. Examine the total
before accidentally tipping twice.

Making Reservations

Make a reservation for Friday or Saturday night at any restaurant that takes them. If you already know where you want to eat, try to call before you leave home. If the night you want is booked, call when you reach Boston and ask if there have been any cancellations. At lunch, a party of two usually shouldn't have trouble landing a table, but a reservation is a good idea for larger groups.

Boston is an early city, even on weekends. Don't count on dropping in and getting a table at what seems to you to be an off-peak hour. "Early" is 5:30 or 6 p.m., and "too late" can be as early as 9:30 p.m.

Some places let you eat at the bar without a reservation, but the location is not ideal — the menu may not be the same as in the dining room, and you'll probably be breathing smoke — but it works if you're desperate to check out a particular restaurant. Make sure the host or hostess knows you're willing to move if there's a last-minute cancellation.

Look, up in the sky — it's a restaurant

Boston has not one, but two high-altitude restaurants that attract tourists and people celebrating special occasions. The food at The Bay Tower and Top of the Hub is quite good, but what you're paying for is the view. Ask for a table by the window when you make your reservation (The Bay Tower has more front-row seats than Top of the Hub). If the person you talk to can't guarantee a seat with a view, just enjoy a drink in the lounge, and eat somewhere else.

The Bay Tower (☎ 617-723-1666; Internet: www.baytower.com) is on the 33rd floor of 60 State St., overlooking Faneuil Hall Marketplace, downtown, and the airport. The Bay Tower serves dinner Monday through Saturday. Men must wear jackets in the dining room. **Top of the Hub (☎ 617-536-1775)** is on the 52nd floor of the Prudential Tower, 800 Boylston St., Back Bay. Top of the Hub serves lunch Monday through Saturday, Sunday brunch, and dinner daily.

Chapter 14

Boston's Best Restaurants

• •

In This Chapter

▶ Reviews of my favorites

▶ Indexes by price, location, and cuisine

• •

By now you're probably pretty hungry, so I'll jump right in. This chapter lists and reviews my favorite restaurants. Here you also find suggestions of neighborhoods to wander when you're hungry but not set on where you want to eat.

The Kid-Friendly symbol indicates restaurants your family will like, and that will like your family. Most have children's menus; all offer friendly service and not-too-challenging fare that can make any homesick youngster feel a little more settled. (Adventurous palates will find reasonable options, too.) As with hotels, the absence of the icon doesn't mean kids aren't welcome — but think twice if they tend to get rambunctious. If you're unsure, describe your family (including the kids' ages) before you make a reservation, to be sure the restaurant can handle you.

Keep in mind that when reservations are recommended, it means for dinner.

The $ symbols that accompany each review give an idea of the price of dinner for one. That covers an appetizer, main course, dessert, and one nonalcoholic drink, not including tax and tip. The listings also include a price range for main courses. The price ranges are estimates — adjust accordingly if you order truffles, lobster, and wine from Château d'Expensive, or if you split an appetizer, drink water, stick to pasta, and skip dessert.

The $ symbols correspond with the following price ranges:

$	less than $20
$$	$20–$30
$$$	$30–$45
$$$$	$45 and up

For restaurant locations, see the "Boston Dining" or "Cambridge Dining" maps in this chapter. (Eateries described in Chapters 13 and 15 are also listed on the maps in this chapter.)

My Favorite Boston-area Restaurants

Aujourd'hui

$$$$ Back Bay CONTEMPORARY AMERICAN

The restaurant that puts the "special" in "special occasion" and the "expense" in "expense account" occupies a striking space on the second floor of the luxurious Four Seasons hotel. The excellent cuisine incorporates seasonal ingredients and inventive preparations, but this *is* a hotel dining room, so don't expect anything too wild. Seafood is a marvelous choice (perhaps roasted lobster with pineapple compote and crabmeat wontons), and the desserts are amazing. The element that makes the experience unforgettable is service so good that "superlative" doesn't cover it.

In the Four Seasons Hotel, 200 Boylston St. (opposite the Public Garden). ☎ 617-351-2071. Reservations suggested (required on holidays). T: Arlington (Green Line); walk one block on Boylston St. opposite the Public Garden. Parking: Valet. Main courses: $35–$45. AE, CB, DC, DISC, MC, V. Open: Mon–Fri 6:30–11 a.m., Sat–Sun 7–11 a.m. (breakfast); Sun–Fri 11:30 a.m.–2:30 p.m. (lunch; brunch Sun); Mon–Sat 5:30–10:30 p.m., Sun 6–10:30 p.m (dinner).

Bartley's Burger Cottage

$ Cambridge/Harvard Square AMERICAN

Down-to-earth burger joints are scarce in Harvard Square, which is more retail haven than college campus. But even Harvard students need their ground beef (and turkey) sometimes, and this hanguot is a great place for it. The college-town atmosphere is authentic, from the vintage posters to the chummy wait staff. Although meat is the main event, vegetarians can eat surprisingly well. Sublime onion rings round out a perfect burger-joint meal.

1246 Massachusetts Ave. (between Plympton and Bow Sts.). ☎ 617-354-6559. Reservations not required. T: Harvard (Red Line); with the Harvard Coop at your back, follow Mass. Ave. 3½ blocks. Main courses: $8 or less. No credit cards. Open: Mon–Wed, Sat 11 a.m.–9 p.m.; Thurs–Fri 11 a.m.–10 p.m.

Billy Tse Restaurant

$$ Downtown/North End CHINESE/PAN-ASIAN

The edge of the Italian North End may seem an odd place for an Asian restaurant, but hey, noodles are noodles. The noodles here are quite good, as are the stir-fries, sushi, and fresh seafood dishes. Lunch specials, served until 4 p.m., are a great deal. If you don't mind some smoke from the bar, you can ask for a table near the French doors that open to the street.

240 Commercial St. (at Fleet St.). ☎ *617-227-9990. Reservations recommended for dinner on weekends. T: Haymarket (Green or Orange Line); cross under Expressway, turn right, follow Cross St. to Hanover St., and turn left. Follow Hanover St. to Fleet St., turn right, walk 4 blocks (to traffic light), and turn right. (Whew!) Main courses: $5–$20; lunch specials: $5.50–$7.50. AE, DC, DISC, MC, V. Open: Mon–Thurs 11:30 a.m.–11:30 p.m.; Fri–Sat 11:30 a.m.–midnight; Sun 11:30 a.m.–11 p.m.*

The Blue Room

$$$$ Cambridge/Kendall Square   ECLECTIC

The trek to the Blue Room is more like a pilgrimage for diners who seek out unusual cuisine in unusual locations. Tech-heavy East Cambridge is not a fine-dining mecca, but the Blue Room is a revelation: Steve Johnson grills, roasts, and braises up a storm, creating gutsy, flavorful food in a sleek but comfortable setting. Among the inventive main courses (which always include admirable vegetarian options), you'll find the best roast chicken in town. In warm weather, seating on the brick patio is available.

1 Kendall Sq. (off Hampshire St.). ☎ *617-494-9034. Reservations recommended. T: Kendall (Red Line); cross through the Marriott lobby, turn left, follow Broadway 2 long blocks (across the train tracks), bear right onto Hampshire St., and walk ½ block. Parking: Validated self. Main courses: $16–$26. AE, CB, DC, DISC, MC, V. Open: Sun–Thurs 5:30–10 p.m., Fri–Sat 5:30–11 p.m. (dinner); Sun 11 a.m.–2:30 p.m. (brunch).*

Border Café

$$ Cambridge/Harvard Square   SOUTHWESTERN

Huge crowds don't necessarily mean high quality, but they do when the crowds have been this huge for this long (since the mid-80s). The nonstop party at the Border Café runs on heaping portions of Tex-Mex, Cajun, and occasionally Caribbean food — and, of course, beer and margaritas. The cheerful but frantic staff keeps the peace with plenty of chips and salsa. Except at off-hours, there are no quick meals here (the wait for a table can stretch out), so be in the mood to linger and join the party.

32 Church St. (at Palmer St.). ☎ *617-864-6100. Reservations not accepted. T: Harvard (Red Line); use Church St. exit (at front of Alewife-bound train), go right at turnstiles, and walk 1 block. Main courses: $7–$15. AE, MC, V. Open: Mon–Thurs 11 a.m.–1 a.m.; Fri–Sat 11 a.m.–2 a.m.; Sun noon–11 p.m.*

Boston Dining

Aujourd'hui **26**
The Bay Tower **45**
Ben & Jerry's **11**
Bertucci's (Back Bay) **15**
Bertucci's (Faneuil Hall) **44**
Biba **25**
Billy Tse Restaurant **35**
The Bristol Lounge **26**
Buddha's Delight **58**
Café Jaffa **7**
Caffe dello Sport **33**
Caffè Graffiti **39**
Caffè Vittoria **31**
Casa Romero **4**
China Pearl **56**
Clio **2**
Cosí Sandwich Bar
  (Federal St.) **51**
Cosí Sandwich Bar
  (Milk St.) **50**
Cosí Sandwich Bar
  (State St.) **46**
Daily Catch **38**
Durgin–Park **44**
The Elephant Walk **1**

Emack & Bolio's **6**
Empire Garden Restaurant **59**
The Federalist **43**
Giacomo's **37**
Golden Palace Restaurant **55**
Grand Chau Chow **57**
Grill 23 & Bar **16**
Grillfish **18**
Hamersley's Bistro **20**
Hard Rock Café **14**
Herrell's **10**
Icarus **19**
Il Panino Express **30**
JP Licks **3**
Kingsfish Hall **44**
La Summa **34**
Legal Sea Foods
  (Copley) **13**
Legal Sea Foods
  (Park Square) **22**
Legal Sea Foods
  (Prudential) **8**
Legal Sea Foods
  (Waterfront) **49**
Le Gamin Café **21**

L'Espalier **5**
Les Zygomates **54**
Mamma Maria **36**
Mike's Pastry **32**
Mistral **17**
Olives **29**
Paradiso Caffè **41**
Piccola Venezia **40**
Pignoli **24**
Pizzeria Regina **29**
Radius **53**
Ritz Lounge **27**
Salamander **12**
Savenor's
  Supermarket **28**
Sel de la Terre **48**
Souper Salad
  (Center Plaza) **42**
Souper Salad
  (State St.) **47**
Souper Salad
  (Summer St.) **52**
Swans Court **23**
Top of the Hub **9**
Zita **14**

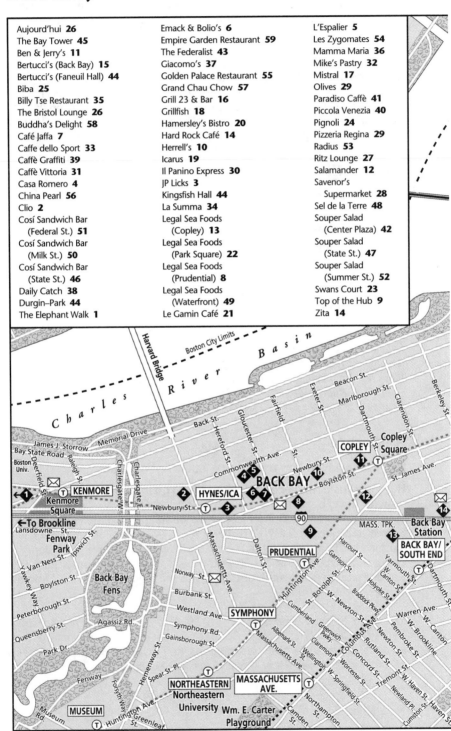

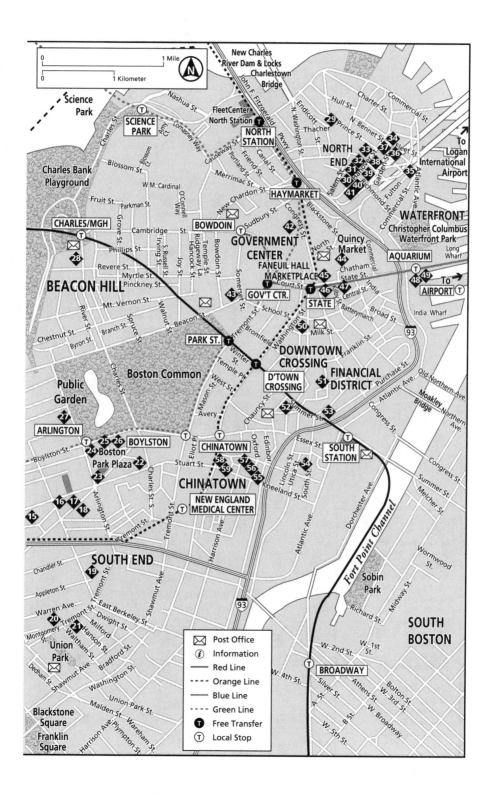

Cambridge Dining

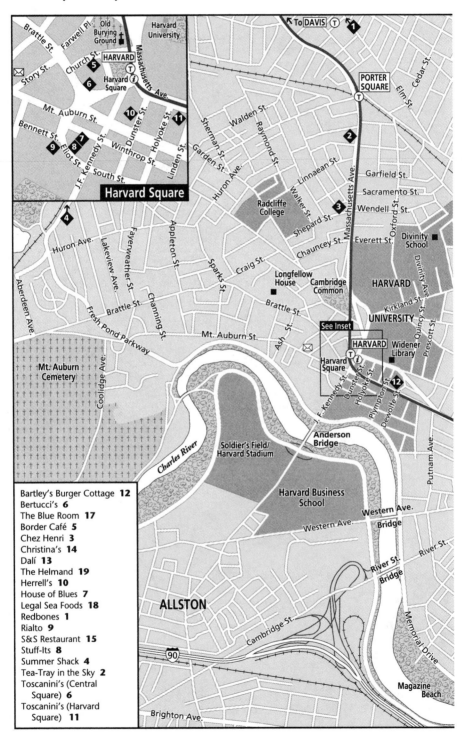

Harvard Square

See Inset

Bartley's Burger Cottage **12**
Bertucci's **6**
The Blue Room **17**
Border Café **5**
Chez Henri **3**
Christina's **14**
Dalí **13**
The Helmand **19**
Herrell's **10**
House of Blues **7**
Legal Sea Foods **18**
Redbones **1**
Rialto **9**
S&S Restaurant **15**
Stuff-Its **8**
Summer Shack **4**
Tea-Tray in the Sky **2**
Toscanini's (Central Square) **6**
Toscanini's (Harvard Square) **11**

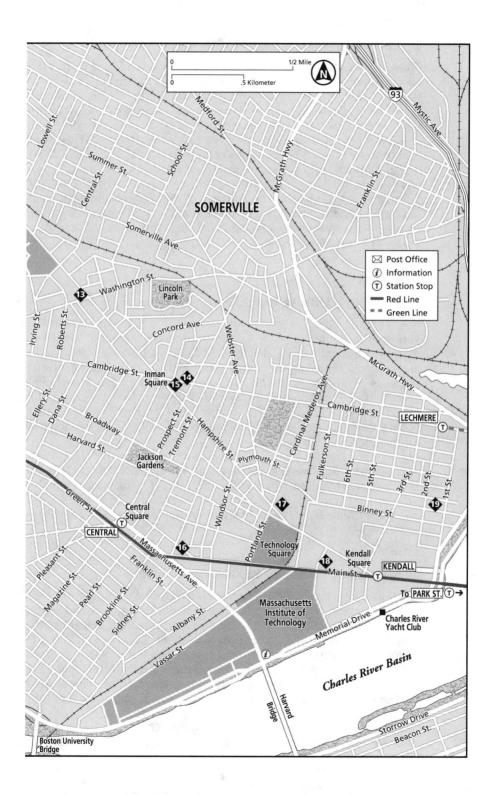

0   1/2 Mile

0   .5 Kilometer

Lowell St.

Medford St.

93

Mystic Ave.

McGrath Hwy.

Summer St.

School St.

Central St.

Franklin St.

SOMERVILLE

Somerville Ave.

⊠ Post Office

ⓘ Information

Ⓣ Station Stop

━ Red Line

╍ Green Line

Washington St.

13

Lincoln Park

Irving St.

Roberts St.

Concord Ave.

Webster Ave.

McGrath Hwy.

Cambridge St.

Inman Square

15 14

Cardinal Medeiros Ave.

Cambridge St.

LECHMERE Ⓣ

Ellery St.

Dana St.

Broadway

Prospect St.

Tremont St.

Hampshire St.

Fulkerson St.

6th St.

5th St.

3rd St.

2nd St.

1st St.

Harvard St.

Plymouth St.

Jackson Gardens

Green St.

Windsor St.

17

Binney St.

19

Central Square

CENTRAL Ⓣ

Massachusetts Ave.

16

Portland St.

Technology Square

18

Kendall Square

KENDALL

Pleasant St.

Franklin St.

Main St. Ⓣ

To **PARK ST.** Ⓣ →

Magazine St.

Pearl St.

Brookline St.

Sidney St.

Albany St.

Massachusetts Institute of Technology

Memorial Drive

■ Charles River Yacht Club

Vassar St.

ⓘ

Charles River Basin

Harvard Bridge

Storrow Drive

Beacon St.

Boston University Bridge

Buddha's Delight

$ Chinatown VEGETARIAN VIETNAMESE

Things are not what they seem: A dingy staircase leads to a comfortable second-floor dining room, the sleek décor belies the friendly service, and the delicious food is actually good for you. Buddha's Delight doesn't serve meat, poultry, fish, or dairy (some beverages are made with condensed milk). Instead, the chefs transform tofu and gluten into chicken, pork, beef, shrimp, and even lobster taste-alikes. This restaurant produces bounteous portions of unusual but delicious food. Try the delightful fresh spring roll appetizer; then start experimenting.

5 Beach St. (at Washington St.), 2nd Floor. ☎ *617-451-2395. Reservations not required. T: Chinatown (Orange Line); follow Washington St. (past the China Trade Center) 1 block. Main courses: $6–$12. MC, V. Open: Sun–Thurs 11 a.m.–9:30 p.m.; Fri–Sat 11 a.m.–10:30 p.m.*

Café Jaffa

$ Back Bay MIDDLE EASTERN

Newbury and Boylston Streets are consumer central, and the last thing you want in the middle of a shopping spree is a meal that weighs you down — physically or financially. Café Jaffa is a favorite with shoppers and students, who come here for low prices, high quality, and good-sized portions. Traditional Middle Eastern dishes such as falafel, baba ghanoush, and hummus make a not-too-filling break from bargain hunting; lamb, beef, and chicken kabobs, burgers, and steak tips are heartier and equally tasty. The exposed-brick, glass-fronted room makes a good setting for midafternoon coffee, too.

48 Gloucester St. (between Boylston and Newbury Sts.). ☎ *617-536-0230. Reservations not required. T: Hynes/ICA (Green Line B, C, or D); use Newbury Street exit, turn right, walk 2 blocks, and turn right. Main courses: $5–$13. AE, DC, DISC, MC, V. Open: Mon–Thurs 11 a.m.–10:30 p.m.; Fri–Sat 11 a.m.–11 p.m.; Sun 1–10 p.m.*

Casa Romero

$$$ Back Bay CLASSIC MEXICAN

Hidden away in an alley, Casa Romero is a romantic destination a stone's throw from busy Newbury Street. The peaceful atmosphere and dimly lit rooms almost make the food secondary, but this food demands attention. The authentic Mexican cuisine is nothing like what you find at the Tex-Mex drive-through — it's fresh, savory, and not too heavy. Unusual ingredients (cactus salad is an unexpectedly good starter) and flavor-layered sauces make meat, poultry, and seafood shine. The enclosed garden is pleasant in warm weather, but seating is on plastic furniture.

30 Gloucester St. (off Newbury St.; entrance in alley). ☎ *617-536-4341. Reservations recommended. T: Hynes/ICA (Green Line B, C, or D); use Newbury St. exit, turn right,* *walk 2 blocks, and turn left. Main courses: $13–$24. DISC, MC, V. Open: Sun–Thurs 5–10 p.m.; Fri–Sat 5–11 p.m.*

Chez Henri

$$$$ Cambridge/Harvard Square FRENCH AND CUBAN

Chez Henri represents an enjoyable combination of destination restaurant and neighborhood hangout, elegant cuisine and down-to-earth bar food, and French technique and Cuban flavors. Chef-owner Paul O'Connell shakes up his bistro menu according to what's fresh and seasonal, creating classic dishes (like superb roast chicken) with a Cuban flair that's especially apparent in creative side dishes (like tasty empanadas). Save room for dessert — the crème brûlée is the best around. The dark, inviting room can get a little noisy. The Cuban bar food complements the strong specialty drinks.

1 Shepard St. (off Mass. Ave.). ☎ 617-354-8980. Reservations recommended; accepted only for parties of six or more. T: Harvard (Red Line); follow Mass. Ave. north 4 blocks, past Cambridge Common. Main courses: $19–$27; bar food: $5–$8. AE, DC, MC, V. Open: Mon–Thurs 6–10 p.m., Fri–Sat 5:30–11 p.m. (dinner; bar food until midnight); Sun 11 a.m.–2 p.m. (brunch) and 5:30–9 p.m. (dinner; bar food until 10 p.m.).

Daily Catch

$$ Downtown/North End SEAFOOD AND SOUTHERN ITALIAN

For a true North End experience, seek out this tiny storefront under an awning that reads "Calamari Café." The open kitchen cranks out hearty, garlicky food that often revolves around squid, right down to the garlic-and-oil pasta sauce (which includes chopped calamari) and the black pasta (which includes squid ink). The casual atmosphere — some dishes land on the table still in the cooking skillet — is part of the fun.

323 Hanover St. (between Richmond and Prince Sts.). ☎ 617-523-8567. Reservations not accepted. T: Haymarket (Green or Orange Line); cross under Expressway, turn right, follow Cross St. to Hanover St., turn left, and go 1½ blocks. Main courses: $10–$18. No credit cards. Open: Sun–Thurs noon–10:30 p.m.; Fri–Sat noon–11 p.m.

Dalí

$$ Cambridge/Somerville SPANISH

A good dinner-party menu at home is all appetizers, no main course — and it can be even better at a restaurant. The main attraction at this boisterous place is delectable *tapas*. The appetizer-like plates of hot or cold meat, seafood, vegetables, and cheeses are so tasty that you won't miss the big platter of one boring old thing. Instead you'll want to ask for another order or two of sausages, cold potato salad, salmon croquettes, or whatever catches your fancy. The wait at the bar can be long, but the atmosphere is festive and the payoff huge — unlike the bill. (A conventional meal of Spanish classics will push the tab into $$$ territory.)

415 Washington St., Somerville. ☎ 617-661-3254. Internet: www.DaliRestaurant. com. Reservations not accepted. T: Harvard (Red Line); cross through Harvard Yard and follow Kirkland St. from back of Memorial Hall to intersection of Washington and Beacon Sts. (A $5 cab ride.) Tapas: $3.50–$7.50. Main courses: $17–$21. AE, DC, MC, V. Open: Daily 6–11 p.m. in summer; 5:30–11 p.m. in winter.

Durgin-Park

$$ Downtown/Faneuil Hall Marketplace   NEW ENGLAND

If you prefer hearty food and sassy service to fancy ingredients and unpronounceable dishes, Durgin-Park is the classic New England experience you're looking for. Bostonians and out-of-towners seek out its long, multiple-party tables (smaller ones are available) for generous helpings of delicious, down-to-earth fare. The cornbread and baked beans are famous, the prime rib and fresh seafood are delicious, and the strawberry shortcake is as fresh as some of the waitresses. That's right — like a 19th-century theme restaurant, Durgin-Park (founded in 1827) has a shtick: borderline-belligerent service. Far from being cranky, many waitresses are actually pleasant, but a trip into the orbit of someone who takes her job seriously can be an eye-opening experience.

340 Faneuil Hall Marketplace (in the North Market building). ☎ 617-227-2038. Reservations not accepted. T: Government Center (Green or Blue Line) or Haymarket (Orange Line); follow the crowds. Main courses: $5–$18; specials $16–$25. AE, DC, DISC, MC, V. Open: Mon–Thurs 11:30 a.m.–10 p.m., Fri–Sat 11:30 a.m.–10:30 p.m., Sun 11:30 a.m.–9 p.m. (lunch menu until 2:30 p.m.).

The Elephant Walk

$$$ Back Bay/Kenmore Square   FRENCH AND CAMBODIAN

This restaurant is the worst-kept "secret" on the Boston culinary scene, but excuse the people who try to pass it off as a discovery — it does feel like a great find. The unique combination of French and Cambodian isn't the mishmash that plagues fusion cuisine; rather, each side of the menu stands alone and complements the other. On the French side, you may find pan-seared filet mignon. On the Cambodian side, *curry de crevettes* (yup, that's French) is a perfect shrimp dish. The accommodating staff offers excellent advice, and tofu can replace animal protein in many dishes.

900 Beacon St. (at St. Mary's St.; 4 blocks past Kenmore Sq.). ☎ 617-247-1500. Reservations suggested at dinner Sun–Thurs, not accepted Fri–Sat. T: St. Mary's (Green Line C). Parking: Valet at dinner only. Main courses: $10–$24. AE, DISC, MC, V. Open: Mon–Sat 11:30 a.m.–2:30 p.m.; Mon–Thurs 5–10 p.m.; Fri 5–11 p.m.; Sat 4:30–11 p.m.; Sun 4:30–10 p.m.

Giacomo's

$$$ Downtown/North End   SEAFOOD AND SOUTHERN ITALIAN

For pure inconvenience — long lines, no credit cards, improbably cramped space — you can't beat Giacomo's. So why the crowds? You also can't beat the food. Go early, before the queue gets too long. Check the board for outstanding daily specials, take the chef's advice, or create your own dish from the list of ingredients and sauces. Salmon with sundried tomatoes over fettuccine is my favorite, but I've never had anything that wasn't fabulous. Portions are large, and even dainty eaters who declare themselves stuffed can't help trying just one more mouthful.

355 Hanover St. (near Fleet St.). ☎ *617-523-9026. Reservations not accepted. T: Haymarket (Green or Orange Line); cross under Expressway, turn right, follow Cross St. to Hanover St., turn left, and walk 3 full blocks. Main courses: $15–$24. No credit cards. Open: Mon–Thurs 5–10 p.m.; Fri–Sat 5–10:30 p.m.; Sun 4–10 p.m.*

Grand Chau Chow

$$ Chinatown   CANTONESE AND CHINESE

Everyone has their favorites among Chinatown's apparently interchangeable restaurants, and this is one of mine. Grand Chau Chow is a great place to come with a group — the menu is so long that anybody who can't find *something* is just trying to cause trouble. Fresh seafood (those fish tanks aren't just for show) is a wise choice. If you're feeling adventuresome, ask your server for suggestions. Lunch specials are a bargain.

45 Beach St. (at Harrison Ave.). ☎ *617-292-5166. Reservations accepted only for parties of 10 or more. T: Chinatown (Orange Line); walk 1 block on Washington St. (past the China Trade Center), turn left, and go 2½ blocks on Beach St. Main courses: $5–$22. AE, DC, DISC, MC, V. Open: Sun–Thurs 10 a.m.–3 a.m.; Fri–Sat 10 a.m.–4 a.m.*

Grill 23 & Bar

$$$$ Back Bay   AMERICAN

The best steakhouse in Boston earns that title with an irresistible mix of macho atmosphere and splendid food. Grill 23 is a favorite business destination with a raucous crowd that seems to have sealed a deal minutes before — all the time. (If they're smart, the young turks give a moment's thought to their plates.) The steak and chops are magnificent, and the more inventive options — for instance, top-notch meat loaf — are equally satisfying but not as *Flintstones*-like. As at any self-respecting steakhouse, the side dishes (à la carte) and desserts are diet-busting delights.

161 Berkeley St. (at Stuart St.). ☎ *617-542-2255. Internet:* www.gril123.com. *Reservations recommended. T: Arlington (Green Line); follow Boylston St. 1 block away from the Public Garden, turn left, and walk 2 full blocks. Parking: Valet. Main* *courses: $22–$30. AE, CB, DC, DISC, MC, V. Open: Mon–Thurs 5:30–10:30 p.m.; Fri–Sat 5:30–11 p.m.; Sun 5:30–10 p.m.*

Grillfish

$$ Back Bay/South End   SEAFOOD

The specialty at this cavernous, clamorous restaurant is grilled seafood, a somewhat neglected option in Boston. Prepared over an open fire, menu standards and daily specials pick up a hint of smoke; each comes with sweet onion or garlic-tomato sauce. Marsala or piccata sauce accompanies sautéed dishes, and pasta comes with several kinds of grilled shellfish (including shrimp scampi with tomatoes). The jovial crowd can get noisy, so ask for a table near the windows or on the small seasonal patio if you're in the mood for conversation. Grillfish is part of a small chain with roots in the Miami area and some locations around Washington, D.C.

162 Columbus Ave. (between Arlington and Berkeley Sts.). ☎ 617-357-1620. Internet: www.grillfish.com. *Reservations accepted only for parties of six or more. T: Arlington (Green Line); follow Arlington St. away from the Public Garden, cross Columbus Ave., turn right (at the Park Plaza Castle), and walk ½ block. Main courses: $10–$21. AE, DISC, MC, V. Sun–Mon 5:30–10 p.m.; Tues–Thurs 5:30–11 p.m.; Fri–Sat 5:30–midnight.*

The Helmand

$$ Cambridge/Kendall Square   AFGHAN

In Cambridge's United Nations of dining, the Helmand stands out. This restaurant offers the tasty food, friendly service, and reasonable prices of an ethnic restaurant in an elegant setting that might make you wonder what the catch is. (It's *too* popular, would be my grumpy answer.) Afghan cuisine is Middle Eastern with Indian and Pakistani influences, filling but not heavy, redolent of spices. Vegetarians will be happy here; meat accents many dishes rather than dominating. My favorite is baked pumpkin with meat sauce, but that's a tough decision — everything is flat-out delicious.

143 First St. (at Bent St.). ☎ 617-492-4646. Reservations recommended. T: Lechmere (Green Line); walk past rear of trolley, pass through tunnel on right, and go 6½ short blocks on First St., passing CambridgeSide Galleria mall. Main courses: $9–$17. AE, MC, V. Open: Sun–Thurs 5–10 p.m.; Fri–Sat 5–11 p.m.

Icarus

$$$$ South End   ECLECTIC

The most romantic restaurant in town (an insanely competitive category) is this subterranean hideaway, a grand space that abounds with personal touches. The regularly changing menu is equally quirky and equally enjoyable. Chef-owner Christopher Douglass simply transforms his fresh local ingredients. The no-nonsense descriptions (lemony grilled chicken with garlic and herbs, polenta with braised exotic mushrooms) can't do justice to the imaginative interplay of flavors and textures. Save room for an unbelievable dessert; even chocolate fiends love the fruit sorbets.

3 Appleton St. (off Tremont St.). ☎ *617-426-1790. Reservations recommended. T: Arlington (Green Line); follow Arlington St. away from the Public Garden, across the Mass. Pike. (about 6 blocks), bear right onto Tremont St., and go 1 long block. Or Back Bay (Orange Line); use Clarendon St. exit (at back of Forest Hills–bound train), turn right, walk 4 blocks, turn left onto Appleton St., and go 2 blocks. Parking: Valet. Main courses: $20–$33. AE, CB, DC, DISC, MC, V. Open: Mon–Thurs 6–10 p.m.; Fri 6–10:30 p.m.; Sat 5:30–10:30 p.m.; Sun 5:30–10 p.m. Closed Sun July–Aug.*

La Summa

$$ Downtown/North End   SOUTHERN ITALIAN

As newcomers push the North End up the *nouveau* scale, neighborhood favorites like La Summa tick along, offering homey food in a welcoming atmosphere. House-made pasta and desserts attract locals and savvy passersby to La Summa, which also serves terrific seafood and meat dishes. Check the specials board on the way in, and if lobster ravioli is on it, don't hesitate. Just be sure to save room for sweets.

30 Fleet St. ☎ *617-523-9503. Reservations recommended. T: Haymarket (Green or Orange Line); cross under Expressway, turn right, and follow Cross St. to Hanover St. Follow Hanover St. to Fleet St., turn right, and go 1½ blocks. Main courses: $11–$17. AE, CB, DC, DISC, MC, V. Open: Daily 4:30–10:30 p.m.*

Legal Sea Foods

$$$ Back Bay, Downtown/Waterfront, other locations   SEAFOOD

Out-of-towners arrive in Boston, unpack, and demand seafood. The ones who wind up here are in for a treat: the freshest seafood around. From its roots as a counter in a fish store, "Legal's" has grown into a sprawling chain that incorporates no-frills fillets and inventive preparations. This is the place for perennial favorites (lobsters the size of a laptop, every species of fish that's available fresh on the day you eat here) and seasonal specials (shad roe, soft-shelled crabs). Legal Sea Foods is the place for do-believe-the-hype clam and fish chowder, sublime raw-bar offerings, and even scrumptious desserts. This eatery is never quiet, and service is pleasant but somewhat slapdash — that's part of the experience.

Also part of the experience, until recently, was the long wait for a table. The Prudential Center branch takes reservations at lunch only, so if you can't abide waiting, go there. Or put your name on the list and see what *not* being an out-of-towner feels like.

Also at 255 State St. (☎ **617-227-3115**), 1 block from the New England Aquarium, Waterfront; 36 Park Sq., between Columbus Avenue and Stuart

Street, Back Bay (☎ **617-426-4444**); Copley Place, second level, Back Bay (☎ **617-266-7775**); and 5 Cambridge Center, Kendall Square, Cambridge (☎ **617-864-3400**).

800 Boylston St., in the Prudential Center. ☎ *617-266-6800. Internet:* www. legalseafoods.com. *Reservations recommended at lunch, not accepted at dinner. T: Prudential (Green Line E) or Copley (Green Line); follow Boylston St. 3 blocks, past the Boston Public Library. Main courses: Dinner $14–$25; lobster is market price. AE, CB, DC, DISC, MC, V. Open: Mon–Thurs 11 a.m.–10:30 p.m.; Fri–Sat 11 a.m.–11:30 p.m.; Sun noon–10 p.m.*

Le Gamin Cafe

$ South End   FRENCH

Everything old really is new again: Here's a classic French café in the trendy South End. The combination of top-notch food and reasonable prices makes Le Gamin a neighborhood favorite. Everything from ultra-rich hot chocolate to crackling-fresh salad is just what you'd expect; sandwiches with fillings you choose are just what you want. The loiterer-friendly atmosphere also makes Le Gamin a good choice for coffee or a glass of wine with a friend. This location is the first out-of-town branch of a small New York chain.

550 Tremont St. (at Waltham St.). ☎ *617-654-8969. Internet:* www.legamin.com. *Reservations not recommended. T: Back Bay (Orange Line); use Clarendon St. exit (at back of Forest Hills–bound train), turn right, and walk 5 blocks. Main courses: $4–$12. MC, V. Open: Mon–Fri 10 a.m.–midnight; Sat–Sun 8 a.m.–midnight.*

L'Espalier

$$$$ Back Bay   NEW ENGLAND AND FRENCH

Diners disappear into this elegant town house off Newbury Street like guests arriving at a dinner party, and in a way, that's just what they are. (Well, except for the pesky matter of money.) The gorgeous 19th-century dining rooms contrast pleasingly with chef and co-owner Frank McClelland's innovative, deliriously good food. French techniques and fresh local ingredients — seafood or game, unusual produce or artisan cheese — collide to produce unusual dishes that never cross the line into brain-teaser territory. The dessert cart is always worth a look, and this is one of the only places in town where the after-dinner cheese tray gets the attention it deserves.

30 Gloucester St. (off Newbury St.). ☎ *617-262-3023. Internet:* www.lespalier. com. *Reservations required. T: Hynes/ICA (Green Line B, C, or D); use Newbury St. exit, turn right, walk 2 blocks, and turn left. Parking: Valet. Prix fixe: $65 (four courses). Degustation menu (seven courses; full tables only): $82. AE, DISC, MC, V. Open: Mon–Sat 6–10 p.m.*

Les Zygomates

$$$ Downtown FRENCH BISTRO

A Parisian accent in the middle of the Big Dig, Les Zygomates *(lay zee-go-mat)* is a loose, lively antidote to the pandemonium outside. Primarily a wine bar, it serves an excellent selection by the bottle, glass, and 2-ounce taste. Classic but original, the food is an artful mix of local ingredients and bistro favorites, such as braised lamb shank with garlic puree. The quirky neighborhood (technically the Leather District) attracts business lunchers and a stylish dinner crowd that lingers for live jazz.

129 South St. (between Tufts and Beach Sts.; 2 blocks from South Station). ☎ *617-542-5108. Internet:* www.winebar.com. *Reservations recommended. T: South Station (Red Line); cross Atlantic Ave., turn left, walk 1 block to East St., turn right, and walk 1 block to South St. Or ask a construction worker. Parking: Valet at dinner only. Main courses: $12–$20; prix fixe lunch: $13; prix fixe dinner: (Sun–Thurs only) $19. AE, CB, DC, DISC, MC, V. Open: Mon–Fri 11 a.m.–1 a.m. (lunch menu until 2 p.m.); Sat 6 p.m.–1 a.m.*

Mamma Maria

$$$$ Downtown/North End NORTHERN ITALIAN

A fine-dining destination in a pasta-and-pizza neighborhood, Mamma Maria is the best restaurant in the North End. Plenty of competitors serve excellent food in no-frills settings, but they can't compete with this elegant town house a stone's throw from the Paul Revere House. The romantic atmosphere makes it a popular place for marriage proposals and anniversary dinners. The exquisite cuisine, which changes seasonally, always includes fabulous seafood dishes, daily pasta specials, and fork-tender osso buco. You won't even miss the pizza.

3 North Sq. (at Prince St.). ☎ *617-523-0077. Internet:* www.mammamaria.com. *Reservations recommended. T: Haymarket (Green or Orange Line); cross under Expressway, turn right, follow Cross St. to Hanover St., and turn left. Walk 2 full blocks, go right onto Prince St., and walk 1 block. Parking: Valet. Main courses: $19–$35. AE, DC, DISC, MC, V. Open: Sun–Thurs 5–9:30 p.m.; Fri–Sat 5–10:30 p.m.*

Piccola Venezia

$$ Downtown/North End SOUTHERN ITALIAN

Piccola Venezia probably loses some business because it's on the first block of the North End's main drag. Banish "maybe we'll find something better" from your mind — you won't be sorry. The menu combines home-style specialties with less red-sauce–intensive options, all in generous quantities. To give you some idea of the scope, tripe is a house specialty, polenta with mushrooms is a great starter, and a recent daily special of seafood lasagna made a delectable dinner *and* a filling lunch the next day. It's a cliché, but spaghetti and meatballs is a good choice, too.

263 Hanover St. ☎ *617-523-3888. Reservations suggested at dinner. T: Haymarket (Green or Orange Line); cross under Expressway, turn right, follow Cross St. to Hanover St., turn left, and walk ½ block. Main courses: $10–$20; lunch specialties: $5–$8. AE, DISC, MC, V. Open: Daily 11 a.m.–10 p.m. (lunch menu weekdays until 4 p.m.).*

Pizzeria Regina

$ North End ITALIAN

The only Boston pizza place that competes with New York in quality and ambience is Regina's. True, this restaurant is hard to find and the line can be long (though it moves quickly). The too-good-to-be-true atmosphere is the real thing, though, right down to waitresses who call you "honey" when they warn you not to burn your mouth on the bubbling-hot pie that just arrived. The pizza, fresh from the brick oven, is that hot. And that good.

11½ Thacher St. (at N. Margin St.). ☎ *617-227-0765. Internet:* www. pizzeriaregina.com. *Reservations not accepted. T: Haymarket (Green or Orange Line); cross under Expressway, go straight onto Salem St. for 3 blocks, turn left onto Cooper St., take next right onto N. Margin St., and go 2 blocks to Thacher St. Pizza: $9–$16. No credit cards. Open: Mon–Thurs 11 a.m.–11:30 p.m.; Fri–Sat 11 a.m.–midnight; Sun noon–11 p.m.*

Redbones

$$ Cambridge/Somerville BARBECUE

"New England barbecue" — doesn't exactly roll off the tongue, does it? But you'll want it rolling right into your mouth after just one whiff of this place. The festive crowd and whimsical decor make an appealing first impression, and the down-home food backs it up. Expatriate Southerners, ravenous college students, and celebratory families relish the lively atmosphere and authentic fare. Barbecue in all its incarnations shares the menu with Southern specialties like catfish and pecan pie — all in abundant portions. Try to get a table at street level, not in the barlike space downstairs. Suck down a beer, make a dent in a pile of pulled pork or baby back ribs, and you'll understand why there's a stack of paper napkins on every table.

55 Chester St. (off Elm St.), Somerville. ☎ *617-628-2200. Internet:* www. redbonesbbq.com. *Reservations accepted only for parties of 11 or more, Sun–Thurs. T: Davis (Red Line); right at turnstiles, right at exit, walk 3 blocks on Elm St., and turn right onto Chester St. Main courses: $7–$15. No credit cards. Open: Sun–Thurs noon–10:30 p.m., Fri–Sat noon–11:30 p.m. (lunch menu until 4 p.m.).*

Rialto

$$$$ Cambridge/Harvard Square MEDITERRANEAN

Rialto is my favorite Boston-area restaurant (*Gourmet* magazine's, too, as of October 2000). This restaurant has the sleek-chic vibe you'd expect at the Charles Hotel, but never to the point of feeling snooty. Rialto assembles the elements that make a memorable dining experience unforgettable: a glamorous but comfortable space, attentive service, and, most important, Jody Adams's amazing food. She makes good use of seasonal local products, creating an overall effect of a sun-drenched field overlooking the Mediterranean. Try any seafood dish, any vegetarian option — anything, really. Now you're *so* cutting edge.

1 Bennett St. (in the Charles Hotel). ☎ *617-661-5050. Reservations suggested. T: Harvard (Red Line); follow Brattle St. 2 blocks, bear left onto Eliot St., and go 2 blocks. Parking: Valet and validated. Main courses: $20–$33. AE, DC, MC, V. Open: Sun–Thurs 5:30 p.m.; Fri–Sat 5:30–11 p.m.*

S&S Restaurant

$ Cambridge/Inman Square   AMERICAN

The best brunch in the area draws huge crowds to this Inman Square standby, which is also a fine place for a tasty meal during the week. Never mind the long walk from the T — on the way back, you'll be working off calories from the huge omelets, inventive pancakes and waffles, and excellent baked goods. On weekends, arrive early or schedule your day to allow for waiting time (and people watching). During non-brunch hours, the traditional deli menu includes breakfast anytime.

1334 Cambridge St. (at Hampshire St.). ☎ *617-354-0777. Reservations not accepted. T: Central (Red Line); turn right on Prospect St. (at Starbucks), go 5 blocks to Cambridge St., and turn left. Or Harvard (Red Line); use Church St. exit (at front of Alewife-bound train), and turn left at turnstiles; then take no. 69 (Harvard–Lechmere) bus to Inman Square or walk 7/10 mile up Cambridge St. (A $5 cab ride.) Main courses: $3–$11. No credit cards. Open: Mon–Sat 7 a.m.–midnight, Sun 8 a.m.–midnight (brunch weekends until 4 p.m.).*

Sel de la Terre

$$$ Downtown/Waterfront   MEDITERRANEAN

The atmosphere at this upscale-but-not-too-upscale cousin of L'Espalier may be the neatest trick in town: It's smack in the middle of the Big Dig, and you'd never know it. Not that you'll imagine you're in Provence, but that's clearly where executive chef Geoff Gardner's heart is. He transforms fresh local ingredients (especially seafood) into luscious food that's flavor-packed but never overwhelming. The crowd is businesslike at lunch, chic at dinner. And you don't even need to ruin your appetite by filling up on the delicious breads — they're available for purchase at the *boulangerie* near the entrance.

255 State St. (at Atlantic Ave.; 1 block from the New England Aquarium). ☎ *617-720-1300. Internet:* www.seldelaterre.com. *Reservations suggested. T: State (Blue or Orange Line) or Aquarium (Blue Line), if it's open; walk 4 blocks toward the harbor on State St. Main courses: $21. AE, DISC, MC, V. Open: Daily 11:30 a.m.–2:30 p.m. and 5:30–10 p.m.*

Hunting grounds: Restaurant-rich neighborhoods

Boston and Cambridge each boast a number of areas where hungry people can scout around and emerge well fed. You don't want to be the first one through the door in these neighborhoods (trust me, the empty places are empty for a reason), but don't let a less-than-full room stop you, especially on a weeknight. Here's a list of Boston's neighborhoods and what to expect in each area's eateries:

✔ Head to the **North End** (Haymarket stop on the Green or Orange Line) for Italian food of every description in every price range. Ordinarily I can't abide waiting, but in this area, lines are good. You'll see some locals in restaurants on high-traffic Hanover and Salem streets, but the neighborhood places are on the little side streets.

✔ **Chinatown** (which has its own Orange Line stop) is another promising neighborhood, and not just for Chinese food. Reasonably priced Asian cuisine abounds on Beach Street and the narrow streets that branch off it between Washington Street (where the T stop is) and the Surface Artery (where the landmark Chinatown Arch is).

✔ Generally more expensive and more upscale is the **South End** (Back Bay stop on the Orange Line), home to some big names and big budgets. Still, the South End is a neighborhood like any other, and people who live here need to eat, too — check out the area around Tremont and Clarendon Streets, or stroll over to Washington Street.

✔ In Cambridge, **Harvard Square** (Red Line to Harvard) offers a good mix of places where students go with other students and places where visiting parents give their kids a break from the dining hall.

✔ **Central Square** is a social and culinary melting pot, with food from almost every corner of the globe. Follow Mass. Ave. in either direction from the T stop (Red Line to Central) and you'll probably find something that gets your nose's attention.

✔ Take the Red Line to Central and walk up Prospect Street (turn the corner at Starbucks) to **Inman Square,** where you'll find everything from Brazilian barbecue to Korean food within about 5 blocks.

Tea-Tray in the Sky

$ Cambridge AMERICAN

Just walking into this little tearoom gives me a buzz, and I'm never sure if it's the caffeine or the trippy, *Alice's Adventures in Wonderland* décor. The mind-blowing selection of tea includes the pedestrian and the unusual, and it complements scrumptious food and baked goods (made in-house). The pastries can substitute for "real" food, but they don't have to — unlike the pedestrian fare at some beverage-oriented places, the soups, salads, and focaccia sandwiches are outstanding. If you're shopping in Harvard and Porter squares, a stop here is a must.

1796 Mass. Ave. (at Lancaster St.). ☎ 617-492-8327. Reservations not accepted. T: Porter (Red Line); walk 4 blocks south on Mass. Ave. Main courses: $5–$13. AE, DISC, MC, V. Open: Tues–Fri 10 a.m.–10 p.m.; Sat 10 a.m.–11 p.m.; Sun 10 a.m.–7 p.m. (closed Sun in summer).

Index of Restaurants by Neighborhood

Back Bay

Aujourd'hui (Contemporary American, $$$$)
Café Jaffa (Middle Eastern, $)
Casa Romero (Classic Mexican, $$$)
The Elephant Walk (French and Cambodian, $$$)
Grill 23 & Bar (American, $$$$)
Legal Sea Foods (Seafood $$$)
L'Espalier (New England and French, $$$$)

Cambridge

Bartley's Burger Cottage (American, $)
The Blue Room (Eclectic, $$$)
Border Café (Southwestern, $$)
Chez Henri (French and Cuban, $$$$)
Dalí (Spanish, $$)
The Helmand (Afghan, $$)
Legal Sea Foods (Seafood, $$$)
Redbones (Barbecue, $$)
Rialto (Mediterranean, $$$$)
S&S Restaurant (American, $)
Tea-Tray in the Sky (American, $)

Chinatown

Buddha's Delight (Vegetarian Vietnamese, $)
Grand Chau Chow (Cantonese and Chinese, $$)

Downtown

Durgin-Park (New England, $$)
Legal Sea Foods (Seafood, $$$)
Les Zygomates (French Bistro, $$$)
Sel de la Terre (Mediterranean, $$$)

North End

Billy Tse Restaurant (Chinese/Pan-Asian, $$)
Daily Catch (Seafood and Southern Italian, $$)
Giacomo's (Seafood and Southern Italian, $$$)
La Summa (Southern Italian, $$)
Mamma Maria (Northern Italian, $$$$)
Piccola Venezia (Southern Italian, $$)
Pizzeria Regina (Italian, $)

South End

Grillfish (Seafood, $$)
Icarus (Eclectic, $$$$)
Le Gamin Café (French, $)

Index of Restaurants by Cuisine

American

Aujourd'hui (Back Bay, $$$$)
Bartley's Burger Cottage (Cambridge Harvard Square, $)
Durgin-Park (Downtown, $$)
Grill 23 & Bar (Back Bay, $$$$)
L'Espalier (Back Bay, $$$$)
Redbones (Cambridge/Somerville, $$)

S&S Restaurant (Cambridge/Inman
    Square, $)
Tea-Tray in the Sky (Cambridge, $)

Asian

Billy Tse Restaurant (North End, $$)
Buddha's Delight (Chinatown, $)
The Elephant Walk (Back Bay/Kenmore
    Square, $$$)
Grand Chau Chow (Chinatown, $$)

Eclectic

The Blue Room (Cambridge/Kendall
    Square, $$$)
Icarus (South End, $$$$)

French

Chez Henri (Cambridge/Harvard
    Square, $$$$)
The Elephant Walk (Back Bay/Kenmore
    Square, $$$)
Le Gamin Café (South End, $)
L'Espalier (Back Bay, $$$$)
Les Zygomates (Downtown, $$$)

Italian

Daily Catch (North End, $$)
Giacomo's (North End, $$$)
La Summa (North End, $$)
Mamma Maria (North End, $$$$)
Piccola Venezia (North End, $$)
Pizzeria Regina (North End, $)

Mediter-ranean

Dalí (Cambridge/Somerville, $$)
Rialto (Cambridge/Harvard
    Square, $$$$)
Sel de la Terre (Downtown, $$$)

Seafood

Daily Catch (North End, $$)
Giacomo's (North End, $$$)
Grillfish (South End, $$)
Legal Sea Foods (Back Bay and other
    locations, $$$)

South of the Border

Border Café (Cambridge/Harvard
    Square, $$)
Chez Henri (Cambridge/Harvard
    Square, $$$$)
Casa Romero (Back Bay, $$$)

Other Ethnic

Café Jaffa (Middle Eastern, Back Bay, $)
The Helmand (Afghan,
    Cambridge/Kendall Square, $$)

Index of Restaurants by Price

$$$$

Aujourd'hui (Contemporary American,
    Back Bay)
Chez Henri (French and Cuban,
    Cambridge/Harvard Square)

Grill 23 & Bar (American, Back Bay)
Icarus (Eclectic, South End)
L'Espalier (New England and French,
    Back Bay)
Mamma Maria (Northern Italian,
    North End)
Rialto (Mediterranean,
    Cambridge/Harvard Square)

$$$

The Blue Room (Eclectic,
    Cambridge/Kendall Square)
Casa Romero (Classic Mexican, Back Bay)

The Elephant Walk (French and Cambodian, Back Bay/Kenmore Square)

Giacomo's (Seafood and Southern Italian, North End)

Legal Sea Foods (Seafood, Back Bay and other locations)

Les Zygomates (French Bistro, Downtown)

Sel de la Terre (Mediterranean, Downtown/Waterfront)

$$

Billy Tse Restaurant (Chinese/Pan-Asian, North End)

Border Café (Southwestern, Cambridge/Harvard Square)

Daily Catch (Seafood and Southern Italian, North End)

Dalí (Spanish, Cambridge/Somerville)

Durgin-Park (New England, Downtown)

Grand Chau Chow (Cantonese and Chinese, Chinatown)

Grillfish (Seafood, South End)

The Helmand (Afghan, Cambridge/Kendall Square)

La Summa (Southern Italian, North End)

Piccola Venezia (Southern Italian, North End)

Redbones (Barbecue, Cambridge/Somerville)

$

Bartley's Burger Cottage (American, Cambridge/Harvard Square)

Buddha's Delight (Vegetarian Vietnamese, Chinatown)

Café Jaffa (Middle Eastern, Back Bay)

Le Gamin Café (French, South End)

Pizzeria Regina (Italian, North End)

S&S Restaurant (American, Cambridge/Inman Square)

Tea-Tray in the Sky (American, Cambridge)

Chapter 15

On the Lighter Side: Top Picks for Snacks and Meals on the Go

● ●

In This Chapter

▶ Get out! Picnic food (and where to eat it)

▶ Chain links: Local favorites

▶ Culinary history: Your Boston tea party

▶ Midday madness: Dim sum

▶ Addictive substances: Coffee and ice cream

● ●

*M*ultiple courses, starched tablecloths, and courtly service have their time and their place; that's usually *not* in the middle of a busy day of sightseeing. Here you'll get the scoop on grabbing a bite (outdoors and indoors), plus pointers on afternoon tea, dim sum, coffee, and ice cream.

For the locations of the places mentioned in this chapter, see the "Boston Dining" or "Cambridge Dining" maps in Chapter 14.

Picking the Picnic Option

With the harbor here and the river there, Boston and Cambridge offer acres of waterfront space that's perfect for picnicking, and plenty of places to outfit your metaphorical picnic basket. Here are some airy options:

> ✔ Gathering your food for your outdoor feast is a "picnic" (sorry 'bout that one) at the **Colonnade food court** at Faneuil Hall Marketplace (T: Government Center [Green or Blue Line] or Haymarket [Orange Line]), which offers enough variety to satisfy

even a large group. When you're set, cross Atlantic Avenue (under the Expressway) and seek out the plaza at the end of Long Wharf or the benches and lawns of **Christopher Columbus Park.**

✔ In the North End, **Il Panino Express,** 266 Hanover St. (T: Haymarket [Green or Orange Line]; ☎ 617-720-5720), cranks out superb sandwiches as well as pasta dishes and pizza. Cross Hanover Street to Richmond Street and follow it 4 blocks downhill to **Christopher Columbus Park.**

✔ At the foot of Beacon Hill (near the Esplanade, a destination for concerts and movies all summer), you'll find **Savenor's Super-market,** 160 Charles St. (T: Charles/MGH [Red Line]; ☎ 617-723-6328). Load up on gourmet provisions and head across the footbridge to the **Charles River Basin.**

✔ Harvard Square also affords easy access to the Charles. **Stuff-Its,** 8½ Eliot St. (near Mt. Auburn St.; T: Harvard [Red Line]; ☎ 617-497-2220), is a great place to load up on "strollers." Sandwiches rolled up in pita bread were the specialty here long before they were trendy — in fact, they're so good they might have started the trend. Stake out a bench on the riverbank or a comfy spot at **John F. Kennedy Park,** at Kennedy Street and Memorial Drive.

Bound for Chains

National chains abound, but really, can't you do that at home? Two exceptions are especially useful if you're traveling with teenagers:

✔ The **Hard Rock Cafe,** 131 Clarendon St. (off Stuart Street, in the Back Bay; T: Back Bay [Orange Line]; ☎ 617-424-ROCK) is what it is. If you don't know what to expect, the kids can fill you in.

✔ The original **House of Blues** is at 96 Winthrop St. (off John F. Kennedy Street, Harvard Square, Cambridge; T: Harvard [Red Line]; ☎ 617-491-BLUE). Live music by talented locals and big-name visitors is the drawing card here; the eclectic menu includes pizza and inventive pasta dishes, with Southern specialties at the Sunday gospel brunch. (See the listing in Chapter 23 for a more complete review.)

Local chains offer a somewhat less generic experience. Check out my favorite picks:

✔ The upscale pizzerias of **Bertucci's** appeal to both adults and kids. The little ones can concentrate on the wood-burning brick ovens, and their caddies can exclaim over the plain and fancy pizzas and pastas. Handy branches are at Faneuil Hall Marketplace (behind Abercrombie & Fitch; ☎ 617-227-7889); 43 Stanhope St. (around the corner from the Hard Rock Café, Back Bay; T: Back Bay

[Orange Line]; ☎ **617-247-6161**), and 21 Brattle St. (Harvard Square, Cambridge; T: Harvard [Red Line]; ☎ **617-864-4748**).

✔ **Cosí Sandwich Bar** is a New York–based chain with a European flair. The pick-your-own-fillings sandwich creations aren't cheap (expect to spend at least $6 a head), but they're filling and delicious. Find them at 53 State St. (T: State [Blue or Orange Line]; ☎ **617-723-4447**); 14 Milk St. (off Washington Street; T: Downtown Crossing [Red or Orange Line]; ☎ **617-426-7565**); and 133 Federal St. (T: South Station [Red Line]; ☎ **617-292-2674**).

✔ Time-sensitive sightseers and downtown workers benefit equally from the lickety-split self-service salad bars at **Souper Salad,** where you can eat in or take out. Branches near the Freedom Trail are at 3 Center Plaza (T: Governement Center [Green or Blue Line]; ☎ **617-367-6067**); 82 Summer St. (T: Downtown Crossing [Red or Orange Line]; ☎ **617-426-6834**); and 103 State St. (T: State [Blue or Orange Line]; ☎ **617-227-9151**).

Taking Tea Time

The original Boston Tea Party, a colonial rebellion, couldn't be further from the experience of proper afternoon tea in a posh hotel. Finger sandwiches, pastries, scones, clotted cream, and other niceties make this the most polite way I know to make a pig of yourself. All three of these hotels are within easy walking distance of the Arlington T stop (Green Line). You'll need a reservation for the first two, especially on weekends. Put on your daintiest attitude and "tea" off at one or more of the following:

✔ The Four Seasons Hotel, 200 Boylston St., serves tea in **The Bristol Lounge** (☎ **617-351-2053**) daily from 3 to 4:30 p.m. Expect to pay $20 per person.

✔ The Ritz-Carlton, 15 Arlington St. (☎ **617-536-5700**), may be closed for renovations when you visit. If it's open, put on your best behavior and head to the refined **Ritz Lounge** between 3 and 5:30 p.m. Tea service will cost you about $20 a person.

✔ For about half the price of the others but nearly as much elegance, try **Swans Court,** 64 Arlington St. (in the lobby of the Boston Park Plaza Hotel; ☎ **617-426-2000**), daily from 3 to 5 p.m.

Bao, Wow: Dim Sum

Dim sum, a traditional Chinese midday meal, is a perfect way to sample a variety of small dishes. To get the most out of it, go on a weekend with at least one other person. Waitresses make the rounds, pushing carts loaded with *bao* (steamed buns), steamed and fried dumplings, spring rolls, sweets, and more. Point at what you want (unless you know Chinese), and the waitress stamps your check with the symbol of the dish; most cost about $1 to $3. For around $10 per person, it's a satisfying experience — but if you don't care for fried food, pork, or shrimp, you might feel more deprived than satisfied.

The top three dim sum destinations, all near the Chinatown T stop (Orange Line):

- **Empire Garden Restaurant,** 690–698 Washington St., 2nd floor (☎ 617-482-8898).

- **Golden Palace Restaurant,** 14 Tyler St. (☎ 617-423-4565).

- **China Pearl,** 9 Tyler St., 2nd floor (☎ 617-426-4338).

Espresso Express

Boston and Cambridge overflow with congenial coffee outlets (college and stimulants just seem to go together), but the classic caffeine-related experience is a spell in a North End *caffè*. Check out the pastries, order an espresso or cappuccino (decaf, if you insist), sit back, and watch the world go by. All of these coffeehouses keep long hours; all but Mike's permit smoking. To get to the North End, take the T to Haymarket (Green or Orange Line) and cross under the Expressway.

My favorite destinations include **Caffè Graffiti,** 307 Hanover St. (☎ 617-367-3016); **Caffè dello Sport,** 308 Hanover St. (☎ 617-523-5063); and **Caffè Vittoria,** 296 Hanover St. (☎ 617-227-7606). **Paradiso Caffè,** 255 Hanover St. (☎ 617-742-1768), is *the* place to watch big European soccer matches. **Mike's Pastry,** 300 Hanover St. (☎ 617-742-3050), is a popular bakeshop with table service. Find what you want in the case; then sit down and order.

Ice Cream

The New Yorker in me still can't believe the year-round popularity of ice cream all over the Boston area. (That's not a complaint, mind you.) After encyclopedic research and great personal sacrifice, I can attest to the quality of all of the following.

In the Back Bay:

- **Emack & Bolio's,** 290 Newbury St. (T: Hynes/ICA [Green Line B, C, or D]; ☎ 617-247-8772).

- **Herrell's,** 224 Newbury St. (T: Hynes/ICA [Green Line B, C, or D]; ☎ 617-236-0857).

- ✓ **JP Licks,** 352 Newbury St. (T: Hynes/ICA [Green Line B, C, or D]; ☎ **617-236-1666**).

- ✓ **Ben & Jerry's,** 174 Newbury St. (T: Copley [Green Line]; ☎ **617-536-5456**).

In Cambridge:

- ✓ **Herrell's,** 15 Dunster St., Harvard Square (T: Harvard [Red Line]; ☎ **617-497-2179**).

- ✓ **Toscanini's,** 899 Main St., Central Square (T: Central [Red Line]; ☎ **617-491-5877**) and 1310 Mass. Ave., Harvard Square (T: Harvard [Red Line]; ☎ **617-354-9350**).

- ✓ **Christina's,** 1255 Cambridge St., Inman Square (T: Central [Red Line], turn right onto Prospect St. (at Starbucks) and go 5 blocks; ☎ **617-492-7021**).

Part V
Exploring Boston

"We've seen the 'Cheers' bar, the 'St. Elsewhere' hospital, and the court house featured in 'The Practice'. I'm not sure why, but I feel like just going back to the hotel and watching TV."

In this part . . .

Now I reach the heart of the matter, the singular experiences and activities that led you to choose Boston over every other potential destination. (And if the meeting planners, the bride and groom, or your parents chose for you, think of this as the "maybe it won't be so bad" section.)

You can approach Boston as a history lesson, an art gallery, a seafood buffet, or even a giant shopping center. You can concentrate on a specific interest or skip around. You can spend a day, a weekend, or a month, and only scratch the surface. Weigh the innumerable options, don't try to do too much, and soon you'll be on your way to a good time. Here's the information that will help you mix and match a trip that's just right for you.

Chapter 16

Boston's Top Sights

●　●

In This Chapter

▶ The most popular destinations and entertaining activities

▶ All the details to help you plan a rewarding visit

▶ A road map for the Freedom Trail

●　●

*B*oston stimulates all your senses: You see great paintings and sculpture, hear classical and popular music, taste ocean-fresh seafood, smell the perfume of the Public Garden flowerbeds, and feel the breeze off the harbor ruffling your hair. The chapters preceding this one addressed getting to Boston and finding shelter and food after you arrive. Now, how will you spend your time? This chapter describes the most popular attractions and contains a separate section on the world-famous Freedom Trail. (Turn to Chapter 17 for descriptions of more specialized experiences.) Also included is an index that organizes the city's top sights by neighborhood.

The best thing you can do for yourself at this stage is to forget that you know the words *should* and *ought*. Yes, you can immerse yourself in history, art, science, or any number of other topics. But if a certain subject feels more obligatory than fun, it's probably not a great option.

Listen to yourself (and me, of course), not to the friends who say that you *must* see or do something that sounds, to you, as dull as watching paint dry. You may want to practice smiling and saying, "That sounded great, but there just wasn't time." (Your well-meaning neighbor doesn't need to know that you're thinking, "and there won't be, even if I live to be 100.")

For locations of the various attractions described below, see the "Boston Attractions" or "Cambridge Attractions" maps in this chapter, unless otherwise noted. (There are also attractions from Chapter 17 listed on these maps as well.)

Time- and money-saving suggestions

Here are two good options for visitors spending more than a day or two:

✔ The **Boston CityPass** includes tickets to the Isabella Stewart Gardner Museum, Kennedy Library, John Hancock Observatory, New England Aquarium, Museum of Fine Arts, and Museum of Science. The price — at press time, adults $30.25; seniors $22.25; youths 12 to 17 $14 — offers a 50 percent savings if you visit all six attractions (and you don't need to wait in line!). The passes, good for 9 days from the date of purchase, are on sale at participating attractions, at the Boston Common and Prudential Center visitors information centers, through the Greater Boston Convention & Visitors Bureau (☎ **800-SEE-BOSTON**), through some hotel concierge desks, and from www.citypass.net.

✔ The **Arts/Boston coupon book** (☎ **617-482-2849**; Internet: www.boston.com/artsboston) includes discounts to museums and attractions such as the Museum of Fine Arts, New England Aquarium, Kennedy Library, Massachusetts Bay Lines cruises, and Beantown and Old Town trolley tours. The coupon book isn't worth the money (currently $9) for single travelers because many of the coupons are two-for-one deals. Arts/Boston coupon books are on sale at BosTix booths at Faneuil Hall Marketplace (on the south side of Faneuil Hall) and in Copley Square (at the corner of Boylston and Dartmouth Streets).

The Top Attractions

Dreams of Freedom

Downtown

Explore Boston's immigrant history at the city's newest attraction, a multimedia experience that covers everyone from the Puritans to the folks alighting from planes today. The artifacts, photographs, backdrops, and re-creations of other elements of immigration (such as a ship's hold) make the center as entertaining as it is informative. Set aside at least 90 minutes to make your way through the exhibits with virtual host Benjamin Franklin.

Pause as you enter or leave to check out the second-floor facade, which honors your tour guide: It reads "Birthplace of Franklin."

1 Milk St. (off Washington St.). ☎ *617-338-6022. Internet:* www.dreamsoffreedom. org. *T: Downtown Crossing (Red or Orange Line); follow Washington St. past Filene's for 2 blocks. Admission: $7.50 adults, $3.50 children 6–16, free for children under 6. Open: Daily 9:30 a.m.–6 p.m.*

Faneuil Hall Marketplace

Downtown

The city's most popular attraction is this agreeable amalgam of recreation, retail, and restaurants. Brick plazas and plenty of outdoor seating surround the five-building "festival market" complex, which buzzes with activity from just past dawn till well past dark in pleasant weather year-round. Dozens of stores, shops, boutiques, and pushcarts share space with restaurants, bars, and food counters.

The marketplace is busiest in the summer and fall; these seasons are peak travel times when street performers and musicians make the rounds. The shopping ranges from generic to quirky, the dining from fast to fancy. The central building, **Quincy Market,** contains a food court that runs the length of the building. You don't need to spend a penny to enjoy the fun, though: Between buskers and visitors from all over the world, the marketplace also offers great people watching. True, it's touristy, especially in warm weather — but sometimes you just need to relax and let your inner tourist look around.

See "The Freedom Trail" section in this chapter for information about **Faneuil Hall.**

Between North, Congress, and State Sts. and I-93. ☎ *617-338-2323. T: Government Center (Green or Blue Line); cross the plaza, walk down the stairs, and cross Congress St. Or Haymarket (Orange Line); follow Congress St. (with I-93 on your left) for 2 to 3 blocks. Open: Marketplace Mon–Sat 10 a.m.–9 p.m.; Sun noon–6 p.m. Food court opens earlier; restaurant hours vary.*

Harvard University

Cambridge

It's old, it's famous, it educated a lot of notable people — that describes dozens of institutions, including this one. What draws visitors to the Harvard campus is the mystique of the country's oldest (1636) and best-known college, alma mater of **five** American presidents. The heart of the campus, two hopelessly picturesque quadrangles known as **Harvard Yard** (or simply, the Yard), sits behind the brick walls that run along Mass. Ave. and Quincy and Cambridge Streets.

The Yard is the oldest part of the campus and contains Harvard's oldest building, **Massachusetts Hall** (1720), home to the university president's office. Also in the Yard, in front of University Hall, you'll find the **John Harvard Statue** (1884), a magnet for photographers from all over the world. Campus legend gives the nickname "the Statue of Three Lies" to the sculpture, whose inscription reads "John Harvard — Founder — 1638." The truth: The college dates to 1636; Harvard bestowed money and his library on the fledgling institution, but wasn't *the* founder; and this isn't John Harvard, anyway. Sculptor Daniel Chester French's model reputedly was either a descendant of Harvard's or a student.

Across Mass. Ave., the Events & Information Center distributes maps and self-guided tour directions and has a bulletin board that lists campus activities. You may also want to visit the university's art and science museums; see Chapter 17 for more information.

Boston Attractions

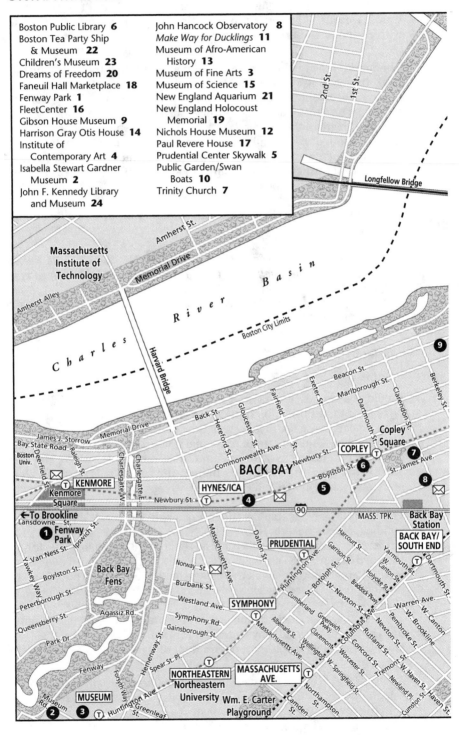

Boston Public Library **6**
Boston Tea Party Ship
& Museum **22**
Children's Museum **23**
Dreams of Freedom **20**
Faneuil Hall Marketplace **18**
Fenway Park **1**
FleetCenter **16**
Gibson House Museum **9**
Harrison Gray Otis House **14**
Institute of
Contemporary Art **4**
Isabella Stewart Gardner
Museum **2**
John F. Kennedy Library
and Museum **24**

John Hancock Observatory **8**
Make Way for Ducklings **11**
Museum of Afro-American
History **13**
Museum of Fine Arts **3**
Museum of Science **15**
New England Aquarium **21**
New England Holocaust
Memorial **19**
Nichols House Museum **12**
Paul Revere House **17**
Prudential Center Skywalk **5**
Public Garden/Swan
Boats **10**
Trinity Church **7**

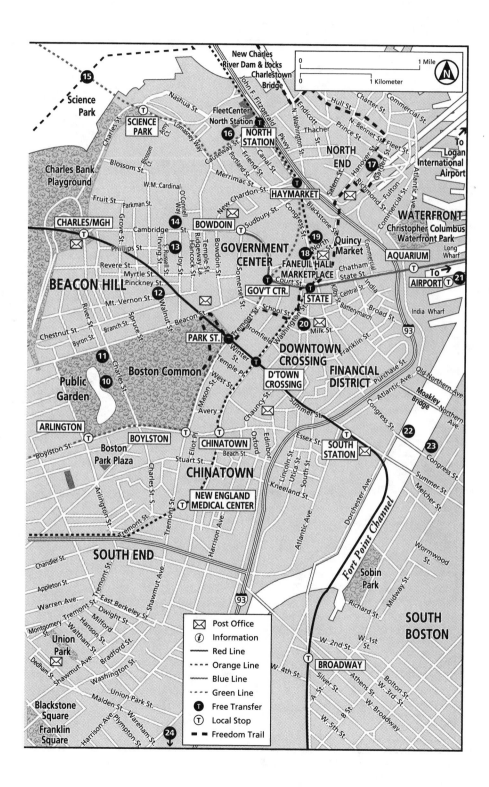

New Charles
River Dam & Locks
Charlestown
Bridge

0   1 Mile
0   1 Kilometer

15 Science Park

SCIENCE PARK

FleetCenter
North Station
16 NORTH STATION

NORTH END

17 To Logan International Airport

Charles Bank Playground

HAYMARKET

CHARLES/MGH

14 BOWDOIN

GOVERNMENT CENTER

13

19 Quincy Market

18 FANEUIL HALL MARKETPLACE

WATERFRONT
Christopher Columbus Waterfront Park
Long Wharf

AQUARIUM

BEACON HILL

12

GOV'T CTR.

STATE

To AIRPORT **21**

India Wharf

PARK ST.

20 Milk St.

DOWNTOWN CROSSING

FINANCIAL DISTRICT

11

Boston Common

Public Garden **10**

ARLINGTON

D'TOWN CROSSING

Moakley Bridge

BOYLSTON
Boston Park Plaza

CHINATOWN

SOUTH STATION

22

23

CHINATOWN

NEW ENGLAND MEDICAL CENTER

SOUTH END

Fort Point Channel

Sobin Park

SOUTH BOSTON

Union Park

Blackstone Square

Franklin Square

BROADWAY

24

⊠ Post Office
ⓘ Information
— Red Line
---- Orange Line
— Blue Line
---- Green Line
● Free Transfer
Ⓣ Local Stop
■ ■ Freedom Trail

Cambridge Attractions

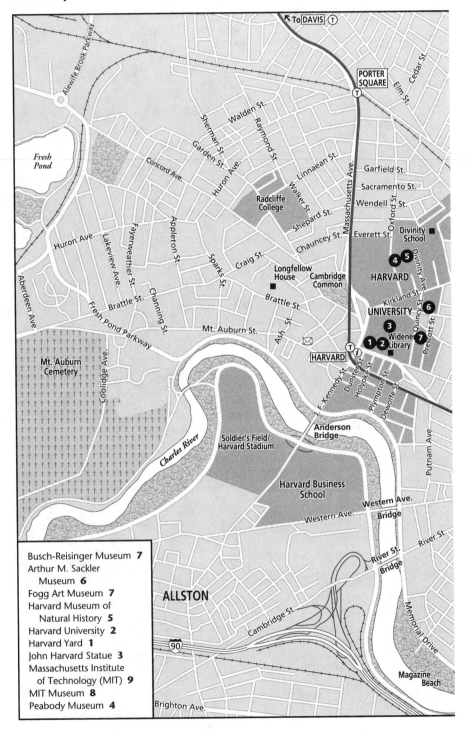

Busch-Reisinger Museum **7**
Arthur M. Sackler
 Museum **6**
Fogg Art Museum **7**
Harvard Museum of
 Natural History **5**
Harvard University **2**
Harvard Yard **1**
John Harvard Statue **3**
Massachusetts Institute
 of Technology (MIT) **9**
MIT Museum **8**
Peabody Museum **4**

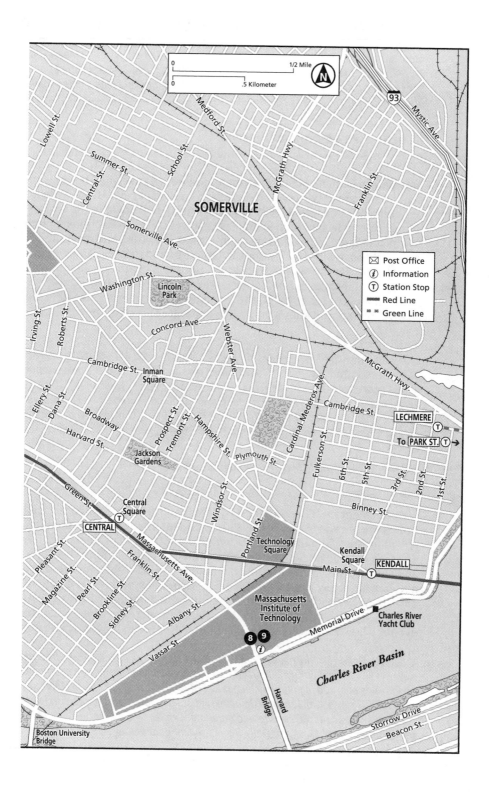

Events & Information Center: Holyoke Center, 1350 Mass. Ave. ☎ 617-495-1573. Internet: www.harvard.edu. *T: Harvard (Red Line). Open: Information Center Mon–Sat 9 a.m.–5 p.m.; Sun noon–5 p.m. Free guided tours four times a day Mon–Sat and twice on Sun during the summer; during school year (except vacations), twice a day on weekdays and once on Sat. Call for exact times; reservations aren't necessary.*

Isabella Stewart Gardner Museum

Fenway

Arts patron Isabella Stewart Gardner (1840–1924) designed her magnificent home in the style of a 15th-century Venetian palace. After her death, her home became a gorgeous museum — and a testament to the timeless judgment of a fascinating, iconoclastic woman. The collections include European, American, and Asian painting and sculpture, and furniture and architectural details from European churches and palaces. Allow at least 2 hours to peruse works by Titian, Botticelli, Raphael, Rembrandt, Matisse, James McNeill Whistler, and John Singer Sargent. Under the terms of Mrs. Gardner's will, the arrangement of the galleries does not change, but special shows go up in a separate space two or three times a year.

280 The Fenway (at Museum Rd., off Huntington Ave.). ☎ 617-566-1401. Internet: www.boston.com/gardner. *T: Museum (Green Line E); walk 2 blocks straight ahead (away from Huntington Ave.). Admission: $11 adults weekends, $10 adults weekdays, $7 seniors, $5 college students with ID, $3 college students on Wed, and free for children under 18. Open: Tues–Sun 11 a.m.–5 p.m. and some Mon holidays. Closed Mon, Jan 1, Thanksgiving, and Dec 25.*

John F. Kennedy Library and Museum

Dorchester

A magnificent building designed by I. M. Pei, the Kennedy Library celebrates the life and legacy of the 35th president. History buffs will want to spend at least 90 minutes exploring exhibits that recall "Camelot." The displays include audio and video recordings, replicas of the Oval Office and the attorney general's office, a film about the Cuban missile crisis, and imaginatively displayed documents and memorabilia. A 17-minute film about Kennedy's early life introduces the museum, which regularly updates its displays and schedules special exhibits, lectures, and other events. Allow for travel time — 30 minutes from or to downtown Boston.

Columbia Point (off Morrissey Blvd.). ☎ 877-616-4599 or 617-929-4500. Internet: www.jfklibrary.org. *T: JFK/UMass (Red Line); then take the free shuttle bus, which runs every 20 minutes. By car: Take I-93/Route 3 south to Exit 15 (Morrissey Blvd./JFK Library), turn left onto Columbia Rd., and follow signs to free parking lot. Admission: $8 adults, $6 seniors and students with ID, $4 children 13–17, and free for children under 13. Open: Daily 9 a.m.–5 p.m. (last film at 3:55). Closed Jan 1, Thanksgiving, and Dec 25.*

John Hancock Observatory

Back Bay

The dizzying view from the 60th floor leaves an unforgettable impression of Boston, and the multimedia exhibits give a sense of how it got that way. The displays make the John Hancock Observatory my pick, by a tiny margin, over the Prudential Center Skywalk (see later in this section), which has a slightly better view. A light-and-sound show recounts the events that preceded the Revolutionary War and illustrates how the city's size and shape have changed. Allow at least 45 minutes.

200 Clarendon St. (at St. James Ave.). ☎ *617-572-6429. Internet:* www. cityviewboston.com. *T: Copley (Green Line); walk diagonally across Copley Square. Admission: $6 adults, $4 seniors, and $4 children 5–15. Open: Daily April–Oct 9 a.m.–11 p.m.; Nov–March Mon–Sat 9 a.m.–11 p.m., Sun 9 a.m.–6 p.m. Ticket office closes 1 hour before observatory.*

Museum of Fine Arts

Fenway

Out-of-towners typically hear about the MFA because of its special exhibitions and traveling shows, not because of its real appeal: an unbeatable combination of the familiar and the unexpected. The galleries contain so many classic pieces that you'll probably feel as if you bumped into an old friend at least once during your visit. The collections span the centuries and the globe — from Old Kingdom Egyptian collections (that means "mummies") to contemporary photography. The celebrated Impressionist paintings include 43 Monets. And you'll always run across something, ancient or modern, that leaves you glad you made the trip.

Schedule at least half a day to explore; art fiends should allow more time. The best way to get an overview is to take a free **guided tour.** These tours start on weekdays (except Monday holidays) at 10:30 a.m. and 1:30 p.m.; Wednesdays at 6:15 p.m.; and Saturdays at 10:30 a.m. and 1 p.m. If you prefer to explore the sprawling galleries on your own, pick up a floor plan or family activity booklet at the information desk. Check ahead for special family- and child-friendly activities, which take place year-round.

The main lobby, in the West Wing, is a madhouse at busy times. To save time, follow Huntington Avenue about half a block and enter from the curved driveway. This entrance is farther from the main gift shop, restaurants, garage, and special exhibits, but usually has no line.

465 Huntington Ave. (at Museum Rd.). ☎ *617-267-9300. Internet:* www.mfa.org. *T: Museum (Green Line E). Or Ruggles (Orange Line); walk 2 blocks on Ruggles St. Admission: Adults $12 entire museum, $10 when only West Wing is open; students and seniors $10 entire museum, $9 when only West Wing is open. Children 7–17 $5 on school days before 3 p.m., otherwise free. Voluntary contribution ($5 suggested), Wed 4–9:45 p.m. Surcharges may apply for special exhibitions. No fee to visit only shop, library, or auditoriums. Open: Entire museum Mon–Tues 10 a.m.–4:45 p.m.;*

Wed 10 a.m.–9:45 p.m.; Thurs–Fri 10 a.m.–5 p.m.; Sat–Sun 10 a.m.–5:45 p.m. Open: West Wing only Thurs–Fri 5–9:45 p.m. Closed Thanksgiving, Dec 25.

Museum of Science

Science Park (between Boston and East Cambridge)

A superb destination for both children and adults, the Museum of Science introduces principles and theories so painlessly that it's almost sneaky. Hands-on displays and exhibits explore every scientific field you can imagine, but — I can't emphasize this enough — always in a fun, accessible way.

Allow at least a couple of hours; if you plan to take in a show (see the next paragraph), you might want to set aside a day. One of the most popular exhibits, acquired when the science museum joined forces with the Computer Museum, is the Virtual FishTank for which you can "build" your fish using your home computer (visit www.virtualfishtank.com) or on the scene, then watch as it interacts with other people's creations.

A show at one of the museum's theaters, which charge separate admission, is well worth your time. The Mugar Omni Theater shows IMAX movies on a five-story domed screen; the Charles Hayden Planetarium schedules daily star shows, weekend rock-music laser extravaganzas, and shows on special astronomical topics.

Buy all your tickets at once, not only because it's cheaper, but because shows sometimes sell out. You must buy tickets to daytime shows in person. For evening shows, you can order tickets (with a service charge) over the phone using a credit card.

Science Park (off Route 28). ☎ *617-723-2500. Internet: www.mos.org. T: Science Park (Green Line); follow signs along elevated walkway onto bridge. Admission: Exhibit halls $10 adults, $7 seniors and children 3–11, free for children under 3. Mugar Omni Theater, Hayden Planetarium, or laser shows $7.50 adults, $5.50 seniors and children 3–11, free for children under 3. Discounted admission tickets for two or three attraction combinations. Open: Museum July 5–Labor Day Sat–Thurs 9 a.m.–7 p.m., Fri 9 a.m.–9 p.m.; day after Labor Day–July 4 Sat–Thurs 9 a.m.–5 p.m., Fri 9 a.m.–9 p.m. Shows during museum hours and some evenings; call or check the Web site for the schedule. Closed Thanksgiving, Dec 25.*

New England Aquarium

Waterfront

Expect to see construction around this popular complex, which is in the process of expanding its exhibit space and adding an IMAX theater. The Aquarium currently contains more than 7,000 fish and aquatic mammals, including sea lions that perform every 90 minutes in the floating pavilion Discovery. (The expansion will likely displace them, so sea lion fans may want to call ahead and make sure they're still in residence.) The center-piece is the 187,000-gallon Giant Ocean Tank; other exhibits focus on local ecology, the Aquarium medical center, and a roster of regularly changing special topics. Allow at least 2½ hours.

"Science at Sea" harbor tours operate daily in the spring, summer, and fall. Tickets are $9 for adults, $7 for seniors and youths 12 to 18, and $6.50 for children under 12. Discounts are available when you combine a visit to the aquarium with a harbor tour or a whale watch (see Chapter 18).

At busy times, the Aquarium can be uncomfortably crowded and the lines unbearably long. The Boston CityPass nearly pays for itself — in time even more than money — on hot summer days when having a ticket allows you to go straight to the entrance. Seriously consider investing in the pass, especially if you're traveling with restless children. If you don't buy a pass, try to make this your first stop of the day, and arrive when the doors open.

Central Wharf (off Atlantic Ave. at State St.). ☎ *617-973-5200. Internet:* www.neaq. org. *T: State (Blue or Orange Line) or Aquarium, if it's open; walk 4 blocks toward the harbor (downhill). Admission: Summer weekends and holidays $14 adults, $12 seniors, $7.50 children 3–11, free for children under 3. Weekdays and off-season weekends $12.50 adults, $10.50 seniors, $6.50 children 3–11, free for children under 3. No fee to visit only outdoor exhibits, cafe, and gift shop. Open: July–Labor Day Mon–Tues and Fri 9 a.m.–6 p.m.; Wed–Thurs 9 a.m.–8 p.m.; Sat–Sun and holidays 9 a.m.–7 p.m. Day after Labor Day–June Mon–Fri 9 a.m.–5 p.m.; Sat–Sun and holidays 9 a.m.–6 p.m. Closed Thanksgiving, Dec 25, and until noon Jan 1.*

Prudential Center Skywalk

Back Bay

Although the 50-story Prudential Tower is shorter than the John Hancock Tower (see earlier in this section), it affords the city's only 360-degree view. I find the displays here less enjoyable, but the panorama can't be beat; visit at twilight on slightly overcast days to enjoy especially spectacular sunsets. The 52nd-floor hosts the Top of the Hub restaurant and lounge (see Chapters 14 and 23).

800 Boylston St. (at Fairfield St.). ☎ *617-859-0648. T: Prudential (Green Line E) or Copley (Green Line B, C, or D); walk toward tower. Admission: $4 adults, $3 seniors and children 2–10. Open: Mon–Sat 10 a.m.–10 p.m.; Sun noon–10 p.m.*

Public Garden/Swan Boats

Back Bay

One of the most pleasant spots in the whole city is the Public Garden, 8-square blocks of peaceful greenery surrounding an agreeable body of water. The oldest botanical garden in the country boasts thriving blooms from spring through late fall, and the action on the lagoon is always diverting. Children love to feed the geese, ducks, and swans. Adults should get a kick out of the sculptures and monuments, which commemorate George Washington, the first use of ether as an anesthetic, and other apparently random people and events.

The **swan boats** have been synonymous with Boston since 1877. Still operated by the same family, the fiberglass birds on pedal boats (the attendants pedal, not the passengers) make a great low-tech break. Fans of *The Trumpet of the Swan,* by E. B. White, can't miss these vessels. Allow 30 minutes.

Near the corner of Charles and Beacon Streets, nine little bronze figures immortalize Robert McCloskey's book **Make Way for Ducklings.** Nancy Schön's renderings of Mrs. Mallard and her babies inspire delighted shrieks from small visitors.

Between Arlington, Boylston, Charles, and Beacon Sts. T: Arlington (Green Line). Or Charles/MGH (Red Line); follow Charles St. 5 blocks to Beacon St. Open: Daily year-round. As in any park, be careful at night, especially if you're alone.

Swan boats ☎ 617-522-1966. Internet: www.swanboats.com. *Admission: Adults $1.75, children under 13 95 cents. Open: Daily, third Mon of Apr–mid-September. Summer 10 a.m.–5 p.m.; spring 10 a.m.–4 p.m.; fall weekdays noon–4 p.m., weekends 10 a.m.–4 p.m.*

The Freedom Trail

Just to say "sixteen historic sights make up the 3-mile Freedom Trail" gives no sense of the role the trail (Internet: www.thefreedomtrail.org) plays for visitors to Boston. Not only are the attractions interesting, but the trail — a red line on the sidewalk from Boston Common to Charlestown — makes finding your way around downtown considerably less confusing than it would be otherwise.

This section lists the stops along the trail starting with Boston Common and ending with the Bunker Hill Monument — this is the order that usually appears in pamphlets, maps, and other publications. That doesn't mean you have to speed-walk from one end to the other, go in exact order, or even see everything. Start in Charlestown and work backward, skip a stop or two, or even get "lost" — this area is too small for you to go too far astray. I insist on just one thing: Wear comfortable walking shoes.

The Freedom Trail takes at least 2 hours, even if you don't linger too long at any one stop. If that's too much time, consider a free 90-minute walking tour of the "heart" of the trail with a National Park Service ranger (see Chapter 17). To head out on your own, start at the Visitors Information Center at 146 Tremont St., on Boston Common. Take the T to Park Street (Red or Green Line).

The Freedom Trail

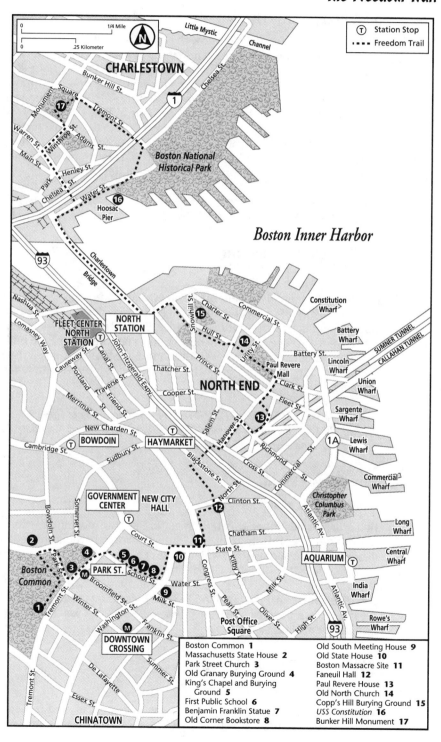

CHARLESTOWN

Little Mystic Channel

Bunker Hill St.

Monument Square

Tremont St.

Warren St.

Winthrop St.
Adams St.

Main St.

Park St.

Henley St.

Chelsea St.

Water St.

Hoosac Pier

Boston National Historical Park

Chelsea St.

Charlestown Bridge

Boston Inner Harbor

93

Nashua St.

Lomasney Way

FLEET CENTER NORTH STATION

NORTH STATION

Causeway St.

Canal St.

Portland St.

Merrimac St.

Traverse St.

Friend St.

John Fitzgerald Expy.

New Charden St.

BOWDOIN

HAYMARKET

Cambridge St.

Sudbury St.

Blackstone St.

Snowhill St.

Charter St.

Hull St.

Prince St.

Thatcher St.

Cooper St.

Salem St.

Hanover St.

NORTH END

Commercial St.

Unity St.

Paul Revere Mall

Clark St.

Fleet St.

Richmond St.

Cross St.

North St.

Commercial St.

Constitution Wharf

Battery Wharf

Battery St.

Lincoln Wharf

Union Wharf

Sargente Wharf

Lewis Wharf

Commercial Wharf

Long Wharf

SUMNER TUNNEL
CALLAHAN TUNNEL

1A

GOVERNMENT CENTER

NEW CITY HALL

Somerset St.

Bowdoin St.

Court St.

Clinton St.

Chatham St.

State St.

Christopher Columbus Park

Atlantic Av.

AQUARIUM

Central Wharf

Boston Common

Park St.

PARK ST.

Broomfield St.

School St.

Winter St.

Washington St.

Tremont St.

Water St.

Milk St.

Congress St.

Kilby St.

Pearl St.

Milk St.

Oliver St.

High St.

Post Office Square

Atlantic Av.

India Wharf

Rowe's Wharf

93

DOWNTOWN CROSSING

Franklin St.

De Lafayette

Summer St.

Essex St.

CHINATOWN

Legend
- T Station Stop
- Freedom Trail

Boston Common **1**
Massachusetts State House **2**
Park Street Church **3**
Old Granary Burying Ground **4**
King's Chapel and Burying Ground **5**
First Public School **6**
Benjamin Franklin Statue **7**
Old Corner Bookstore **8**

Old South Meeting House **9**
Old State House **10**
Boston Massacre Site **11**
Faneuil Hall **12**
Paul Revere House **13**
Old North Church **14**
Copp's Hill Burying Ground **15**
USS Constitution **16**
Bunker Hill Monument **17**

Boston Common

Downtown/Beacon Hill

In 1634, Boston bought what's now the country's oldest park. In 1640, the land became common ground, and later served as a cow pasture (until 1830), military camp, and all-purpose municipal gathering place. Plaques and memorials abound. One of the loveliest is up the hill from the T station, on Beacon Street across from the State House. Augustus Saint-Gaudens designed the bas-relief **Robert Gould Shaw Memorial,** which honors Colonel Shaw and the Union Army's 54th Massachusetts Colored Regiment, who fought in the Civil War. (The 1989 movie *Glory,* with Matthew Broderick and Denzel Washington, told the story of the first American army unit made up of free black soldiers.)

Between Beacon, Park, Tremont, Boylston, and Charles Sts. Visitors Information Center ☎ 800-SEE-BOSTON or 617-536-4100. T: Park Street (Red or Green Line).

Massachusetts State House

Beacon Hill

Governor Samuel Adams laid the cornerstone of the state capitol in 1795. The great Federal-era architect Charles Bulfinch designed the imposing central building and its landmark golden dome. Free tours — guided and self-guided — leave from the second floor. Visit the rear of the building, off Bowdoin Street, to see a 60-foot monument that illustrates the hill's original height (material from the top went into 19th-century landfill projects).

Beacon St. (at Park St.). ☎ 617-727-3676. T: Park Street (Red or Green Line); walk up Park St. 1 block. Admission: Free. Open: Weekdays 9 a.m.–5 p.m.; Sat 10 a.m.–4 p.m. Tours Mon–Sat 10 a.m.–3:30 p.m.

Park Street Church

Downtown/Beacon Hill

Henry James described this 1809 structure as "the most interesting mass of bricks and mortar in America." Plaques arrayed around the entrance describe its storied history, which includes the first public performance of "America" ("My Country 'Tis of Thee") on July 4, 1831.

1 Park St. (at Tremont St.). ☎ 617-523-3383. T: Park Street (Red or Green Line). Admission: Free. Open: Late June–Aug Tues–Sat 9:30 a.m.–4 p.m. Year-round services Sun 9 a.m.; 10:45 a.m.; 5:30 p.m.

Old Granary Burying Ground

Downtown

This cemetery, which dates to 1660, was once part of Boston Common. The graveyard contains the final resting places of patriots Samuel Adams,

Paul Revere, John Hancock, and James Otis; merchant Peter Faneuil (spelled "FUNAL"); the victims of the Boston Massacre; and Benjamin Franklin's parents. Also buried here is the wife of Isaac Vergoose; historians believe she was "Mother Goose" of nursery rhyme fame.

Gravestone rubbing is illegal in Boston's historic cemeteries. (And pretty bad karma, if you ask me.)

Tremont St. (at Bromfield St.). T: Park Street (Red or Green Line); walk 1 block on Tremont St. Open: Daily 8 a.m.–5 p.m. (until 3 p.m. in the winter).

King's Chapel and Burying Ground

Downtown

A squat granite structure, King's Chapel is historically and architecturally interesting. The first Anglican church in Boston, it replaced a wooden chapel and construction (from 1749 to 1754) went on *around* the previous building. After the Revolution, in a rejection of the royal religion, King's Chapel became the first Unitarian church in America.

The **burying ground,** on Tremont Street, is the oldest in the city (1630). Elaborate colonial headstones dot the graveyard, the final resting place of John Winthrop, the first governor of the Massachusetts Bay Colony; William Dawes, who rode with Paul Revere; and Mary Chilton, the first female colonist to step ashore on Plymouth Rock.

58 Tremont St. (at School St.). ☎ 617-523-1749. T: Government Center (Green or Blue Line); walk 1 block on Tremont St. Open: Chapel Tues–Sat 10 a.m.–2 p.m. Services Sun 11 a.m. Burying ground daily 8 a.m.–5:30 p.m. (until 3 p.m. in winter).

First Public School/Benjamin Franklin Statue

Downtown

A colorful folk-art mosaic marks the site of the first public school in the country, which opened in 1634 (2 years before Harvard). The school's illustrious alumni include John Hancock, Benjamin Franklin, Charles Bulfinch, Ralph Waldo Emerson, George Santayana, and Leonard Bernstein. Now called Boston Latin School, it still exists in the Fenway neighborhood.

Inside the fence is a statue of Boston native **Benjamin Franklin** (1706–1790). The plaques on the base describe his numerous accomplishments. The elegant granite building behind the statue is **Old City Hall,** built in 1865 and designed in Second Empire style by Arthur Gilman (who laid out the Back Bay) and Gridley J. F. Bryant.

School St. (at Province St.). T: State (Orange or Blue Line); walk 2 blocks on Washington St. and turn right.

Old Corner Bookstore

Downtown

This land once held the home of religious reformer Anne Hutchinson, who wasted no time in ticking off the church authorities — in 1638, a mere 8 years after the establishment of Boston, they excommunicated her and expelled her from town. In the middle of the 19th century, the little brick building (which dates to 1712) held the publishing house of Ticknor & Fields. Publisher James "Jamie" Fields's wide circle of friends included Longfellow, Thoreau, Emerson, Hawthorne, and Harriet Beecher Stowe.

3 School St. (at Washington St.). T: State (Orange or Blue Line); walk 2 blocks up Washington St.

Old South Meeting House

Downtown

The Boston Tea Party started in this building, which remains a religious and political gathering place today. On December 16, 1773, revolutionaries protesting the royal tea tax assembled here and wound up dumping the cargo of three ships into the harbor. An interactive multimedia exhibit tells the building's fascinating story. This structure, with its landmark clock tower, dates to 1729; the original went up in 1670.

310 Washington St. ☎ 617-482-6439. Internet: www.oldsouthmeetinghouse. org. *T: State (Orange or Blue Line); walk 3 blocks up Washington St. Admission: $3 adults, $2.50 seniors, $1 children 6–12, free for children under 6. Open: Daily Apr–Oct 9 a.m. to 5:30 p.m.; Nov–March weekdays 10 a.m.–4 p.m., weekends 10 a.m.–5 p.m.*

Old State House

Downtown

Built in 1713, the Old State House served as the seat of the colony's government before the Revolution and as the state capitol until 1797. The gilded lion and unicorn that adorn the exterior are replicas — the original symbols of British rule went into a bonfire on July 18, 1776, the day Bostonians first heard the Declaration of Independence read from the balcony. Inside you'll find the Bostonian Society's **museum of the city's history.** Displays include an introductory video on the history of the building, and changing exhibits that showcase the society's enormous collection of documents, photographs, and artifacts. Plan on at least 45 minutes if you enjoy history, considerably less if you're more interested in architecture (or in getting to Faneuil Hall Marketplace for some shopping and eating).

206 Washington St. (at State St.). ☎ *617-720-3290. Internet:* www.bostonhistory. org. *T: State (Blue or Orange Line). Admission: $3 adults, $2 seniors and students, $1 children 6–18, free for children under 6. Open: Daily 9 a.m.–5 p.m.*

Boston Massacre Site

Downtown

Look for the ring of cobblestones on the traffic island in the middle of State Street behind the Old State House. This spot marks the approximate site of the Boston Massacre, a conflict that took place on March 5, 1770 and helped launch the colonial rebellion. Angered at the presence of royal troops in Boston, colonists threw snowballs, garbage, rocks, and other debris at a group of soldiers. The redcoats panicked and fired into the crowd, killing five men (their graves are in the Old Granary Burying Ground).

State St. at Devonshire St. T: State (Blue or Orange Line).

Faneuil Hall

Downtown

The "Cradle of Liberty" was a gift to the city from prosperous merchant Peter Faneuil. Built in 1742, it grew to more than twice its original size in 1805, using a Charles Bulfinch design. Note the statue on the Congress Street side; it's Samuel Adams (yes, as in the beer), one of the countless orators whose declamations shook the building in the years before the Revolution. Faneuil Hall also played host to abolitionists, temperance advocates, and women's suffragists. Because of the terms of Faneuil's will, the building remains a public meeting (and sometimes concert) hall, and the ground floor holds retail space. National Park Service rangers give free 20-minute talks every half-hour in the second-floor auditorium and operate a visitors center on the first floor.

The French Huguenot name "Faneuil" more or less rhymes with "Daniel"; it's also pronounced _Fan-yoo-ul._

Across North Street on Union Street, you'll see a series of glass towers in a small park; this is the **New England Holocaust Memorial.** Built in 1995, this memorial is a moving reminder, in the midst of attractions that celebrate freedom, of the consequences of a world without it. The pattern on the glass is 6 million random numbers, one for each Jew who died during the Holocaust.

Dock Square (Congress St. off North St.). ☎ *617-242-5675. T: Government Center (Green or Blue Line) or Haymarket (Orange Line). Admission: Free. Open: Second floor daily 9 a.m.–5 p.m.; ground floor Mon–Sat 10 a.m.–9 p.m., Sun noon–6 p.m.*

Paul Revere House

North End

Remember "Listen my children and you shall hear / Of the midnight ride of Paul Revere"? Paul Revere's ride started here, in what's now one of the most enjoyable stops on the Freedom Trail. On April 18, 1775, Revere set out for Lexington and Concord and into the American imagination (courtesy of Henry Wadsworth Longfellow) from his home, which he had bought in 1770. The oldest house in downtown Boston, it dates to around 1680. The self-guided tour permits a glimpse of 18th-century life and many family heirlooms.

19 North Square (at North Street between Richmond and Prince Sts.). ☎ *617-523-2338. Internet:* www.paulreverehouse.org. *T: Haymarket (Green or Orange Line). Cross under elevated highway and follow Freedom Trail. Admission: $2.50 adults, $2 seniors and students, $1 children 5–17. Open: Daily Apr 15–Oct 9:30 a.m.–5:15 p.m., Nov–Apr 14 9:30 a.m.–4:15 p.m. Closed Mon Jan–March, Jan 1, Thanksgiving, Dec 25.*

Old North Church

North End

Christ Church (its formal name) is the oldest church in Boston; it dates to 1723. In the original steeple, sexton Robert Newman hung two lanterns on the night of April 18, 1775, alerting Paul Revere to the movement of British troops. The second beacon told Revere the redcoats were crossing the Charles River by boat, not on foot ("One if by land, two if by sea"). Markers and plaques dot the building and its gardens; note the bust of George Washington, reputedly the first memorial to the first president. The quirky gift shop and museum (☎ **617-523-4848**), in a former chapel, is open daily 9 a.m. to 5 p.m., and all proceeds go to support the church.

Robert Newman was a great-grandson of George Burroughs, one of the victims of the Salem witch trials of 1692.

193 Salem St. (at Hull St.). ☎ *617-523-6676. Internet:* www.oldnorth.com. *T: Haymarket (Green or Orange Line); cross under elevated highway and walk 6 blocks on Salem St. Admission: Free; donations appreciated. Open: Daily 9 a.m.– 5 p.m. Services (Episcopal) Sun 9 a.m.; 11 a.m.; 4 p.m.*

Copp's Hill Burying Ground

North End

The Mather family of Puritan ministers, Robert Newman, and Prince Hall lie in the second-oldest graveyard (1659) in the city. Hall, a prominent member of the free black community that occupied the hill's north slope in colonial times, fought at Bunker Hill and established the first black Masonic lodge. The highest point in the North End enjoys a great view of the Inner Harbor, the northern part of the Big Dig construction, and Charlestown (look for the masts of USS *Constitution*).

Between Hull, Snowhill, and Charter Sts. T: North Station (Green or Orange Line). Follow Causeway St. to North Washington St., where it becomes Commercial St. Walk 2 blocks, turn right, and climb the hill. Open: Daily 9 a.m.–5 p.m. (until 3 p.m. in winter).

USS Constitution

Charlestown

In modern terms, "Old Ironsides" retired undefeated. Launched in 1797 as one of the U.S. Navy's six original frigates, USS *Constitution* never lost a battle. The tour guides are active-duty sailors in 1812 dress uniforms, in homage to the ship's prominent role in the War of 1812. The frigate earned its nickname during an engagement on August 19, 1812, with the French warship *Guerriere,* whose shots bounced off its thick oak hull as if it were iron. "Old Ironsides" sailed under its own power in 1997 for the first time since 1881, drawing international attention. Tugs tow it into the harbor every Fourth of July and turn it to ensure that the ship weathers evenly.

The nearby **Constitution Museum** (☎ **617-426-1812;** Internet: www.ussconstitutionmuseum.org) contains participatory exhibits that illustrate the history and operation of the ship. Also at the navy yard, National Park Service rangers (☎ **617-242-5601**) staff an information booth and give free 1-hour guided tours of the base.

Charlestown Navy Yard (off Constitution Rd.). ☎ 617-242-5670. T: North Station (Green or Orange Line); follow Causeway St. to North Washington St., turn left, and cross bridge. Total walking time: About 15 minutes. Admission for tours and museum: Free. Open: Museum daily May–Oct 9 a.m.–6 p.m.; Nov–April 10 a.m. to 4 p.m. Constitution tours daily 9:30 a.m.–3:50 p.m. Closed Jan 1, Thanksgiving, Dec 25.

Bunker Hill Monument

Charlestown

One of Boston's best-known landmarks, this 221-foot granite obelisk honors the colonists who died in the Battle of Bunker Hill on June 17, 1775. The win was a costly victory for the British, who lost nearly half of their troops to death or injury. The battle led directly to the British decision to abandon Boston 9 months later. A flight of 294 stairs leads to the top — there's no elevator, but the view affords a look at the Charles River end of the Big Dig. The ranger-staffed lodge at the base holds dioramas and exhibits.

Monument Square (at Tremont St.). ☎ 617-242-5644. T: Ferry between Long Wharf or North Station and navy yard, and then follow Freedom Trail up the hill. Or Community College (Orange Line); cross Rutherford Ave. and walk toward the monument. Or no. 92 or 93 bus along Main St. (foot of the hill) to and from Haymarket. Admission: Free. Open: Monument daily 9 a.m.–4:30 p.m.; visitors center daily 9 a.m.–5 p.m.

Neighborhood Watch

Boston and Cambridge are famous for their neighborhoods, which make good destinations for out-of-towners interested in exploring beyond the usual attractions. I particularly enjoy these three locations (two in Boston, one in Cambridge), but if you're visiting friends who want to explore an area you never heard of, go for it — this is one of the best ways to get to know a new city.

✔ **Beacon Hill:** West and north of the golden dome of the State House is one of the city's oldest neighborhoods, a festival of brick and brownstone that looks the way you probably think Boston "should." Wander downhill toward Charles Street, making sure to explore the lovely side streets and tiny parks. One of the oldest black churches in the country, the African Meeting House, is at 8 Smith Court.

Between Beacon St., Embankment Rd., Cambridge St., and Park St. T: Charles/ MGH (Red Line) or Park St. (Green Line).

✔ **The North End:** Traditionally an Italian-American neighborhood, the North End is now more than half newcomers, but it retains an Italian flavor that makes it great for roaming around. You'll see Italian restaurants, caffès, bakeries, pastry shops, and food stores. This detour is easy from the Freedom Trail, and worth more than just a quick trip for a pasta dinner. Hanover and Salem Streets are the main drags; plenty of action is available on the side streets, too.

Between I-93, Commercial Street, and North Washington Street. T: Haymarket (Green or Orange Line); cross under the elevated highway.

✔ **Harvard Square:** Cambridge's best-known intersection attracts a kaleidoscopic assortment of students, shoppers, street musicians, and sightseers. This area is a retail playground (see Chapter 19) that's especially lively on weekend afternoons. Stop at the information booth near the main T entrance (☎ 617-497-1630; open Monday to Saturday 9 a.m. to 5 p.m., Sunday 1 to 5 p.m.), visit Harvard University (see listing under "The Top Attractions" in this chapter), or explore on your own. The area's three main thoroughfares and the side streets that connect them make great places for wandering.

Intersection of Mass. Ave., John F. Kennedy Street, and Brattle Street. T: CambridgeHarvard (Red Line).

Index of Top Attractions by Neighborhood

Back Bay

Beacon Hill
Boston Common
John Hancock Observatory
Massachusetts State House
Park Street Church
Prudential Center Skywalk

Public Garden/Swan Boats
Robert Gould Shaw Memorial

Cambridge

Harvard University/John Harvard
  Statue

Charlestown
Bunker Hill Monument
USS *Constitution*/Charlestown Navy
  Yard

Dorchester
John F. Kennedy Library and Museum

Downtown
Benjamin Franklin Statue
Boston Massacre Site
Dreams of Freedom/Benjamin
  Franklin's Birthplace
First Public School Site
King's Chapel and Burying Ground
Old City Hall
Old Corner Bookstore
Old Granary Burying Ground
Old South Meeting House
Old State House

Faneuil Hall Marketplace
Faneuil Hall
New England Holocaust Memorial

Fenway
Isabella Stewart Gardner Museum
Museum of Fine Arts

North End
Copp's Hill Burying Ground
Old North Church
Paul Revere House

Science Park
Museum of Science

Waterfront
New England Aquarium

Index of Top Attractions by Type

Churches and Burying Grounds
Copp's Hill Burying Ground
King's Chapel and Burying Ground
Old Granary Burying Ground
Old North Church
Park Street Church

Gardens
Boston Common
Public Garden/Swan Boats

Historic Buildings and Sites
Benjamin Franklin Statue
Boston Massacre Site
Bunker Hill Monument
Faneuil Hall
First Public School Site
Massachusetts State House
Old City Hall
Old Corner Bookstore
Old State House
Old South Meeting House
Paul Revere House
USS Constitution

Memorials
New England Holocaust Memorial
Robert Gould Shaw Memorial

Museums and Other Cultural Centers
Dreams of Freedom
Faneuil Hall Marketplace
Isabella Steward Gardner Museum
John F. Kennedy Library and Museum
Museum of Fine Arts
Museum of Science
New England Aquarium

Observation Areas
John Hancock Observatory
Prudential Center Skywalk

Universities
Harvard University

Chapter 17

More Cool Things to See and Do

* *

In This Chapter

▶ Entertaining the kids

▶ Finding special-interest attractions and activities

▶ Getting into the swing: Sports

* *

*W*ell-known, high-profile attractions are great — that's why they're so popular, right? Once you get comfortable with Boston, you may feel ready for something more offbeat. The sights and activities in this chapter don't have the same broad appeal, but they're equally fun. In fact, if you're particularly interested, they might be even more fun. Here you'll find suggestions for keeping the kids (small and large) happy, entertaining travelers with specific interests, and captivating sports fans.

For locations of the various attractions described in this chapter, see the "Boston Attractions" or "Cambridge Attractions" maps in Chapter 16, unless otherwise noted.

Especially for Kids

Nearly every attraction in the area appeals to children, and I'm not just saying that — they clearly enjoy themselves all over town. That doesn't mean every single kid loves every single destination, however. The little ones feeding the birds at the Public Garden may find the Museum of Science overwhelming, for instance; meanwhile, an older sibling may only be interested in the Aquarium. Make sure that you know what they're looking forward to, and that they know what to expect.

Children's Museum

Waterfront/Museum Wharf

Visitors under 13 or so usually enjoy a great time here, and most older travelers admit that they have fun, too. The novelty of raising your voice in a place with "museum" in its name is just the beginning; the exhibits combine recreation and education to good effect. The displays include "Science Playground," where every-day objects like golf balls and soap bubbles illustrate principles of physics; "Boats Afloat," where kids operate model vessels on a giant water tank; the "Dress-Up Shop," with enough costumes for any aspiring thespian; and the "New Balance Climb," a kids-only two-story maze. A room is reserved just for toddlers, and the gift shop is literally and figuratively tremendous. Allow at least 2 hours plus travel time (the route from South Station passes some entertaining construction equipment).

Museum Wharf, 300 Congress St. (at Fort Point Channel). ☎ *617-426-8855. Internet:* www.bostonkids.org. *T: South Station (Red Line); walk north on Atlantic Ave. 1 block (past the Federal Reserve Bank), turn right onto Congress St., follow it 1 long block, and cross the bridge. Admission: $7 adults, $6 children age 2–15 and seniors, $2 children age 1, free for children under 1; Fri 5–9 p.m. $1 for all. Open: June–Aug Mon–Thurs 10 a.m.–7 p.m., Fri 10 a.m.–9 p.m., Sat–Sun 10 a.m.–5 p.m.; Sept–June Sat–Thurs 10 a.m.–5 p.m., Fri 10 a.m.–9 p.m. Closed: Jan 1, Thanksgiving, and Dec 25.*

Boston Tea Party Ship & Museum

Waterfront/Museum Wharf

One of the most famous tax protests ever, the Boston Tea Party lives on as a hands-on family activity. Not far from the site of the real uprising, a replica of the infamous *Beaver II* sits at anchor. On December 16, 1773, laden with tea, this vessel became a symbol of the British government's repressive policies — until a band of rebellious colonists emptied its cargo into the water. The museum contains audio and video displays (including a 15-minute film), dioramas, and informational panels that tell the story of the uprising. You can dump a bale of tea into Boston Harbor (a museum staffer retrieves it) and drink complimentary tax-free tea. Allow about an hour for your visit. The attraction makes a good stop on the way to the Children's Museum.

Congress Street Bridge (off Dorchester Ave.). ☎ *617-338-1773. Internet:* www. historictours.com/boston/teaparty.htm. *T: South Station (Red Line); walk north on Atlantic Avenue 1 block (past the Federal Reserve Bank), turn right onto Congress St., and walk 1 block. Admission: $8 adults, $7 students, $4 children 4–12, free for children under 4. Open: Daily Mar–Nov 9 a.m.–dusk (about 6 p.m. in summer; 5 p.m. in spring and fall). Closed: Thanksgiving, Dec–Feb.*

Especially for Teens

Occupying teenagers can be tricky, but keeping the lines of communication open can pay off for everyone. If the adolescents in your group cheerfully go anywhere, count yourselves among the lucky. (Humbly grin at the jealous parents of disgruntled teenagers that are booked in the hotel room next door.) But is your teen committed to sightseeing? Will he or she be more open to different types of attractions if one of the sights is in a mall or club? Does a campus tour count as fun or as pressure? Talk it out.

Shopping options abound. Two excellent malls — the **Shops at Prudential Center** and **Copley Place** — connect through a skybridge so you don't even need to go outside. Also, the **CambridgeSide Galleria** mall offers almost nothing unusual, but it's about 5 minutes on foot from the Museum of Science. For information on these places and other stores, see Chapter 19.

The shopping in **Harvard Square** also tends toward the generic, but with plenty of unconventional items, too. And the neighborhood scene — especially in "the Pit," near the main T entrance — is always, well, let's just call it eye-opening. For more information, see Chapter 19.

Nightlife may not be the first thing that springs to mind when you're thinking about teen diversions, but a trip to a theme restaurant or the theater can be a great family excursion. Kids love the food and music at the **House of Blues** and **Hard Rock Cafe,** and the interactive theater of **Shear Madness** and **Blue Man Group.** During the day (kids are not allowed at night), teens also enjoy the high-tech games at **Jillian's Boston** (a top destination for pool players). For family-oriented nightlife suggestions, turn to Part 6 and look for the kid-friendly icon.

Finally, consider a **campus tour.** The Boston area is home to dozens of schools. Every admissions office worth its salt is eager to show you around, and every college-oriented high school student knows where to find a few top choices on the Web. Tours are fun, free, and potentially eye-opening for the younger kids in your party. Among the many schools in the Boston area are Bentley College, Boston College, Boston University, Brandeis University, Emerson College, Harvard University, Lesley College, Massachusetts Institute of Technology, Northeastern University, Simmons College, Suffolk University, Tufts University, University of Massachusetts, and Wellesley College.

Some Specialty Museums

Museum of Afro-American History

Beacon Hill

This museum highlights the history of blacks in Boston and Massachusetts. The complex includes the **African Meeting House** (1806), 8 Smith Court; also known as the "Black Faneuil Hall." This place of worship is the oldest standing black church in the United States.

46 Joy St. ☎ *617-742-1854. Internet:* www.afroammuseum.org. *T: Park Street (Red or Green Line); climb the hill, walk around the State House to the left, and* *follow Joy Street 3½ blocks. Admission: Free; suggested donation $5 for adults, $3 for seniors, students, and children. Open: Mon–Sat 10 a.m.–4 p.m.*

Harvard Museum of Natural History and Peabody Museum of Archaeology & Ethnology

Cambridge

These museums house world-famous collections of items related to the natural world. The natural history museum comprises three collections: botanical, zoological (from insects to dinosaurs), and mineralogical. The best-known display is the Glass Flowers, 3,000 eerily lifelike models of more than 840 plant species. The Peabody mounts great displays on international people and cultures; the Native American collections are especially noteworthy.

Museum of Natural History, 26 Oxford St. ☎ 617-495-3045. Internet: www.hmnh. harvard.edu. *Peabody Museum, 11 Divinity Ave. ☎ 617-496-1027. Internet:* www.peabody.harvard.edu. *T: Harvard (Red Line); cross Harvard Yard, keeping the John Harvard statue on your right, turn right at the Science Center, and take the first left onto Oxford St. Admission: Covers both museums $5 for adults, $4 for students and seniors, $3 for children 3 to 13, free for children under 3; free to all on Sundays before noon. Open: Mon–Sat 9 a.m.–5 p.m.; Sunday 1–5 p.m. Closed: January 1, July 4, Thanksgiving, and December 25.*

Especially for Art Lovers

Art galleries cluster on **Newbury Street** in the Back Bay and dot many other Boston and Cambridge neighborhoods. If you enjoy seeing workspaces as well as the final product, check the *Globe* when you arrive to see if any of the area's artist-intensive neighborhoods has scheduled "open studios" during your visit. Or just head to Newbury Street; the big names tend to be near the Public Garden end, but the whole street is worth wandering. When strolling along Newbury Street, remember to look above the first floor where you're sure to find many more galleries.

Institute of Contemporary Art

Back Bay

This museum has no permanent collection, so it's different every time you visit. The rotating exhibits concentrate on 20th- and 21st-century art. The broad-minded curatorial approach doesn't confine the shows to one medium or era, or even to what most people typically consider art. For example, a recent installation focused on classic automobiles: "Customized: Art Inspired by Hot Rods, Low Riders & American Car Culture."

955 Boylston St. ☎ 617-266-5152. Internet: www.icaboston.org. *T: Hynes/ICA (Green Line B, C, or D); use the Boylston St. exit. Admission: $6 for adults, $4 for* *students and seniors, free for children under 12; free to all Thurs after 5 p.m. Open: Wed and weekends noon–5 p.m.; Thurs noon–9 p.m.; Fri noon–7 p.m.*

Harvard University Art Museums

Cambridge

Harvard is home to three art museums; together they house some 150,000 works. The **Fogg Art Museum** consists of 19 rooms, which concentrate on topics that range from 17th-century Dutch landscapes to contemporary sculpture. The **Busch–Reisinger Museum** is the only museum in North America devoted to the art of northern and central Europe — specifically Germany. The **Arthur M. Sackler Museum** houses the university's collections of Asian, ancient, and Islamic art.

Fogg Art Museum, 32 Quincy St. (near Broadway); Busch–Reisinger Museum, enter through the Fogg; Arthur M. Sackler Museum, 485 Broadway, (at Quincy St.). ☎ *617-495-9400. Internet:* www.artmuseums.harvard.edu. *T: Harvard (Red Line); cross Harvard Yard diagonally, and then cross Quincy St. Or turn your back on the Coop and follow Mass. Ave. to Quincy St., and then turn left. Admission: Covers all three museums $5 for adults, $4 for seniors, $3 for students, free for children under 18; free to all on Sat before noon and all day Wed. Open: Mon–Sat 10 a.m.–5 p.m.; Sun 1–5 p.m. Closed: all major holidays.*

Architectural Highlights

Sheer variety makes Boston a unique treat for architecture buffs. Some areas boast fairly consistent style — notably Beacon Hill, where Federal-era construction abounds (and draconian zoning keeps it that way), and the Back Bay, which didn't exist until the 1830s and remains a 19th-century showpiece. Elsewhere in Boston and Cambridge, the most enjoyable feature is the juxtaposition of classic and cutting-edge.

Here's a convenient twist: Two of the city's architectural gems face each other across Copley Square.

Boston Public Library

Copley Square

This library is home to a museum-quality art collection — and that's just in the main entrance. The 1895 building, an Italian Renaissance–style design by Charles F. McKim, overflows with gorgeous doors, murals, frescoes, sculptures, and paintings. Pick up a brochure or take a free **Art & Architecture Tour.** The 30-minute excursions focus on the McKim building, which boasts ornamentation by such end-of-the-century giants as John Singer Sargent, Daniel Chester French, and Pierre Puvis de Chavannes.

700 Boylston St. ☎ *617-536-5400. Internet:* www.bpl.org. *T: Copley (Green Line) or Back Bay (Orange Line). Admission: Free. Open: Mon–Thurs 9 a.m.–9 p.m.;*

Fri–Sat 9 a.m.–5 p.m.; Sun (Oct–May only) 1–5 p.m. Tours: Mon 2:30 p.m.; Tues and Wed 6:30 p.m.; Thurs and Sat 11 a.m.; Sun (Sep–May only) 2:00 p.m.

Trinity Church

Copley Square

This Romanesque masterwork by H. H. Richardson is across the square from the Boston Public Library. Completed in 1877, the church sits on a foundation of 4,502 vertical supports called pilings (remember, most of the Back Bay is landfill). Brochures and guides can direct you around the building, one of the finest examples of American church architecture. On Fridays, you can enjoy an organ recital, beginning at 12:15 p.m.

545 Boylston St. ☎ 617-536-0944. Admission: Free. Open: Daily 8 a.m.–6 p.m. Sunday services (Episcopal): 8 a.m.; 9 a.m.; 11 a.m.; 6 p.m.

Historic Houses

The **Paul Revere House** (see the Freedom Trail listings in Chapter 16) is the foremost example, but hardly the only one. Charles Bulfinch, the renowned Federal-era architect, designed two Beacon Hill houses that are open for tours; another residence nearby offers a look at a later era.

You must take a tour to visit any of the house museums listed below.

Harrison Gray Otis House

Beacon Hill

Charles Bulfinch designed this house in 1796 for a promising lawyer who was later mayor of Boston. The historic furnishings and anecdote-laden tour give a sense of the life of a prosperous family in the young republic.

141 Cambridge St. ☎ 617-227-3956. Internet: www.spnea.org. T: Charles/MGH (Red Line); follow Cambridge St. away from the river. Tour charges: $4 for adults, $3.50 for seniors. Tours: Wed–Sun hourly from 11 a.m.–4 p.m.

Nichols House Museum

Beacon Hill

The furnishings and fine art at the 1804 reflect the taste of several generations of the Nichols family. Charles Bulfinch designed the building (and its neighbor at no. 57), which was a family home until it became a museum in 1960. It offers a singular chance to see how the upper crust lived: It's the neighborhood's only private house museum.

55 Mount Vernon St. ☎ 617-227-6993. T: Park St. (Red or Green Line); climb the hill, walk around the State House to the left, follow Joy St. 1 long block, and turn left. Tour charge: $5. Tours: May–Oct Tues–Sat; Nov–Apr Mon, Wed, and Sat (open days may vary; call ahead); every half-hour from 12:15 p.m–4:15 p.m.

Under construction

The renovation process was dragging at two interesting destinations that remained closed at press time. The **Longfellow National Historic Site**, 105 Brattle St., Cambridge (☎ **617-876-4491**; Internet: www.nps.gov/long), was poet Henry Wadsworth Longfellow's home for many years. An extensive refurbishment should be complete by late 2001. The 30-foot glass **Mapparium** (☎ **617-450-3790**; Internet: www.tfccs.com), a hollow, walk-through globe, is an unusual combination — an educational novelty. Look for it to reopen in 2002 at the world headquarters of the First Church of Christ, Scientist, 275 Huntington Ave. (entrance on Mass. Ave.).

Gibson House Museum

Back Bay

This 1859 house overflows with elaborate decorations that personify the word Victorian. To modern eyes, that seems synonymous with "over the top." The only design element more outrageous than the ornamentation is the accessories — including a little pink pagoda for the cat.

137 Beacon St. ☎ _617-267-6338. T: Arlington (Green Line); follow Arlington St. past the Public Garden and turn left on Beacon St. Tour charges: $5. Tours: May–Oct Wed–Sun 1 p.m., 2 p.m., 3 p.m.; Nov–Apr weekends only 1 p.m., 2 p.m., 3 p.m. Closed: major holidays._

A Famous Park

The **Public Garden** (see "The Top Attractions" in Chapter 16) will probably satisfy most of your horticultural cravings. The garden's gorgeous seasonal plantings (which change as soon as they start looking tired) complement a variety of trees and shrubs arranged to allow aimless strolling and quiet contemplation. Nature fans can also visit the following attraction:

Arnold Arboretum

Jamaica Plain

Devoted green thumbs may want to set aside half a day for a trip to this arboretum. Founded in 1872, it's one of the country's oldest parks, with about 15,000 ornamental trees, shrubs, and vines from all over the world on its 265 acres.

125 The Arborway (Jamaica Plain is southwest of downtown Boston). ☎ _617-524-1718. Internet:_ www.arboretum.harvard.edu. _T: Forest Hills (Orange Line); follow signs to the entrance. Admission: Free. Open: Daily sunrise–sunset. Visitors Center open: Weekdays 9 a.m.–4 p.m.; weekends noon–4 p.m._

More Cambridge Destinations

Massachusetts Institute of Technology (MIT)

Cambridge

MIT is the most prestigious technical college in . . . well, anywhere that doesn't have a Cal Tech alum nearby. Science gets top billing, but the techies care about more than just practical matters. Picasso, Alexander Calder, Eero Saarinen, and I. M. Pei are among the big names represented in the school's outdoor sculpture collection and architecture. Stop by the Information Center to take a free tour or pick up maps and brochures. The campus of the of MIT lies a mile or so down Mass. Ave. from Harvard Square, across the Charles River from Beacon Hill and the Back Bay.

MIT Information Center, 77 Mass. Ave. ☎ ***617-253-4795.*** *Internet:* http://web.mit.edu. *Tours: Weekdays 10 a.m.; 2 p.m.*

MIT Museum

Cambridge

This museum shows holography and more conventional works. Exhibits don't always have an MIT connection, but some of the most interesting — for example, an interactive installation on artificial intelligence, and a look at the work of pioneering photographer Harold "Doc" Edgerton — come straight from campus.

265 Mass. Ave. ☎ ***617-253-4444.*** *Internet:* http://web.mit.edu/museum. *T: No. 1 (Dudley–Harvard) bus; exit at first stop across bridge. Or Kendall/MIT (Red Line); follow the campus map at street level. Admission: $5 for adults, $2 for seniors, $1 for students and children under 12. Open: Tues–Fri 10 a.m.–5 p.m.; weekends noon–5 p.m. Closed: major holidays.*

Whale Watching

The waters off New England are choice whale-migration territory, and Boston is a center of whale watching. The magnificent mammals seek out the feeding grounds of **Stellwagen Bank,** which extend from Gloucester to Provincetown about 27 miles east of Boston. The most common species are the finback and humpback, and you may see minke whales and rare right whales. These aquatic mammals often "perform for spectators by jumping out of the water, and dolphins sometimes join in. Trained naturalists serve as tour guides, identifying animals and interpreting their activities.

The trip to the bank is long. (If your children aren't accustomed to immediate gratification, they may not appreciate the journey.) The tedium vanishes in an instant when the first whale appears.

Dress in plenty of layers to fend off the cool sea air, and sunglasses, a hat, and rubber-soled shoes. Don't forget sunscreen and, of course, a camera. If you tend to get motion sick, take precautions before you leave the dock.

New England Aquarium whale-watching expeditions (☎ **617-973-5281**; Internet: www.neaq.org) operate daily from May through mid-October and on weekends in April and late October. On-board hands-on exhibits help pass the time and prepare passengers for spotting duty. The trips take 4 to 5 hours; check exact departure times when you make reservations. Tickets are $26 for adults, $21 for seniors and college students, $19 for youths 12 to 18, and $16.50 for children 3 to 11. Children must be 3 years old and at least 30 inches tall. Reservations are strongly recommended. The T stop is State (Blue or Orange Line) or Aquarium, if it's open; walk 4 blocks toward the harbor (downhill). For information on attractions at the aquarium, see Chapter 16.

Boston Harbor Whale Watch (☎ **617-345-9866**; Internet: www. bostonwhale.com) promises more time watching whales than trying to find them. Trips run Friday through Sunday in late June, then daily from July through early September. Tours depart from Rowes Wharf (behind the Boston Harbor Hotel, off Atlantic Avenue near Northern Avenue). T: South Station (Red Line), then walk two long blocks north on Atlantic Avenue; or Aquarium (Blue Line), if it's open, then walk two long blocks south on Atlantic Avenue. Tour times are 10 a.m. on weekdays, 9 a.m. and 2 p.m. on weekends. Expect to spend about 4½ hours at sea. Tickets are $21 for adults, $18 for seniors and children under 13. Reservations are suggested.

Especially for Sports Fans

The hot Boston sports topic is the future of Fenway Park, the oldest facility in major league baseball (1912), followed closely by the future of the Boston Red Sox. Plans to replace the legendary park include tearing down at least part of it, and the franchise itself is for sale as I write this. The team won the 1918 World Series, and then took a break (82 years, at press time), which only adds to the aura. For diehard fans who want to say they saw the old Fenway, there really is no time like the present.

Boston's sports scene offers more than just the Red Sox. Included here are a few other teams and places to round out your sports tour.

Fenway Park

Kenmore Square

The **Red Sox** play from April until at least early October. Tickets go on sale in January; prices start at $14 for the bleachers. Just about every seat in the place is narrow, cramped, and delightfully close to the action.

If you didn't plan your trip months in advance, not to worry: Check with the ticket office when you arrive in town, or visit on the day of the game you want to see. A limited number of standing room tickets go on sale the day of the game, and ticket holders sometimes return those they can't use. Your concierge may be able to lend a hand, too.

Given a choice between a right-field grandstand seat (in sections 1 through 11 or so) and the bleachers, go for the slightly less expensive bleachers and the better view.

You can also take a **tour of Fenway Park,** which includes a walk on the warning track. From May to September, tours begin on weekdays only at 10 a.m., 11 a.m., noon, and 1 p.m. No tours operate on holidays or before day games. Admission is $5 for adults, $4 for seniors, $3 for children under 16. Call ☎ **617-236-6666** for more information.

Red Sox ticket office, 4 Yawkey Way (near the corner of Brookline Ave., in the stadium). ☎ 617-267-8661 for information; 617-267-1700 for tickets; 617-482-4SOX for touch-tone ticketing. Internet: www.redsox.com. *T: Fenway (Green Line D) or Kenmore (Green Line B, C, or D). Games usually begin at 6 p.m. or 7 p.m. weeknights; 1 p.m. on weekends.*

FleetCenter

North Station

The FleetCenter is home to two professional teams and a museum. Boston's championship basketball team, the **Celtics** (www. bostonceltics.com), play from early October to April or May. Prices start as low as $10 for some games. Tickets to the **Bruins** (www. bostonbruins.com) ice hockey games sometimes sell out despite being among the most expensive in the league ($37 and up).

Also at the Fleet, you can get a sense of how the Boston area earned its reputation as a sports paradise — which certainly doesn't rest on any of the current teams' records. The **Sports Museum of New England** (☎ **617-624-1234**) occupies the arena's fifth- and sixth-level concourses. This museum offers a specialized collection, most appealing for devoted fans of regional sports. Admission is $5 for adults, $4 for seniors, students, and children 6 to 17. Hours (subject to change during events) are Tuesday to Saturday 10 a.m. to 5 p.m. and Sunday noon to 5 p.m.

Off Causeway Street at North Station. ☎ 617-624-1000 for general info for every event. Internet: www.fleetcenter.com. *T: Green or Orange Line.*

Foxboro Stadium

Foxboro

The **New England Patriots** (☎ **800-543-1776**; Internet: www.patriots.com) usually sell out their football games at Foxboro Stadium, about an hour south of Boston. CMGI Field, which should open in 2002 to replace Foxboro Stadium, likely will be even more popular because it's new. Plan as far ahead as possible. The team plays from August through December or January.

Route 1. Call the Patriots' number or check their Web site, both listed above, for stadium information. The stadium is not near a T stop, but you can catch a bus from South Station or the Riverside Green Line T station to the stadium (call ☎ 800-23LOGAN for information about the bus).

College sports are much less expensive than their pro counterparts and loads of fun. Ice hockey is the most hotly contested of the dozens of sports in which local teams compete. Check the papers to see what's up during your visit, then call to check ticket availability. The Division I schools are **Boston College** (☎ 617-552-3000), **Boston University** (☎ 617-353-3838), **Harvard University** (☎ 617-495-2211), and **Northeastern University** (☎ 617-373-4700).

Chapter 18

And on Your Left, Quincy Market: Seeing Boston by Guided Tour

· ·

In This Chapter

▶ Deciding whether to take a guided tour

▶ Seeing the sights on land, water, and (wow!) both

▶ Investigating special interests

· ·

*T*he most important question about guided tours (even before "which one?") is "why?" If your time is limited, you have trouble getting around, or you haven't a clue about what to expect from Boston, a general orientation tour may be right for you. Visitors interested in a particular topic often want to seek out a guide who knows it cold. And if you crave something offbeat, Boston has that, too, in the form of tours that cover land *and* water.

Another good question is "why not?" Maybe a day trundling off and on a trolley sounds hopelessly touristy, or you can't bear the cookie-cutter sameness of standard tours. Don't let that turn you off all guided tours, though — a special-interest walking tour may be just the thing. One thing to note: Don't waste your money on a tour ticket that covers a whole day if you think one circuit of a trolley tour is all you need. You'll be cheating yourself out of the rich experiences you can only enjoy at ground level.

Boston offers four main types of guided tours: walking, trolley (a bus with a trolley-style body), cruise, and Duck.

> ✔ **Walking tours** place you face-to-face with the city. Boston abounds with small pleasures — a whiff of ocean air, sunlight through a blown-glass window — and walking tours put you in touch with them. But these tours don't cover everything, they're relatively brief, and they can be tiring. And keep in mind that regularly scheduled walking tours typically don't run in the winter.

✔ For an overview of an attraction or area, a narrated **trolley tour** can be a reasonable option. You can choose specific attractions to focus on, or take advantage of the all-day pass to visit as many places as you can. Some trolley stops, especially in the North End, lie some distance from the attractions. And piling off a trolley with a little sticker on your shirt (it allows you to reboard) is very much a "typical tourist" thing. But these tours do operate year-round.

✔ **Sightseeing cruises** offer sensational scenery and an unusual vantage point. Tours on the Inner Harbor pass the airport (a hit with aviation buffs), include some maritime history, and make pleasant alternatives to walking or driving. But these tours aren't comprehensive, don't last too long, and close for the winter.

✔ **Boston Duck Tours,** the only amphibious operation in town, offers a great deal of fun for a fair amount of money.

Walking Tours

Check the Thursday *Globe* "Calendar" section when you arrive to see whether any operators are offering special-interest or one-shot tours to coincide with events or anniversaries during your visit.

Free 90-minute Freedom Trail walking tours with **National Park Service** rangers as guides start as often as four times a day during busy periods, once daily in the winter. These tours cover the "heart" of the trail — from the Old South Meeting House to the Old North Church. Schedules change seasonally. You don't need reservations, but try to arrive 30 minutes prior to the start of the tour, especially during busy times; groups are no larger than 30. Tours depart from the Visitor Center, 15 State St. (T: State [Orange or Blue Line]; ☎ **617-242-5642;** Internet: www.nps. gov/bost), off Washington Street across from the Old State House. Call to check on tour times and schedules.

The best private walking tour provider is the nonprofit organization **Boston by Foot** (☎ **617-367-2345,** or 617-367-3766 for recorded information; Internet: www.bostonbyfoot.com). From May through October, this company offers historical and architectural tours that concentrate on certain neighborhoods and topics. The volunteer guides love their subjects and welcome questions. The 90-minute tours run rain or shine; you don't need reservations. Buy tickets ($8) from the guide. Excursions that leave from Faneuil Hall meet at the statue of Samuel Adams on Congress Street. The regularly scheduled tours include the following:

✔ The **"Heart of the Freedom Trail"** tour starts at Faneuil Hall Tuesday through Saturday at 10 a.m.

✔ The **Beacon Hill** tour starts at the foot of the State House steps on Beacon Street weekdays at 5:30 p.m.; Saturday at 10 a.m.; Sunday at 2 p.m.

✔ The **"Boston Underground"** tour includes crypts, the subway, and the Central Artery construction. This tour starts at Faneuil Hall Sunday at 2 p.m.

✔ The **Victorian Back Bay** tour starts at the steps of Trinity Church at 10 a.m. Friday and Saturday.

✔ The **Waterfront** tour starts at Faneuil Hall on Friday at 5:30 p.m. and Sunday at 10 a.m.

✔ The **North End** tour starts at Faneuil Hall on Saturday at 2 p.m.

The **Society for the Preservation of New England Antiquities** (☎ 617- 227-3956; Internet: www.spnea.org) offers a 2-hour tour that focuses on life in the upstairs-downstairs world of Beacon Hill in 1800. "Magnificent and Modest" ($10) starts at the Harrison Gray Otis House, 141 Cambridge St. (see Chapter 17), at 11 a.m. on Saturdays and Sundays from May through October. The price includes a tour of the Otis House; reservations are recommended.

The **Boston Park Rangers** (☎ 617-635-7383; Internet: www.ci. boston.ma.us/parks) offer free tours of the "Emerald Necklace," pioneering landscape architect Frederick Law Olmsted's loop of green spaces. These tours include Boston Common, the Public Garden, the Commonwealth Avenue Mall, the Muddy River in the Fenway, Olmsted Park, Jamaica Pond, the Arnold Arboretum, and Franklin Park. The full 6-hour walk happens only a few times a year; one-hour tours that highlight a location or theme take place year-round. Check ahead for topics and schedules.

Trolley Tours

These tours are a popular way to see the sights, and easy ways to "see" everything without getting a good sense of what Boston is really like. Don't fall into that trap — if you can possibly manage it, climb down and look around.

The cutthroat competition between tour operators makes their offerings virtually indistinguishable. Each company offers slightly different stops, but all cover the major attractions. The 90- to 120-minute tours usually include a map and all-day reboarding (so you don't have to do the whole thing at once).

The guide makes or breaks the tour; shop around to find one you particularly like before you pay. Local news outlets periodically "break" the story that guides are embellishing the facts in their narratives (a whole summer of reciting the same stories would probably get to you, too), but most of them are on the level. And some of the most improbable-sounding stories are actually true. (For instance, the true story of a woman and her lover buried alive by her husband inspired Edgar Allan Poe's "Fall of the House of Usher.")

Trolley tickets cost $18 to $24 for adults, $12 or less for kids. Stops usu-
ally are at hotels, attractions, and tourist information centers. To start,
seek out busy waiting areas where you can check out the guides and
see if you click with one. Trolleys line up near the New England
Aquarium and near the corner of Boylston Street and Charles Street
South, where the Common meets the Public Garden.

Each company paints its cars a different color. Orange-and-green **Old
Town Trolleys** (☎ 617-269-7150; Internet: www.historictours.com)
are the most numerous. Minuteman Tours' **Boston Trolley Tours**
(☎ 617-867-5539; Internet: www.historictours.com) are blue and
Beantown Trolleys (☎ 800-343-1328 or 617-236-2148) are red. The
Discover Boston Multilingual Trolley Tours (☎ 617-742-1440) vehicle
is white; these tours are conducted in Japanese, Spanish, French,
German, and Italian.

Sightseeing Cruises

Seeing Boston from the water gives you a sense of the city's storied
maritime history — and confirms that (except in the winter) the water
is cooler than the land. On a sweaty summer day, a breezy cruise
makes an enjoyable break from a march along the tourist track. The
new perspective will help you remember that the city remains an
active port, and the sheer number of sailboats will make you wonder if
every office in the city is empty.

The season for narrated cruises runs from April through October, with
spring and fall offerings usually on weekends only. If you tend to get
seasick, check the size of the vessel before you pay; larger boats are
more comfortable. See Chapter 17 for information on whale watching.

Boston Harbor Cruises, 1 Long Wharf (☎ 617-227-4321; Internet:
www.bostonboats.com), operates 30-minute lunchtime cruises ($2)
on weekdays at 12:15 p.m. Ninety-minute historic tours of the Inner
and Outer Harbor begin at 11 a.m., 1 p.m., 3 p.m., and 7 p.m. (the
sunset cruise). Tickets are $15 for adults, $12 for seniors, $10 for chil-
dren under 12. The 45-minute *Constitution* cruise takes you around the
Inner Harbor and docks at the Charlestown Navy Yard so you can go
ashore and visit "Old Ironsides." Tours start every hour on the half-
hour from 10:30 a.m. to 4:30 p.m., and leave the navy yard on the hour
from 11 a.m. to 5 p.m. Tickets are $8 for adults, $7 for seniors, $6 for
children. Trips leave from Long Wharf, off Atlantic Avenue between the
New England Aquarium and the Marriott.

Massachusetts Bay Lines (☎ 617-542-8000; Internet: www.
massbaylines.com) offers 55-minute harbor tours on the hour
from 10 a.m. to 6 p.m. You'll get a sailor's-eye view of the waterfront,
harbor islands, and airport; the sunset cruise also passes the
Charlestown Navy Yard in time to hear the cannon salute that signals

day's end. The price is $8 for adults, $5 for children and seniors. The 90-minute sunset cruise, at 7 p.m., costs $15 for adults, $10 for children and seniors. Cruises leave from Rowes Wharf, off Atlantic Avenue behind the Boston Harbor Hotel.

The **Charles Riverboat Company** (☎ **617-621-3001**; Internet: www. charlesriverboat.com), operates out of the CambridgeSide Galleria mall, on First Street in East Cambridge. From the Charles, you can enjoy a panoramic view of Boston (including the towers of the Back Bay) and Cambridge (the landmark dome indicates that you're approaching MIT); the harbor cruise traces the Boston waterfront. Its 55-minute cruises around the lower Charles River basin depart on the hour from noon to 5 p.m. Once a day at 10:30 a.m., a 55-minute tour goes in the opposite direction, through the Charles River locks to Boston Harbor. Tickets for either tour are $8 for adults, $6 for seniors, $6 for seniors, $5 for children 2 to 12.

The cheapest "cruise" is the $1.25 ferry ride from Long Wharf to the Charlestown Navy Yard to Lovejoy Wharf, behind North Station. The MBTA visitor pass (see Chapter 11) covers the ferry, which makes a great way to finish the Freedom Trail.

Duck Tours

The most unusual excursions in town are 80-minute **Boston Duck Tours** (☎ **800-226-7442** or 617-723-DUCK; Internet: www.bostonducktours. com), which operate from April through November. They're relatively expensive, but you're paying for novelty, and it's worth the money. The vehicles are reconditioned World War II amphibious landing craft known as "ducks" — and like the real thing, they move easily between land and water. The duck cruises around Boston, passing most of the major sights, and then heads to the Charles River dam and right into the water for a turn around the basin.

Tickets, available inside the Prudential Center (also known as the "Pru"), are $21 for adults, $18 for seniors and students, $11 for children 4 to 12, and 25 cents for children under 4. Boarding is on the Boylston Street side of the Pru. Tours run every 30 minutes from 9 a.m. to 1 hour before sunset. Reservations are not accepted (except for groups of 16 or more), and tickets usually sell out, especially on weekends. Try to buy same-day tickets early in the day, or ask about the limited number of tickets available 2 days ahead. No tours operate from December through March.

Special-Interest Tours

Boston by Foot targets 6- to 12-year-olds (who must be accompanied by an adult) with **Boston by Little Feet.** The 60-minute walking tour concentrates on the architecture along the Freedom Trail and on

Boston's role in the American Revolution. The price ($6) includes a map. Tours run from May through October. Meet at the statue of Samuel Adams on the Congress Street side of Faneuil Hall on Saturday at 10 a.m., Sunday at 2 p.m., and Monday at 10 a.m. — rain or shine.

The **Historic Neighborhoods Foundation** (☎ 617-426-1885) offers a 90-minute "Make Way for Ducklings" tour that entertains both children and adults. The route follows the path of the Mallard family described in Robert McCloskey's beloved book of the same name, ending at the Public Garden. The price is $7 for adults, $5 for children over 4, free for younger children. Call for schedules.

The **Boston History Collaborative** (☎ 617-574-5950), a nonprofit group created to promote historic tourism, coordinates several heritage trails that focus on subjects significant to local history. This group's offerings are still evolving, but all are worth looking into.

The best known special-interest tour is the **Literary Trail** (☎ 617-574-5950; Internet: www.Lit-Trail.org), a 5-hour trolley tour of sites in Boston, Cambridge, and Concord associated with local authors. You can tour on your own, too, using a guide that's available at local bookstores for $4.95. The escorted tour costs $35 for adults, $31.50 for students and children under 18. Check ahead for schedules and reservations.

Other History Collaborative offerings range from simple (a downloadable self-guided tour route) to elaborate (a 90-minute cruise). Each Web site has links to the others. Check ahead for info about **Boston by Sea: The Maritime Trail** (www.bostonbysea.org); **Boston Family History** (www.BostonFamilyHistory.org), which concentrates on immigration; the **Innovation Trail** (www.innovationtrail.org), which focuses on technological, medical, and financial breakthroughs and a trail that follows the African-American community from abolition to civil rights.

National Park Service rangers lead free 2-hour walking tours of the **Black Heritage Trail,** a 1.6-mile route on Beacon Hill that includes stations of the Underground Railroad, homes of famous citizens, and the first integrated public school. Tours leave from the Visitor Center, 46 Joy St. (☎ 617-742-5415; Internet: www.nps.gov/boaf); check ahead for schedules. To explore on your own, pick up a brochure from the Visitor Center; these brochures include maps and descriptions of the buildings.

The **Boston Women's Heritage Trail** includes homes, churches, and social and political institutions associated with 20 influential women. You can buy a guide (make sure it's the most recent, from 1999) at the National Park Service Visitor Center at 15 State St.; you can also check local bookstores and historic sites for these guides. For more detailed information, call ☎ 617-522-2872.

Old Town Trolley (☎ **617-269-7150;** Internet: www.historictours. com) offers specialty tours on a wide and changing variety of subjects. These tours currently include "JFK's Boston," which visits sights related to the president; a brew pub tour; a chocolate-tasting tour; and a seafood tour. Tickets usually cost at least $20 for adults, more if the tour includes refreshments. Call for information, schedules, and reservations.

Chapter 19

A Shop-'Til-You-Drop Guide to Boston

* *

In This Chapter

▶ Checking out the big names and other famous labels

▶ Exploring the main shopping areas

▶ Finding the right place for what you want

* *

*B*efore you feel guilty about shopping when there's still so much sightseeing to do, consider this: Visitors to Boston consistently list the city's stores as their favorite destination, even ahead of its museums. Retail outlets of every description await you, from unusual boutiques to indistinguishable chain stores. In this chapter, I concentrate on the offbeat destinations, with plenty of attention to big national names and retail-intensive neighborhoods. All over town, you'll also find tons of businesses you recognize from the mall at home. Unless otherwise noted, see the "Boston Shopping" map in this chapter for the locations of the stores I mention.

The Shopping Scene

The first thing to know is that the 5 percent Massachusetts sales tax does not apply to clothing priced below $175 or to food items. If you buy an article of clothing for $175 or more, the tax applies only to the amount over $175. But if you're shipping merchandise to a state where the store has a branch, the sales tax for that state usually applies; check before celebrating a bargain that isn't.

Stores usually open at 9:30 or 10 a.m. and close at around 6 or 7 p.m. A few don't open on Sunday, but most do, from noon to 5 or 6 p.m. Exceptions include shopping malls, which stay open later; art galleries, which typically don't open until 11 a.m., and close on Monday; and smaller shops, which often make their own hours. When in doubt, call ahead.

Boston Shopping

Abercrombie & Fitch **22**
Ann Taylor **6 22**
Anthropologie **1**
Artful Hand Gallery **6**
Barnes & Noble **19**
Black Ink **13**
Borders **20**
Boston Antique
  Cooperative I & II **14**
Boston City Store **22**
Brattle Book Shop **15**
Coach **22**
Copley Place **6**
Crate & Barrel **6 22**
Dairy Fresh Candies **25**

FAO Schwarz **8**
Filene's **17**
Filene's Basement **18**
The Gap **22**
Globe Corner Bookstore **7**
Gucci **6**
Hermès of Paris **11**
J. Pace & Son **23**
Koo De Kir **12**
Legal Seafoods **3 6**
Lord & Taylor **5**
Louis Vuitton **6**
Macy's **16**
The Magic Hat **22**
Museum of Fine Arts **6 22**

Neiman Marcus **6**
Newbury Comics **22**
The Nostalgia Factory **24**
Restoration Hardware **2**
Rockport **22**
Saks Fifth Avenue **4**
Salumeria Italiana **26**
Scribes Delight Pen Shop **22**
Shops at Prudential Center **3**
Shop at the Union **9**
Shreve, Crump & Low **10**
Thomas Pink **6**
Tiffany & Co. **6**
Williams-Sonoma **6 22**

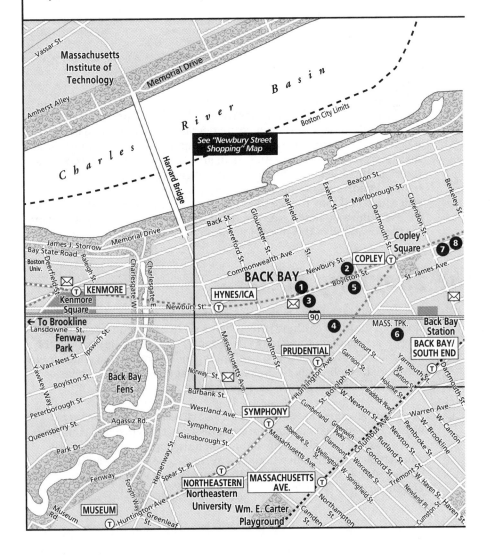

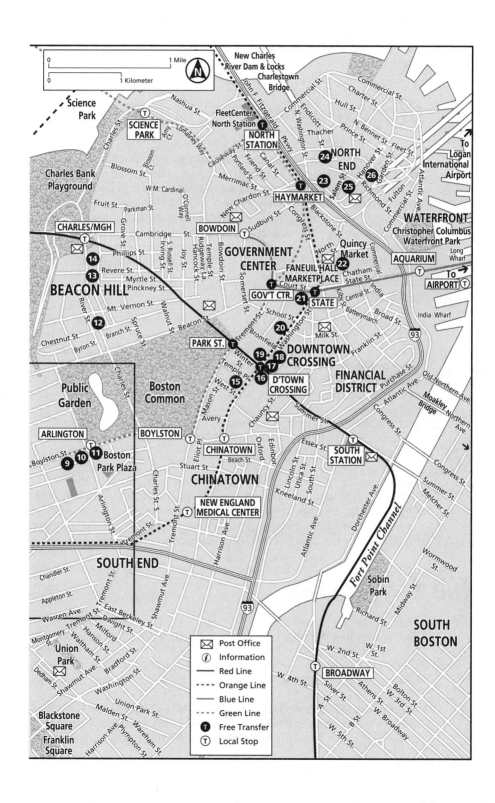

0 ___ 1 Mile
0 ___ 1 Kilometer

New Charles
River Dam & Locks
Charlestown
Bridge
John F. Fitzgerald

Science
Park

Nashua St.

Commercial St.
Charter St.
Hull St.
N. Bennet St.
Fleet St.

FleetCenter
North Station

SCIENCE
PARK

NORTH
STATION

Commercial St.
N. Washington St.
Endicott
Thacher
Prince St.
Hanover St.
Garden St.

To
Logan
International
Airport

Charles Bank
Playground

Blossom St.

Merrimac St.

24 **NORTH
END**

25 26

Atlantic Ave.

W.M. Cardinal

New Chardon St.

23

HAYMARKET

Salem St.
Richmond St.
Fulton

Commercial St.
WATERFRONT
Christopher Columbus
Waterfront Park

Fruit St.
Parkman St.

CHARLES/MGH

Cambridge St.

Grove St.

14

13

Phillips St.
Revere St.
Myrtle St.

BEACON HILL

Pinckney St.

BOWDOIN

Sudbury St.

Blackstone St.

GOVERNMENT
CENTER

North
FANEUIL HALL
MARKETPLACE

Quincy
Market

22

AQUARIUM

Long
Wharf

To
AIRPORT

India Wharf

Mt. Vernon St.

12

Chestnut St.
Byron St.

Branch St.
Spruce St.
Walnut St.
Beacon St.

GOV'T CTR.

21 STATE

School St.

Court St.
Central St.
Battery march
Broad St.

India St.

PARK ST.

Tremont St.
Bromfield
Washington St.

20

Milk St.

Franklin St.

93

Public
Garden

Boston
Common

Charles St.

ARLINGTON

BOYLSTON

Winter St.
Temple Pl.
19 18
17

15 16 **D'TOWN
CROSSING**

DOWNTOWN
CROSSING

FINANCIAL
DISTRICT

Purchase St.
Atlantic Ave.

Old Northern Ave.

Moakley
Bridge
Northern
Ave.

Boylston St.

9 10 11 Boston
Park Plaza

Eliot Pl.

CHINATOWN

Stuart St.
Beach St.

West St.
Avery

Chauncy St.
Oxford
Edinbor
Summer St.

Essex St.

Lincoln St.
Utica St.
South St.

SOUTH
STATION

Congress St.
Summer St.
Melcher St.

Arlington St.

CHINATOWN

Charles St. S.

Tremont St.

NEW ENGLAND
MEDICAL CENTER

Kneeland St.

Atlantic Ave.

Dorchester Ave.

Fort Point Channel

Wormwood
St.

SOUTH END

Chandler St.
Appleton St.

Warren Ave.

E. Berkeley St.
Dwight St.
Milford St.

Shawmut Ave.

Harrison Ave.

93

Sobin
Park

Richard St.
Midway St.

SOUTH
BOSTON

Montgomery St.
Tremont St.
Hanson St.
Waltham St.

Union
Park

Dedham St.
Shawmut Ave.

Bradford St.
Washington St.

Union Park St.

W. 2nd St.
W. 1st
St.

W. 4th St.

BROADWAY

Silver St.
Athens St.
Bolton St.

W. 3rd St.
W. Broadway

Blackstone
Square

Malden St.
Wareham St.

Franklin
Square

Harrison Ave.
Plympton St.

W. 5th St.

✉	Post Office
ⓘ	Information
——	Red Line
----	Orange Line
~~	Blue Line
----	Green Line
●	Free Transfer
Ⓣ	Local Stop

Always check out the gift shop when you visit a museum or other attraction (see Chapters 16 and 17). Prices are competitive, and the merchandise often draws on the museum's collections in its design or inspiration.

The Biggest Name

That would be **Filene's Basement,** 426 Washington St., at Summer Street; enter directly from the station or through Filene's, the department store upstairs. (T: Downtown Crossing [Red or Orange Line]; ☎ 617-542-2011.) After a period when the store's well-known bargains were harder to sniff out (though they never entirely disappeared), "the Basement" seems to be back on track. This store is the flagship of a chain that emerged from bankruptcy in 2000 as part of the Midwestern chain Value City. Somehow it has maintained the cachet accumulated in nearly a century of great deals on men's, women's, and children's clothing and accessories.

The legendary "automatic markdown" policy applies only at this store. After merchandise has been on the racks for 2 weeks, its price drops by 25 percent. Boards hanging from the ceiling bear the all-important dates; the original sale date is on the back of the price tag. Prices continue to fall until, after 5 weeks (and 75 percent off), everything remaining goes to charity. To fit in with the locals, be aggressive and don't be shy about telling people how much — how little, really — you paid for that stunning designer outfit. And if you can't make up your mind about something, just buy it. You can always return merchandise, but you can't always come back and find it the next day. Yes, this is the voice of experience talking.

Open weekdays 9:30 a.m. to 7:30 p.m., Saturday 9 a.m. to 7:30 p.m., Sunday 11 a.m. to 7 p.m. Crowds can be huge at lunch and after work, especially during special sales; try to shop in the morning or midafternoon. T: Downtown Crossing (Red or Orange Line); enter directly from the station or through Filene's, the department store upstairs.

The Big Names

People complain about the rise of chain stores, but when they really need a wedding present, off they go to Crate & Barrel. Many of Boston's high-profile retailers are branches, often of chains based in New York. I single out a few in the neighborhood descriptions that appear later in this chapter; for that only-in-Boston feeling, check out the following:

Shreve, Crump & Low, 330 Boylston St. (☎ 617-267-9100), is the oldest jewelry store in the country (since 1796). Legendary diamonds, traditional silver baby presents, even a superb antiques department (on the second floor). Call it "Shreve's," and remember to check out the estate jewelry.

The **Museum of Fine Arts** operates gift shops at Copley Place (☎ **617-536-8818**) and in the South Market Building at Faneuil Hall Marketplace (☎ **617-720-1266**). The well-stocked satellites can't replace the real thing, but they make a fine substitute.

Filene's, 426 Washington St., at Summer Street, Downtown Crossing (☎ **617-357-2100**), and CambridgeSide Galleria, East Cambridge (☎ **617-621-3800**). Part of a national department-store conglomerate, but with a fine old New England name (fie-*leen's*). Note: This is not Filene's Basement (see the previous section, "The Biggest Name"), which is below Filene's and no longer the same company.

Newbury Comics is a local chain of fantastic music stores that also stock gifts and comics. Three stores are located in Boston: 332 Newbury St., Back Bay (☎ **617-236-4930**); 1 Washington Mall, Washington Street off State Street, Downtown Crossing (☎ **617-248-9992**); and 36 John F. Kennedy St., in the Garage mall, Harvard Square (☎ **617-491-0337**).

Great Shopping Neighborhoods

Here I zero in on some consumer-friendly areas and single out some favorite stops. By no means does that mean that these areas are the only parts of town worth trolling, or that the shops I mention are the only ones to visit. You know what you like, and you can probably track it down. Hey, you turned straight to the shopping chapter (go on, admit it) — trust your instincts.

The Back Bay

From name-dropping socialites to head-banging students, everyone shops in the Back Bay. The main shopping streets are Newbury and Boylston (T: Arlington [Green Line]).

For locations of shops on Newbury Street, see the "Newbury Street Shopping" map in this chapter.

Newbury Street is the Rodeo Drive of New England. Known as the home of the area's toniest boutiques and art galleries, it runs from **Chanel** and **Burberrys** (at Arlington Street) to **Tower Records** and **Urban Outfitters** (at Mass. Ave.). Newbury even has a Web site (www. newbury-st.com). You'll see **Brooks Brothers,** multiple two **Armani** outlets, the alarmingly huge **Niketown,** and an assortment of other famous names.

Newbury Street Shopping

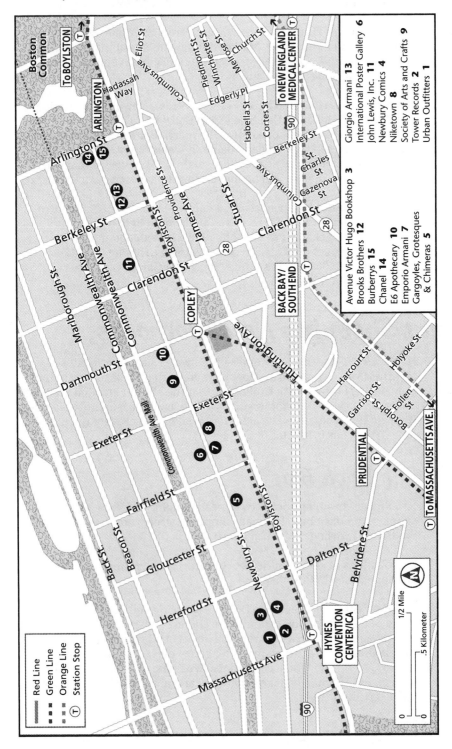

Avenue Victor Hugo Bookshop **3**
Brooks Brothers **12**
Burberrys **15**
Chanel **14**
E6 Apothecary **10**
Emporio Armani **7**
Gargoyles, Grotesques
  & Chimeras **5**

Giorgio Armani **13**
International Poster Gallery **6**
John Lewis, Inc. **11**
Newbury Comics **4**
Niketown **8**
Society of Arts and Crafts **9**
Tower Records **2**
Urban Outfitters **1**

I tend to seek out the smaller retailers who celebrate their specialties in an attitude-free parallel universe. For exquisite jewelry, **John Lewis, Inc.,** 97 Newbury St. (☎ 617-266-6665); for museum-quality artisan work, the **Society of Arts and Crafts,** 175 Newbury St. (☎ 617-266-1810;** Internet: www.societyofcrafts.org); for gothic home accessories (not as far-out as it sounds), **Gargoyles, Grotesques & Chimeras,** 262 Newbury St. (☎ 617-536-2362). Fine cosmetics and friendly service appeal equally at **E6 Apothecary,** 167 Newbury St. (☎ 800-664-6635 or 617-236-8138; Internet: www.e6apothecary.com); the **International Poster Gallery,** 205 Newbury St. (☎ 617-375-0076; Internet: www.internationalposter.com), offers an agreeable mix of high art and low culture; and **Avenue Victor Hugo Bookshop,** 339 Newbury St. (☎ 617-266-7746; Internet: www.avenuevictorhugo-books.com), is an old-time independent bookseller. That's six. I promise you can find a dozen more with hardly any effort.

Newbury Street's other claim to fame is its dozens of art galleries. Pick up a copy of the free *Gallery Guide* (at any gallery and many other businesses) or start at Arlington Street and work your way west. Remember that some of the most interesting collections are above ground level. Don't be afraid to ask questions — the people hanging around the gallery, who often include the manager, love to talk about the art.

Boylston Street gets going at Arlington Street, with **Hermès of Paris** and **Shreve, Crump & Low** (see "The Big Names" earlier in this chapter), and extends past the entrance to the **Shops at Prudential Center** (see later in this section). This street is where you'll find **FAO Schwarz, Restoration Hardware, Anthropologie,** and **Lord & Taylor.**

One exceptional destination is the **Shop at the Union,** 356 Boylston St. (☎ 617-536-5651). It carries a dizzying variety of top-quality gifts, clothing, home accessories, and jewelry — not cheap, but practically guilt free. Proceeds go to the nonprofit Women's Educational and Industrial Union, an educational and social-service organization founded in 1877.

Boylston Street also holds one entrance to the giant consumer wonderland of the **Shops at Prudential Center,** 800 Boylston St. (T: Prudential [Green Line E] or Back Bay [Orange Line]; ☎ 800-SHOP-PRU or 617-267-1002), and **Copley Place,** 100 Huntington Ave. (☎ 617-375-4400). Skybridges link the malls, which incorporate dozens of national chains that allow you to pretend you've never left home, plus a smattering of unique boutiques.

The "Pru" contains a food court, a **Legal Sea Foods** (☎ 617-266-6800) restaurant (see Chapter 14), dozens of shops, an entrance to **Saks Fifth Avenue,** and various pushcarts that sell souvenirs, crafts, and accessories. The **Greater Boston Convention & Visitors Bureau** (☎ 800-SEE-BOSTON or 617-536-4100; Internet: www.bostonusa.com) operates the information booth.

Copley Place is a more upscale complex — entering from the Pru, one of the first stores you see is **Tiffany & Co.** The "anchor" store is **Neiman Marcus,** and its neighbors include the only Boston branches of such big names as **Gucci, Louis Vuitton,** and London haberdasher **Thomas Pink.** Also here are **Williams-Sonoma, Crate & Barrel,** and **Legal Sea Foods** (☎ 617-266-7775). Independent retailers tend not to thrive here; a welcome exception is the **Artful Hand Gallery,** Copley Place (☎ 617-262-9601), which carries a discriminating selection of jewelry, wood and glass pieces, ceramics, and sculpture.

Faneuil Hall Marketplace

Boston's top attraction, Faneuil Hall Marketplace (T: Government Center [Green or Blue Line]; ☎ 617-338-2323) draws much of its appeal from its abundant consumer enticements. Most street-level shops are chain outlets such as **Ann Taylor, Coach, Crate & Barrel,** and **Rockport;** there's also a huge, free-standing **Abercrombie & Fitch.** Exceptions include **The Magic Hat,** Marketplace Center (☎ 617-439-8840), which stocks all the trappings to satisfy would-be magicians, and **Scribes Delight Pen Shop,** South Market Building (☎ 617-523-2572). Second-floor shops (not including the **Gap** and **Williams-Sonoma**) tend to be quirkier independents, as do the pushcarts that cluster between the North Market Building and Quincy Market.

The **Boston City Store** (☎ 617-635-2911), on the lower level of Faneuil Hall, is a must if you enjoy unpredictability. City surplus doesn't sound all that exciting, but the funky merchandise ranges from T-shirts to mounted-police horseshoes to old street signs — and it changes regularly.

Charles Street

Beacon Hill's main street is both a neighborhood hangout and a gift-shopper magnet. Charles Street (T: Charles/MGH [Red Line]) is also home to some excellent antiques shops and a curiously refined 7-Eleven — thanks to the strict zoning laws that cover the landmark district.

Head for a specific destination, or just stroll up one side of the street and down the other. My favorite gift shops are **Koo De Kir,** 34 Charles St. (☎ 617-723-8111), and **Black Ink,** 101 Charles St. (☎ 617- 723-3883). A good place to start antique hunting is the **Boston Antique Cooperative I & II,** 119 Charles St. (☎ 617-227-9810).

Downtown Crossing

Filene's, Macy's, and **Filene's Basement** occupy the corner of Washington and Summer streets, the busiest stretch of the pedestrian mall at the center of Downtown Crossing (T: Downtown Crossing [Red or Orange Line]). The shopping here isn't as highfalutin as in the Back Bay or as touristy as at Faneuil Hall Marketplace. Downtown Crossing is where the locals shop.

Washington and Winter streets overflow with discount clothing and shoe stores, souvenir carts, and places for office workers to grab a quick lunch. Another necessity for real Bostonians is a well-stocked bookstore, and Downtown Crossing has three. **Barnes & Noble** and **Borders** carry a predictably huge range of books. The stock at the **Brattle Book Shop,** 9 West St. (off Washington St.; ☎ **800-447-9595** or 617-542-0210; Internet: www.brattlebookshop.com), is an unpredictably huge assortment of used, rare, and out-of-print titles.

The North End

You already know you'll be coming here for a pasta dinner; if you want to make your own, the North End (T: Haymarket [Green or Orange Line]) is the place to stock up.

Italian groceries and fresh meats and cheeses cram the shelves and cases at **J. Pace & Son,** 42 Cross St. (☎ **617-227-9673**), and **Salumeria Italiana,** 151 Richmond St. (☎ **617-523-8743**). Your sweet tooth can lead you to **Dairy Fresh Candies,** 57 Salem St. (☎ **800-336-5536** or 617-742-2639).

For a non-edible adventure, turn right as you leave Dairy Fresh and follow Salem Street to Cooper Street. Go left, and then take the first right to reach **The Nostalgia Factory,** 51 North Margin St. (☎ **800-479-8754** or 617-720-2211; Internet: www.nostalgia.com). Known nationally for its collection of posters and vintage advertising pieces, this shop is the perfect place to browse between snacks.

Cambridge

Harvard Square (T: Harvard [Red Line]) grows less individualized by the day, but it's still worth a trip if you know where to look. Bookstore enthusiasts and T-shirt collectors will be particularly happy here. (For locations of stores in this section, see the "Harvard Square Shopping" map in this chapter.)

Agreeable chain stores in the neighborhood include **Urban Outfitters, Barnes & Noble** (which runs the book operation at the **Harvard Coop**), **Crate & Barrel,** and **Tower Records.**

"The Square" is great for window-shopping, and the best displays are at **Calliope,** 33 Brattle St. (☎ **617-876-4149**), a terrific children's clothing and toy store. A block away is **Colonial Drug,** 49 Brattle St. (☎ **617-864-2222**), a family business that specializes in hard-to-find fragrances. At **Beadworks,** 23 Church St. (☎ **617-868-9777**), you'll find everything you need to make your own jewelry — an excellent activity if kids are along, and even if they're not.

Harvard Square Shopping

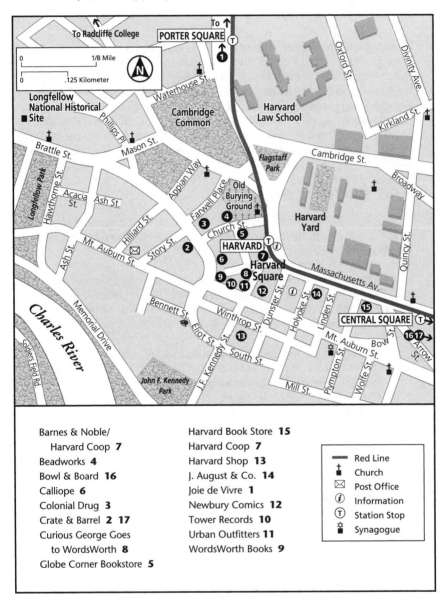

Barnes & Noble/	Harvard Book Store **15**	
Harvard Coop **7**	Harvard Coop **7**	——— Red Line
Beadworks **4**	Harvard Shop **13**	✝ Church
Bowl & Board **16**	J. August & Co. **14**	✉ Post Office
Calliope **6**	Joie de Vivre **1**	ⓘ Information
Colonial Drug **3**	Newbury Comics **12**	Ⓣ Station Stop
Crate & Barrel **2 17**	Tower Records **10**	✡ Synagogue
Curious George Goes	Urban Outfitters **11**	
to WordsWorth **8**	WordsWorth Books **9**	
Globe Corner Bookstore **5**		

Now, how about those bookstores? Two of the area's best general-interest stores are here: **WordsWorth Books,** 30 Brattle St. (☎ **800-899-2202** or 617-354-5201; Internet: `www.wordsworth.com`); and the **Harvard Book Store,** 1256 Mass. Ave. (☎ **800-542-READ** outside 617, or 617-661-1515; Internet: `www.harvard.com`). WordsWorth discounts everything except textbooks at least 10 percent, and the basement of the Harvard Book Store overflows with discounted books and used books.

Two worthwhile special-interest bookstores are **Curious George Goes to WordsWorth,** 1 John F. Kennedy St. (☎ **617-498-0062;** Internet: www.curiousg.com), an excellent children's store, and the **Globe Corner Bookstore,** 28 Church St. (☎ **617-497-6277;** Internet: www.globecorner.com), where you'll find travel books, maps, narratives, and atlases.

Harvard Square also makes a good starting point for a shopping stroll. **Mass. Ave.** runs north to **Porter Square** through boutique country and southeast toward funkier **Central Square.** Heading toward Porter, be sure to leave time for a stop at **Joie de Vivre,** 1792 Mass. Ave., (☎ **617-864-8188**), a superb gift shop with a great kaleidoscope collection. On the way to Central Square, you'll pass **Bowl & Board,** 1063 Mass. Ave. (☎ **617-661-0350**), which specializes in upscale home accessories, and a **Crate & Barrel** furniture store.

In **East Cambridge,** the **CambridgeSide Galleria,** 100 CambridgeSide Place (T: Lechmere [Green Line], and then walk 2 blocks. Or Kendall/ MIT [Red Line], and then the free shuttle bus, which runs every 10–20 minutes Mon–Sat 10 a.m.–9:30 p.m., Sun 11 a.m.–7 p.m.; ☎ **617-621-8666**), is a three-level mall with more than 100 specialty stores, a branch of **Borders,** several restaurants, and a food court. Part of its appeal is how astonishingly generic it is; the Galleria may be just the bargaining chip you need to lure your teenagers to the nearby Museum of Science. T: Lechmere (Green Line), then walk 2 blocks. Or Kendall/ MIT (Red Line), then the free shuttle bus, which runs every 10 to 20 minutes Monday to Saturday from 10 a.m. to 9:30 p.m. and Sunday from 11 a.m. to 7 p.m.

Join the crowd: College bookstores

Anything big enough to hold a college logo is for sale somewhere, and Boston offers a breathtaking variety. The big name is Harvard, of course, but savvy sightseers may prefer something less predictable. If that's you, check out the following:

- ✔ **Barnes & Noble** at Boston University, 660 Beacon St., Kenmore Square (☎ 617-267-8484).
- ✔ **Emerson College Book Store,** 80 Boylston St., Theater District (☎ 617-728-7700).
- ✔ **MIT Coop,** 3 Cambridge Center, Kendall Square (☎ 617-499-3200) and 84 Mass. Ave. (☎ 617-499-2000).
- ✔ **Northeastern University Bookstore,** 360 Huntington Ave., Fenway (between Symphony Hall and the Museum of Fine Arts; ☎ 617-373-2286).
- ✔ **Suffolk University Bookstore,** 148 Cambridge St., Beacon Hill (☎ 617-227-4085).

For Harvard paraphernalia, try the following, all in Harvard Square:

- ✔ **Harvard Coop,** 1400 Mass. Ave. (☎ 617-499-2000).
- ✔ **Harvard Shop,** 52 John F. Kennedy St. (☎ 617-864-3000).
- ✔ **J. August & Co.,** 1320 Mass. Ave. (☎ 617-864-6650).

Index of Stores by Merchandise

Antiques
Boston Antique Cooperative I & II

Art and Posters
International Poster Gallery
The Nostalgia Factory

Books
Avenue Victor Hugo Bookshop
Barnes & Noble
Borders
Brattle Book Shop
Curious George Goes to WordsWorth
Globe Corner Bookstore
Harvard Book Store
The Harvard Coop
WordsWorth Books

Clothing and Accessories
Abercrombie & Fitch
Ann Taylor
Armani
Burberrys
Brooks Brothers
Chanel
Coach
The Gap
Gucci
Hermès of Paris
Louis Vuitton
Thomas Pink
Urban Outfitters

Cosmetics and Perfume
Colonial Drug
E6 Apothecary

Crafts
Artful Hand Gallery
Society of Arts and Crafts

Department Stores
Filene's
Lord & Taylor
Macy's
Neiman Marcus
Saks Fifth Avenue

Discount Clothing
Filene's Basement

Food and Candy
Dairy Fresh Candies
J. Pace & Son
Salumeria Italiana

Footware
Niketown
Rockport

Gifts and Toys
Anthropologie
Black Ink
Boston City Store
Calliope
FAO Schwarz
Joie de Vivre
Koo De Kir
The Magic Hat
Museum of Fine Arts gift shops
Scribes Delight Pen Shop
The Shop at the Union
Urban Outfitters

Home Accessories
Bowl & Board
Crate & Barrel
Gargoyles, Grotesques & Chimeras
Restoration Hardware
Williams-Sonoma

Jewelry

Beadworks
John Lewis, Inc.
Shreve, Crump & Low
Tiffany & Co.

Malls

Copley Place
Shops at Prudential Center

Music

Newbury Comics
Tower Records

Chapter 20

Five Great Boston Itineraries

*F*rom the moment you land in a new city, you can almost hear the clock ticking. The city offers so much for you to see and you never seem to have enough time to explore all its possibilities.

Relax and consider two things: First, Boston is a compact, manageable city, and you can get a good sense of it in just a few days; second, you can't master *any* destination of appreciable size in such a short time, so the pressure is off. Yes, you can see six or eight or a dozen places and things in a day, but what does that get you? (A mediocre-to-unsatisfying trip, that's what.)

Do what you want with the time you have. In this chapter, I suggest outlines for trips of certain durations or focuses; feel free to mix and match as you see fit.

Boston in 3 Days

Day 1: In the morning, follow at least part of the **Freedom Trail** (see Chapter 16). The trail officially starts at Boston Common, but you can start in Charlestown, somewhere in the middle, or at the National Park Service Visitor Center with a ranger tour (see Chapter 18). The trail takes at least 2 hours. (On the first section of the trail, consider a detour to **Filene's Basement,** especially if you can get there before the lunch rush. See the first map in Chapter 19 for the store's location.) Break for coffee, snacks, or lunch at **Faneuil Hall Marketplace,** where takeout counters and sit-down restaurants satisfy nearly every taste. **Durgin-Park** (see Chapter 14) is a good choice for the latter. If the weather is fine, take a picnic — stock up in the sprawling Quincy Market food court — across Atlantic Avenue to the end of Long Wharf (past the Marriott) or to Christopher Columbus Park.

In the afternoon, push on to the **North End.** Between the Paul Revere House and the Old North Church, pause on **Hanover Street** for espresso or cappuccino and a pastry at a *caffè* (see Chapter 15). If you opt to finish the trail — and I'm *not* saying you have to — return downtown on the MBTA **ferry** to Long Wharf from the Charlestown Navy Yard. Once you arrive at Long Wharf, look for a branch of **Legal Sea Foods** across the street from the ferry dock; you can grab some dinner here (but first you may decide to visit your hotel to rest and wash up — the people at the next table certainly will appreciate it). If all this sounds exhausting, pick a restaurant near your hotel instead. If you're still up for more, make evening plans that include a trip to the **John Hancock Observatory** or the **Prudential Center Skywalk** before or after dinner.

Day 2: This is museum day. Be there when the doors open at the **Museum of Fine Arts,** also known as MFA, (10 a.m.) or the **Museum of Science** (9 a.m.) and plan to stay at least through lunch — both museums offer decent options for lunch. If art is your interest, consider spending part of the afternoon at the **Isabella Stewart Gardner Museum,** up the street from the MFA. From the science museum, a strenuous but rewarding walk leads to the **Bunker Hill Monument** (the last stop on the Freedom Trail, in case you didn't get there on Day 1). The walk takes about 30 minutes; it's not long, but mostly uphill.

If none of that appeals to you, start the day at the **John F. Kennedy Library and Museum** or the **Children's Museum.** Any of these options can land you in the Back Bay by midafternoon, the perfect time for a **Duck Tour, swan boat** ride, or just some down time in the **Public Garden.** Collect yourself and do a little **shopping** on Newbury or Boylston Street (see Chapter 19). Freshen up, and then head to the **North End** for a hearty Italian dinner. Follow with dessert and people watching in a Hanover Street *caffè* (especially if you didn't indulge on Day 1). Or plan a visit to a bar or club — maybe the **Comedy Connection** or the **Black Rose,** both at Faneuil Hall Marketplace, or Cambridge's **House of Blues** (see Chapter 23).

Check the weather forecast when you arrive; inclement weather may mean scheduling your museum-visiting day to coincide with nasty outdoor conditions.

Day 3: Now you're off to **Cambridge.** This area can occupy a whole day or just a half (if the latter, use the extra time to further explore one of the options on the Day 1 or 2 itineraries above). Start with breakfast in the heart of **Harvard Square** — continental at **Au Bon Pain,** 1360 Mass. Ave. (☎ 617-497-9797), or full at the **Greenhouse Coffee Shop,** 3 Brattle St. (☎ 617-354-3184). Then tour the Harvard campus (see Chapter 16), visit one or more of the **university museums** (see Chapter 17), or do some serious **shopping** (see Chapter 19). Stroll along picturesque Brattle Street to the **Longfellow National Historic Site,** if it's open (see Chapter 17). For lunch, follow the students to **Bartley's Burger Cottage** (see Chapter 14), or picnic by the river on something tasty from **Stuff-Its** (see Chapter 15). In the afternoon, continue to explore or shop in Cambridge or head back to Boston. Spend this time hitting **Filene's Basement** if you didn't yet (or even if you did). For the evening, consider activities that don't strain your budget, starting with dinner at one of Boston's neighborhood restaurants (see Chapter 14). Follow with a student play or performance or a free concert or film. If you're up for another big night out, consider a **Boston Symphony Orchestra** performance or a pre- or post-Broadway play (see Chapter 22).

Boston in 5 Days

Day 4: Road trip! Turn to Chapter 21 and pick a town or two where you can spend the day. Explore **Lexington, Concord, Salem, Marblehead, Gloucester, Rockport, Plymouth,** or some sensible combination thereof. You don't need to rent a car for this, but you may want to; at busy times, make a reservation. Have dinner at your day-trip destination, or return to Boston or Cambridge. Afterward, you can hear jazz at the **Regattabar** or **Scullers** in Cambridge, or barely hear yourself think at a **club** in Cambridge, Somerville, or Boston (see Chapter 23).

Day 5: Today you tie up the loose ends that would have left you saying, "If only we'd had time for . . ." Leaf through Chapters 16, 17, and 18 to refresh your memory on places you'd like to see — a **historic house?** The **New England Aquarium?** The **Freedom Trail** stops you skipped? A special-interest **walking tour?** One of the **museums** you couldn't fit in on Day 2? In the evening, check out a **sporting event,** one of the earlier nightlife suggestions, or your hotel room (you still need to pack, right?).

Boston with the Kids

Here's an outline of a single kid-centric day in Boston. This itinerary is designed for warm weather; at colder times of the year, you may want to concentrate on indoor destinations like museums and, if you must, malls. It's flexible enough to allow lingering at some stops and trimming (or even eliminating) others, and it cries out to be personalized. Take the parts that help you keep the peace, and integrate them with adult-oriented activities to create a family plan. At all times, make sure the children put in their two-cents worth before you finalize anything.

Order some extra unbuttered toast at breakfast, or hang on to that extra half a bagel; you'll need it later.

Start with a **Boston Duck Tour.** Buy tickets at the Prudential Center (Pru) when the booth opens (no later than 9 a.m.) or be compulsive and snap up some of the limited allotment that goes on sale 2 days ahead. If you face a wait before your tour, wander around the shopping plaza or check out the **Christian Science Center reflecting pool,** across the street from the back of the Pru.

After the tour, use the Boylston Street exit at the front of the Pru, turn right, and walk 3 blocks to Copley Square. The square contains a fountain, benches, and **The Tortoise and Hare at Copley Square,** a two-piece sculpture by Nancy Schön. Where's that camera? Follow Boylston Street 2 blocks to the giant teddy bear in front of **FAO Schwarz** and make sure everyone knows how much time and money the decision-makers consider acceptable.

Continue on Boylston Street 2 more blocks, and you come to the **Public Garden.** The **swan boats** make a good low-tech break. These vessels share the lagoon with live swans, ducks, and geese who want the rest of your breakfast. Near the corner of Beacon and Charles Streets (diagonally across from where you entered the Garden) is **Make Way for Ducklings,** another enchanting work by Nancy Schön.

Kids with liberal TV privileges may want to head across the street for lunch at the "Cheers" bar, also known as the **Bull & Finch Pub** (see Chapter 23). Solid pub fare (including fine burgers) and a children's menu may make up for the fact that the real thing looks nothing like the set of the TV show. Alternatively, walk 2 blocks back on Boylston Street, turn left, and walk 2½ blocks to the **Hard Rock Cafe** (see Chapter 23).

In the afternoon, pick a museum: the **Children's Museum** for the younger set, the **Museum of Science** for older kids.

For dinner, let the children name the restaurant — perhaps the Hard Rock Cafe if you had lunch elsewhere, a **North End** pasta place, or the multiple options at **Faneuil Hall Marketplace.** Finally, if it doesn't blow anyone's bedtime, spend the evening taking in a live performance of **Shear Madness** or **Blue Man Group** (see Chapter 22).

Boston for Art Lovers

Would-be artists and would-be art collectors flock to Boston for inspiration of all sorts, in museums and galleries. From the dazzling Impressionist paintings at the Museum of Fine Arts to work by promising artists and craftspeople in cutting-edge Newbury Street galleries, the city abounds with aesthetic treats.

Check ahead for special museum shows. Short-term exhibits often require separate tickets, sometimes good only at a specific time.

For high-profile traveling exhibitions, many large hotels arrange special packages that include museum tickets. Start investigating as soon as you hear about the show. You may not save much money, but the tickets usually are valid at any time — an invaluable perk if your schedule is uncertain.

Stop one is the **Museum of Fine Arts** (MFA), which opens at 10 a.m. Take a free tour at 10:30 a.m. or help yourself to a floor plan and wander. I could cheerfully spend a day here, but you may not enjoy that kind of freedom with your vacation time. Go in with some sense of what you want to see; the Web site, www.mfa.org, is a great planning tool. When you've had your fill, move on (2 blocks or so) to the **Isabella Stewart Gardner Museum.** Have lunch in the MFA's cafeteria, café, or restaurant (you may need a reservation), or the Gardner's café. Then hop on the Green Line and head for the Copley or Arlington stop. One block away is **Newbury Street,** home to more art galleries than you can possibly see in half a day — or even a whole day. If time allows, plan for an hour or so at one of the **historic houses** nearby (see Chapter 17) before or after you hit the galleries. Wind down with afternoon tea (see Chapter 15) or a drink (see Chapter 23) in the elegant confines of the **Four Seasons** or the **Ritz.** If you've kept your spending under control at the art galleries, you may want to have a little caviar with your tea.

Boston in a Day

If you can spend only one day in Boston, two itineraries leap to mind: You can concentrate on one attraction (such as Boston Common, Cambridge, Faneuil Marketplace, or New England Aquarium) without the smallest pang about not doing more, or you can try to sample enough of the city to get a sense that you actually visited it, not just *seen* it. I am offering suggestions for the latter; this itinerary works in a loop — you can start at the beginning in the morning, or pick it up in the middle and go from there.

Start with an hour or less at **Filene's Basement** (see Chapter 19). Be there when it opens at 9:30 a.m., or earlier if the store is offering a special sale — check the newspapers when you arrive. Then follow the **Freedom Trail** from **Boston Common** to **Faneuil Hall Marketplace,** or take a 90-minute National Park Service ranger tour (see Chapter 18). Have lunch at the marketplace (see Day 1 under "Boston in 3 Days," earlier in the chapter) as you evaluate your options for what to do after lunch. Pick one of these four: Finish the Freedom Trail, take a **sightseeing cruise** (see Chapter 18), explore the **New England Aquarium** (see Chapter 16), or head to the **Children's Museum** (see Chapter 17). In the late afternoon, make your way to the Back Bay and enjoy the view from the **John Hancock Observatory** or the **Prudential Center Skywalk.** Sunset is the perfect time to visit these two attractions; let your appetite and the time of year determine whether you eat dinner before or after. If you can't leave town without a lobster, three branches of **Legal Sea Foods** are close by. If you'd rather stay downtown, enjoy dinner at the waterfront Legal's, and then head to the lounge at the 33rd-floor **Bay Tower** (see Chapter 23) for drinks, dessert, and dancing.

Some Tips for Organizing Your Time

The most important advice I can offer is ridiculously simple: Be realistic. Trying to do too much wastes time, money, and the goodwill of your fellow travelers. For the record, scheduling more than three major destinations in a day is trying to do too much. Scheduling three of anything in one afternoon is madness, especially if you made dinner reservations.

How can you make your plans more practical? You can extend your trip, but it's a bit late for that. If you travel with a group, you can split up. What you sacrifice in togetherness, you more than make up for in maximized satisfaction and minimized boredom. Here are some other suggestions:

- ✔ **Double-check open hours and days.** Setting the alarm, scheduling an early breakfast, and driving your family nuts so you can be at a certain attraction at 9 a.m. sharp is no fun when you arrive and find that it opens at 10.

- ✔ **Double-check a map.** Again, ridiculous — unless you forget. When you catch yourself before you go from Filene's Basement to the North End by way of the Public Garden (hint: not a straight line), it won't seem so silly. But backtracking may be a good idea if, say, your hotel is nearby, and you can drop off the spoils of your trip to the Basement instead of lugging your goods all over town.

- ✔ **Double-check with the kids.** Offer everyone a chance to change his or her mind, even if it messes up your second-by-second itinerary. The sights and attractions that were theoretical at home may hold even more appeal in 3-D — or they may seem disappointing. Better to have the "I'd rather do something else" conversation at the hotel than at the entrance to a distant attraction that (for whatever reason) has lost its luster.

Chapter 21

Exploring Beyond Boston: Four Great Day Trips

* *

In This Chapter

▶ Planning your getaway

▶ Leaving town

▶ Exploring and eating on the road

* *

*P*art of Boston's appeal is its proximity to other fascinating destinations. Seven municipalities that lie within an hour or so of downtown — Lexington, Concord, Salem, Marblehead, Gloucester, Rockport, and Plymouth — make enjoyable day trips. (For the locations of these towns in relation to Boston, see the map on the inside back cover of this book.) Each boasts abundant historic associations and excellent sightseeing, with enough shopping and dining opportunities to keep everyone happy.

In this chapter, I walk you through the process of planning a day trip to each town, and suggest ways to visit them individually and (except Plymouth) in pairs. I start with general pointers, and then offer specific tips on getting there, making the most of your day, and planning sightseeing and dining.

General Pointers

Two items that can inflate the cost of your day trip are a rental car and an overnight stay. If your visit to the Boston area is relatively short, I suggest that you skip the room but consider the car.

Here's why: Packing up and moving for the second time in just a few days is more disruptive than convenient, but having wheels increases your flexibility and touring range. That said, remember that reliable public transportation serves each of the towns in this chapter; if you don't want to deal with a car, you don't need to. (For information about the commuter rail and buses, contact the T at ☎ 800-392-6100 outside Mass. or 617-222-3200; Internet: www.mbta.com.)

If you want to plan an overnight stay, the chamber of commerce or other tourism authorities in each town will eagerly advise you. One good option is a bed and breakfast; see Chapter 6 for suggestions.

 Summer and fall weekends are the day-trip version of rush hour. In pleasant weather, gridlock is a problem. If you can, try to schedule your trip for a weekday, preferably in the spring or fall when car and pedestrian traffic is more manageable and weather slightly more predictable. Some businesses and attractions close for the winter, but if you visit then, the open ones will be practically empty.

Finally, if you don't want to worry about details, consider a guided half- or full-day bus trip. For a good selection and fair prices, contact **Gray Line's Brush Hill Tours,** 435 High St., Randolph, MA 02368 (☎ **800-343-1328** or 781-986-6100; Internet: www.grayline.com).

Where to find out more

Information offices in all seven of the towns can assist walk-in visitors. To receive information in advance (a good way to involve kids in the planning), contact the following:

- **Massachusetts:** Massachusetts Office of Travel & Tourism, 100 Cambridge St., 13th floor, Boston, MA 02202 (☎ **800-227-6277** or 617-727-3201; Internet: www.mass-vacation.com).

- **Lexington and Concord:** Lexington Chamber of Commerce, 1875 Mass. Ave., Lexington, MA 02421 (☎ **781-862-2480**; Internet: www.lexingtonchamber.org); Concord Chamber of Commerce, 2 Lexington Rd., Concord, MA 01742 (☎ **978-369-3120**; Internet: www.ultranet.com/~conchamb); or Greater Merrimack Valley Convention & Visitors Bureau, 9 Central St., Suite 201, Lowell, MA 01582 (☎ **800-443-3332** or 978-459-6150; Internet: www.lowell.org).

- **Salem and Marblehead:** Destination Salem, 10 Liberty St., Salem, MA 01970 (☎ **877-SALEM-MA** or 978-744-363; Internet: www.salem.org); Marblehead Chamber of Commerce, 62 Pleasant St., P.O. Box 76, Marblehead, MA 01945 (☎ **781-631-2868**; Internet: www.marbleheadchamber.org); or North of Boston Convention & Visitors Bureau, 17 Peabody Sq., Peabody, MA 01960 (☎ **800-742-5306** or 978-977-7760).

- **Gloucester and Rockport:** Gloucester Tourism Commission, 22 Poplar St., Gloucester, MA 01930 (☎ **800-649-6839** or 978-281-8865; Internet: www.gloucesterma.com); Rockport Chamber of Commerce and Board of Trade, 3 Main St., Rockport MA 01966 (☎ **978-546-6575**; Internet: www.rockportusa.com); and Cape Ann Chamber of Commerce, 33 Commercial St., Gloucester, MA 01930 (☎ **800-321-0133** or 978-283-1601; Internet: www.capeannvacations.com).

- **Plymouth:** Destination Plymouth, P.O. Box ROCK, Plymouth, MA 02361 (☎ **800-USA-1620** or 508-747-7525; Internet: www.visit-plymouth.com).

Lexington and Concord

The Revolutionary War started in these prosperous suburbs, which were then country villages. With an assist from a Henry Wadsworth Longfellow poem, the events of April 1775 vaulted Lexington and Concord into immortality. On your day trip, you'll understand why.

A visit to both towns makes a reasonable one-day excursion. Lexington is a half-day trip; if Concord appeals to you, you can spend the whole day there. Some attractions close for the winter and reopen after Patriots' Day, the third Monday of April.

Note: No public transportation is available between Lexington and Concord.

Hit the Boston Public Library (Chapter 17) or the Old North Church gift shop (Chapter 16), and track down Longfellow's poem "Paul Revere's Ride." This verse is a classic but historically dubious account of Revere's journey on the nights of April 18 and 19, 1775. You'll hear about it all over Lexington and Concord.

Getting to Lexington

To drive from Boston (9 miles) or Cambridge (6 miles), take Soldiers Field Road or Memorial Drive west to Route 2. Exit at Route 4/225, and follow signs into the center of town. From Route 128 (I-95), use Exit 31A and proceed into town. Parking is available on Mass. Ave., and a public-metered lot is located near the corner of Mass. Ave. and Waltham Street.

Public transportation is more complicated. Start by riding the Red Line to the last stop, Alewife. From there, bus routes no. 62 (Bedford) and no. 76 (Hanscom) serve Lexington. The buses run Monday to Saturday, hourly during the day, and every 30 minutes during rush-hour periods. No service is available on Sunday. The bus trip takes about 25 minutes and costs 75¢ one-way.

Seeing the sights in Lexington

Pick up maps and other information at the **Chamber of Commerce Visitor Center,** 1875 Mass. Ave. (☎ **781-862-2480**). The center is open July through September daily from 9 a.m. to 5 p.m., and October through June daily from 9:30 a.m. to 3:30 p.m. Displays include a diorama that illustrates the battle.

The visitor center is on the **Village Green** or Battle Green, site of the Revolution's first skirmish. The monuments and memorials in this area include the Minuteman Statue (1900) of the militia commander, Captain John Parker. He instructed his troops, "Don't fire unless fired upon, but

Lexington

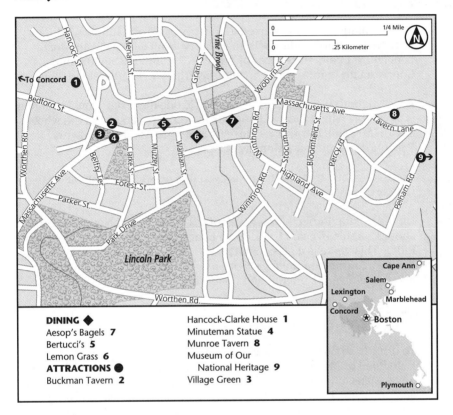

| 0 | | | 1/4 Mile |
| 0 | | .25 Kilometer | |

←To Concord **1**

Hancock St.

Merian St.

Vine Brook

Grant St.

Woburn St.

Bedford St.

Massachusetts Ave. **8**

Tavern Lane

Worthen Rd.

Massachusetts Ave.

Belfry Ter.

Clarke St.

Muzzey St.

Waltham St.

Winthrop Rd.

Stocum Rd.

Bloomfield St.

Percy Rd.

Pelham Rd.

2
3 **4**
5
6
7
9→

Forest St.

Parker St.

Winthrop Rd.

Highland Ave.

Park Drive

Lincoln Park

Worthen Rd.

Cape Ann ○
Salem ○
Lexington ○ ○
○ Marblehead
Concord
✱ **Boston**

Plymouth ○

DINING ◆
Aesop's Bagels **7**
Bertucci's **5**
Lemon Grass **6**
ATTRACTIONS ●
Buckman Tavern **2**

Hancock-Clarke House **1**
Minuteman Statue **4**
Munroe Tavern **8**
Museum of Our
National Heritage **9**
Village Green **3**

---

if they mean to have a war, let it begin here!" Checking out the Visitor Center displays and the outdoor sights on the Battle Green takes about half an hour.

The Lexington Historical Society (Internet: www.lexingtonhistory. org) operates the most compelling attraction on the Green, the **Buckman Tavern,** 1 Bedford St. (☎ 781-862-5598). The tavern is the only building left that stood on the Green on April 19, 1775. Costumed guides lead an outstanding tour that describes the history of the building, the battle, and the details of colonial life. Even if time is short, don't miss this tour.

Tours of the society's other two properties are well worth your time, but are not can't-miss experiences. The **Hancock–Clarke House,** 36 Hancock St. (☎ 781-861-0928), ⅓ of a mile from the Green, houses the Historical Society's museum of the Revolution. About a mile from the Green in the other direction is the 1690 **Munroe Tavern,** 1332 Mass. Ave. (☎ 781-674-9238). During the battle, the tavern fell into British hands and became the headquarters and, later, field hospital.

To see the houses, you must take a guided tour, which lasts 30 to 45 minutes (per house). Open hours are Monday to Saturday 10 a.m. to 4 p.m. and Sunday 1 to 4 p.m. The Buckman Tavern is open from early March to late November; the Hancock–Clarke House and Munroe Tavern are open from April to October. Admission for adults is $4 per house and $10 for all three; children 6 to 16 pay $2 per house and $4 for all three. Group tours run by appointment only.

The other major attraction in Lexington is the **Museum of Our National Heritage,** 33 Marrett Rd. (Route 2A), at Mass. Ave. (☎ 781-861-6559 or 781-861-9638; Internet: www.mnh.org), which takes a fun approach, illustrating history with cultural artifacts.

In recent years, the temporary exhibits included jigsaw puzzles, Navajo rugs, and displays on George Washington and Frank Lloyd Wright, just to name a few. For another look at the Revolution, visit the permanent installation on the Battle of Lexington. The Scottish Rite of Freemasonry sponsors the museum. Admission is free; the museum is open Monday to Saturday from 10 a.m. to 5 p.m. and Sunday from noon to 5 p.m.

Dining in Lexington

The center of town, near the intersection of Mass. Ave. and Waltham Street, offers a number of choices. If you're starting the day in Lexington, **Aesop's Bagels,** 1666 Mass. Ave. (☎ 781-674-2990), is a good place for breakfast. For lunch, you may want to hold out until Concord, where you'll find Guida's, which serves great seafood. If you can't, try **Bertucci's,** 1777 Mass. Ave. (☎ 781-860-9000), for pizza and pasta, or **Lemon Grass,** 1710 Mass. Ave. (☎ 781-862-3530), for tasty Thai food.

Sights en route from Lexington to Concord

Minute Man National Historical Park (Internet: www.nps.gov/mima) spreads over 900 acres in Lexington, Concord, and Lincoln. The park encompasses the scene of the first Revolutionary War battle and a 4-mile piece of the road that the vanquished British troops used in their retreat from Concord to Boston. Artwork and artifacts illustrate the displays at visitor centers in Lexington and Concord, either of which makes an excellent starting point. Visiting the park takes as little as half an hour (to see Concord's North Bridge) or as long as several hours if you include stops at both visitor centers and maybe a ranger-led program.

The park is open daily, year-round. Admission is free; charges for special tours may apply. In Lexington, the **Minute Man Visitor Center** is off Route 2A, ½ mile west of I-95 (Mass. 128) Exit 33B (☎ 781-862-7753).

The center is open daily from 9 a.m. to 5 p.m. (until 4 p.m. in winter). Concord's **North Bridge Visitor Center,** 174 Liberty St. (off Monument Street; ☎ 978-369-6993), overlooks the Concord River and the bridge. The center is open daily from 9 a.m. to 5:30 p.m. (until 4 p.m. in winter).

Walden Pond State Reservation, Route 126, Concord (☎ 978-369-3254; Internet: www.state.ma.us/dem/parks/wldn.htm), preserves the site of the cabin where Henry David Thoreau lived from 1845 to 1847. Besides being a literary pilgrimage site, it's a popular park with visitors who hike around the pond, picnic, swim, and fish. In fine weather, call before heading over to make sure the parking lot has space available (there's no additional parking); between Memorial Day and Labor Day, a parking fee (about $2) applies.

To get to Waldon Pond State Reservation from Lexington, take Mass. Ave. west to Route 2A, bear left onto Route 2, and turn left onto Route 126. From Concord, take Walden Street (Route 126) south, away from Concord Center, cross Route 2, and look for signs pointing to the parking lot.

Getting to Concord

To drive from Lexington, take Mass. Ave. west, across Route 128, and pick up Route 2A. Pass through Lincoln and bear right onto Lexington Road in Concord. Follow HISTORIC CONCORD signs into the center of town. If you miss the turn-off, continue about a ½ mile and take the next right onto Cambridge Turnpike, which turns into the center of town. To go straight to Walden Pond, take what's now Route 2/2A another mile or so and turn left onto Route 126. From Boston and Cambridge, take Soldiers Field Road or Memorial Drive west to Route 2. In Lincoln, stay in the right lane. Where the road makes a sharp left, go straight onto Cambridge Turnpike. Parking is available throughout town and at the attractions.

By public transportation, the commuter rail takes about 45 minutes from North Station in Boston, with a stop at Porter Square in Cambridge. The one-way fare is $4. (No public transportation is available between Lexington and Concord.) The station is about three-quarters of a mile from the town center. The attractions are accessible on foot but not all that close together; in hot or cold weather, make appropriate preparations (hats, water, sunscreen, and such).

If you want to fit in, pronounce it *conquered* (not <u>con</u>-cored).

Taking a tour of Concord

The **Chamber of Commerce** (☎ 978-369-3120) offers 1-hour tours from May through October on Saturday, Sunday, and Monday holidays, and on weekdays by appointment. These tours start at the information booth on Heywood Street, 1 block southeast of Monument Square. Also check to see whether Park Service rangers from the **North Bridge Visitor Center** (☎ **978-369-6993;** Internet: www.nps.gov/mima; see above) are leading tours during your visit.

Seeing the sights in Concord

The monuments and descriptions around and in the North Bridge Visitor Center give a good sense of Concord's best-known event — the Battle of Concord. The town is equally famous for its literary associations, and indications of that abound, too. Visit **Sleepy Hollow Cemetery,** off Route 62 west (☎ **978-318-3233**), and climb to "Author's Ridge." In this area, you'll find the graves of the Alcotts, Ralph Waldo Emerson, Nathaniel Hawthorne, and Henry David Thoreau, among others. The cemetery is open daily 7 a.m. to dusk; call ahead for wheelchair access.

Concord Museum

The Concord Museum offers a fascinating, comprehensive look at the town's storied history. The best feature of the galleries is not the abundant objects and artifacts, although they're impressive; it's the accompanying descriptions and interpretations that place the exhibits in context. For instance, you'll see one of the lanterns that signaled Paul Revere from the steeple of the Old North Church. This display includes just enough explanatory text to show why it's a big deal.

Lexington Road and Cambridge Turnpike. ☎ *978-369-9763. Internet:* www.concordmuseum.org. *Follow Lexington Rd. out of Concord Center and bear right at museum onto Cambridge Turnpike; entrance is on the left. Parking: In lot or on road. Admission: $7 adults, $6 seniors and students, $3 children under 16, $16 families. Open: Apr–Dec Mon–Sat 9 a.m.–5 p.m., Sun noon–5 p.m.; Jan–Mar Mon–Sat 11 a.m.–4 p.m., Sun 1–4 p.m.*

The Old Manse

The Reverend William Emerson, Ralph Waldo Emerson's grandfather, built this house in 1770 and watched the Battle of Concord from the yard. For almost 170 years, it was home to his widow, her second husband, their descendants, and (briefly) newlyweds Nathaniel and Sophia Peabody Hawthorne. The tour traces the history of the house and its occupants, using a rich trove of family memorabilia.

269 Monument St. (at North Bridge). ☎ *978-369-3909. Internet:* www.thetrustees.org. *From Concord Center, follow Monument St. until you see North Bridge parking lot on the right; the Old Manse is on the left. Guided tours: $6 adults, $5 seniors, $4 children 6–12. Open: Mid-Apr–Oct Mon–Sat 10 a.m.–5 p.m.; Sun and holidays noon–5 p.m. Closed Nov–mid-Apr.*

Concord

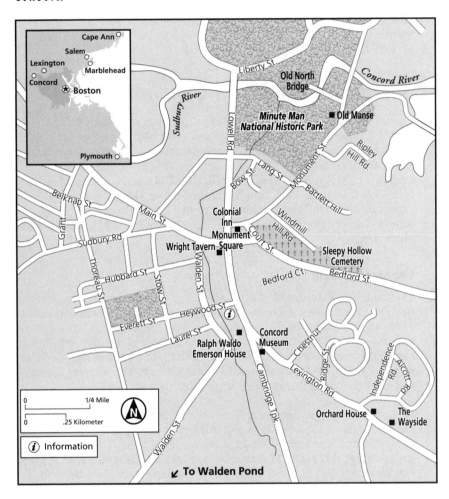

Orchard House

Louisa May Alcott lived and wrote at Orchard House, the setting for her best-known book, *Little Women* (1868). If you loved the book, don't leave town without seeing the house; if you don't understand what the fuss is about, well, this attraction may not be the best use of your time. The tour offers an intriguing look at 19th-century family life, overflowing with anecdotes and heirlooms. If you are or were a preadolescent girl, this stop will be one of the best parts of your trip.

399 Lexington Rd. ☎ *978-369-4118. Internet:* www.louisamayalcott.org. *Follow Lexington Rd. out of Concord Center past Concord Museum; house is on the left. Parking: In lot; overflow parking lot is across street. Guided tours: $7 adults, $6 seniors and students, $4 children 6–17, $16 families (up to 2 adults and 4 children).*

Open: Apr–Oct Mon–Sat 10 a.m.–4:30 p.m., Sun 1–4:30 p.m.; Nov–Mar Mon–Fri 11 a.m.–3 p.m., Sat 10 a.m.–4:30 p.m., Sun 1–4:30 p.m. Closed Jan 1–15.

Ralph Waldo Emerson House

Emerson is not the household name he once was — except in Concord, where he remains such a towering presence that the guides at his home still call him "Mr. Emerson." The philosopher, essayist, and poet lived here from 1835 until he died, in 1882. The tour highlights his domestic life and his house's over-the-top Victorian décor.

28 Cambridge Turnpike. ☎ *978-369-2236. Take Cambridge Turnpike out of Concord Center; just before Concord Museum, house is on the right. Guided tours: $5 adults, $3 seniors and children 7–17; call to arrange group tours. Open: Mid-Apr–Oct Thurs–Sat 10 a.m.–4:30 p.m.; Sun 2–4:30 p.m. Closed Nov–mid-Apr.*

The Wayside

Nathaniel Hawthorne lived at the Wayside from 1852 until his death, in 1864. The Alcott family lived here, too, as did Harriett Lothrop, who wrote the *Five Little Peppers* books under the pen name Margaret Sidney. This house is part of Minute Man National Historical Park; rangers lead the interesting tours, which explore the house's patchwork architecture as well as its famous residents' lives and careers.

455 Lexington Rd. ☎ *978-369-6975. Internet:* www.nps.gov/mima/wayside. *Follow Lexington Rd. past Concord Museum and Orchard House; the Wayside is on the left. Guided tours: $4 adults; free for children under 17. Open: May–Oct Thurs–Tues 10:30 a.m.–4:30 p.m. Closed Nov–Apr.*

Dining in Concord

The **1716 Colonial Inn,** 48 Monument Sq. (☎ **978-369-2372;** Internet: www.concordscolonialinn.com), is a traditional establishment with a fine restaurant and two friendly lounges. The food is hardly adventurous, but you're here to soak up the atmosphere — the fact that the fare is also tasty is a bonus. The inn serves afternoon tea from Wednesday to Sunday (make a reservation).

My favorite Concord restaurant is **Guida's Coast Cuisine,** 84 Thoreau St. (Route 126, at Concord Depot; ☎ **978-371-1333**). Guida's serves succulent seafood, often Portuguese style, in a cozy, elegant space overlooking the train tracks. Service can be slow, but you won't want to rush. This restaurant serves dinner nightly and lunch on weekends and some weekdays; call for reservations and exact open days.

For picnic fixings, visit the **Cheese Shop,** 25–31 Walden St. (☎ 978-369-5778), near the town center.

Salem and Marblehead

The North Shore played a role in the Revolution and attained great prosperity by dominating the China trade in the early Federal era, but that's not why you flipped to this page. When you read "Salem," you said, "Witches!"

The witch trials of 1692 left an indelible mark on Salem, which good-naturedly welcomes the association — while never forgetting that 20 people died in the unfounded hysteria. Once you discover this pleasant city, you may want to hang around and learn about its rich maritime history. Salem shares that legacy with the affluent, picturesque town of Marblehead, which (Newport be hanged) bills itself as the "Yachting Capital of America."

Much like Lexington and Concord, Salem and Marblehead together make a full day trip. Or, you easily can spend an entire day at either location.

Getting to Salem

To drive from Boston (17 miles), take the Callahan Tunnel to Route 1A north past the airport and into downtown Salem. Be careful in Lynn, where the road turns left and immediately right. Or take I-93 or Route 1 to Route 128, and then Route 114 into downtown Salem. From Marblehead, follow Route 114 (Pleasant Street) west. Plenty of on-street parking is available, and a municipal garage is located across from the National Park Service Visitor Center.

Bus route no. 450 runs from Haymarket (Green or Orange Line), and commuter trains operate from North Station (Green or Orange Line). The bus takes an hour, the train 30 to 35 minutes. The one-way fare for either is $2.75. During warm weather, ferries (☎ 617-227-4321; Internet: www.bostonharborcruises.com) from Boston's Long Wharf serve the Blaney Street Ferry Terminal, off Derby Street, not very far from downtown Salem (call for details on getting downtown from here). The ferry service was an experimental program until recently; call ahead for details of the service, which takes about 75 minutes and costs about $10 for adults.

Taking a tour of Salem

The **Salem Trolley** (☎ 978-744-5469) operates daily 10 a.m. to 5 p.m. from April through October and on weekends in March and November. Tickets ($8 adults, $7 seniors, $4 children 5 to 12, family $20) are good all day, and you can get off and on as much as you like at any of the 15 stops. The first stop is at the Essex Street side of the National Park Service Visitor Center on New Liberty Street.

Salem

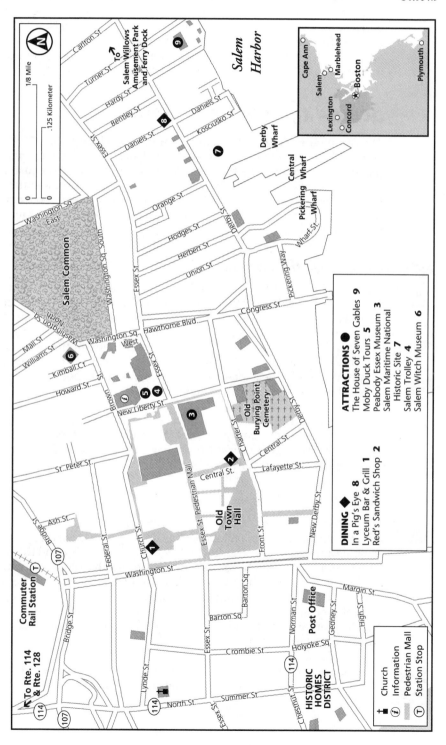

Moby Duck Tours (☎ 978-741-4386; Internet: www.mobyduck.com) are operated on amphibious vehicles that lumber through the streets, then cruise around the harbor. The 55-minute tours leave from New Liberty Street in front of the Visitor Center. Tickets (cash only) cost $14 for adults, $12 for seniors, and $8 for children under 12. Tours operate on weekends in May, daily from Memorial Day to Halloween.

Seeing the sights in Salem

The **National Park Service Visitor Center,** 2 New Liberty St. (☎ 978-740-1650; Internet: www.nps.gov/sama), distributes brochures and pamphlets, including one that describes a walking tour of the historic district. The center is open daily from 9 a.m. to 5 p.m. Architecture buffs will want to see Chestnut Street, a gorgeously preserved example of colonial style; the whole street is a registered National Historic Landmark.

The House of the Seven Gables

Nathaniel Hawthorne visited this house as a child, and legends about the building and its inhabitants inspired his 1851 novel of the same name. If you haven't read it (or even if you have), watch the audiovisual program that tells the story before you start the tour. The six rooms of period furniture in the main house include pieces mentioned in the book, and a steep secret staircase. Costumed guides lead the tour (they sometimes play to the kids in the audience) and can answer just about any question about the novel, the buildings, and the artifacts.

54 Turner St. ☎ *978-744-0991. Internet:* www.7gables.org. *From downtown, follow Derby St. east 3 blocks past Derby Wharf. Guided tours: $8 adults, $5 children 6–17, free for children under 6. Open: May–Nov daily 10 a.m.–5 p.m.; Dec–Apr Mon–Sat 10 a.m.–5 p.m., Sun noon–5 p.m.*

Peabody Essex Museum

This museum illustrates the history of Salem through displays of the objects and artifacts its residents considered worth preserving — a fascinating approach that affords a look at treasures from around the world. The Peabody Museum began as a repository for the spoils of the China trade; the Essex Institute was the county historical society. Between them, the sprawling collections encompass everything from toys to animal specimens to East Asian art. Visitors can tour a historic house or a gallery, or take a self-guided tour using a pamphlet from about a dozen available on various topics.

Parts of the museum may be under renovation by the time you read this; check to see if the planned expansion project affects open hours or areas.

East India Square. ☎ 800-745-4054 or 978-745-9500. Internet: www.pem.org. *Take Hawthorne Blvd. to Essex St., following signs for Visitor Center, and enter on Essex or New Liberty St. Admission: $10 adults, $8 seniors and students with ID, free for children under 17. Open: Mon–Sat 10 a.m.–5 p.m.; Sun noon–5 p.m. Closed Mon Nov–March.*

Salem Maritime National Historic Site

Before the waterfront began to decay in the early 1800s, it linked Salem to the world for many years On this harborfront land, National Park Service buildings and displays recall the port's heyday. The most recent addition to the site is in the water alongside the orientation center: a full-size replica of a 1797 East Indiaman merchant vessel. Fees for visiting the three-masted 171-footer Friendship aren't set, but the price of ranger-led tours probably will include a tour of the ship.

174 Derby St. ☎ 978-740-1660. Internet: www.nps.gov/sama. *Take Derby St. east, just past Pickering Wharf; the orientation center is on the right. Admission: Free; guided tours: $3 adults, $2 seniors and children 6–16. Open: Daily 9 a.m.–5 p.m.*

Salem Witch Museum

The Salem Witch Museum is so memorable that I'm fighting the urge to call it "haunting" (oh, well). As informative as it is frightening, the museum's three-dimensional audiovisual presentation about the witch-craft trials and the accompanying hysteria is illustrated with life-sized figures. That sounds a little corny, but the 30-minute narration does a good job of explaining the historical context and consequences. (One "man" dies when his tormentors pile rocks onto a board on his chest — you may need to remind small children that he's not real.)

The "witch" on the traffic island across from the Witch Museum is really Roger Conant, who founded Salem in 1626. Nice outfit, Roger.

19½ Washington Square. ☎ 978-744-1692. Internet: www.salemwitchmuseum. com. *Follow Hawthorne Blvd. to the northwest corner of Salem Common. Admission: $6 adults, $5.50 seniors, $3.75 children 6–14. Open: July–Aug daily 10 a.m.–7 p.m.; Sept–June daily 10 a.m.–5 p.m.*

Dining in Salem

For a quick bite, try **Red's Sandwich Shop,** 15 Central St. (☎ 978-745-3527). The fare's cheap, good, and served fast, but the shop doesn't take credit cards. **In A Pig's Eye,** 148 Derby St. (☎ 978-741-4436; Internet: www.inapigseye.com), is a neighborhood bar near the House of the Seven Gables that serves delicious Mexican food and bar fare. One of the best restaurants north of Boston is the **Lyceum Bar & Grill,** 43 Church St. (at Washington St.; ☎ 978-745-7665; Internet: www. lyceumsalem.com). This bar and grill serves creative American fare at lunch on weekdays, and at dinner daily; Sunday brunch is also offered. For any meal, make a reservation.

Getting to Marblehead

To drive from Boston, take the Callahan Tunnel and follow Route 1A past the airport north through Revere and Lynn. Bear right where you see signs for Swampscott and Marblehead. Follow Lynn Shore Drive into Swampscott, bear left onto Route 129, and follow it into Marblehead. Or take I-93 or Route 1 to Route 128, and then Route 114 through Salem into Marblehead. Parking is limited — grab the first spot you see and be sure you know your time limit.

Bus route no. 441/442 runs from Haymarket (Green or Orange Line) in Boston to downtown Marblehead. During rush periods on weekdays, the no. 448/449 connects Marblehead to Downtown Crossing (Red or Orange Line). The 441 and 448 buses detour to Vinnin Square shopping center in Swampscott; otherwise, the routes are the same. The trip takes about an hour and costs $2.75 one-way.

Seeing the sights in Marblehead

The **Marblehead Chamber of Commerce** operates an information booth on Pleasant Street near Spring Street. The booth is open daily from May through October, 10 a.m. to 6 p.m. (In the off-season, visit the office at 62 Pleasant St., just up the hill.) You can pick up pamphlets and a map, but the town is ideal for wandering, especially around "Old Town," the historic district. Be sure to visit Crocker Park or Fort Sewall, on the harbor at opposite ends of Front Street; the view from either place is amazing.

Marblehead is a top-notch shopping destination. Shops, boutiques, and galleries dot Washington and Front Streets, with another prime area on Atlantic Avenue.

Abbot Hall

The Selectmen's Meeting Room houses Archibald M. Willard's painting *The Spirit of '76*. That title may not ring a bell, but the painting will when you see the widely imitated drummer, drummer boy, and fife player. Cases in the halls contain objects and artifacts from the collections of the Marblehead Historical Society; a stop here takes 5 or 10 minutes at most.

Washington Square. ☎ *781-631-0528. From the historic district, follow Washington St. up the hill toward the clock tower. Admission: Free. Open: Nov–Apr Mon, Tues, Thurs 8 a.m.–5 p.m., Wed 7:30 a.m.–7:30 p.m., Fri 8 a.m.–1 p.m.; May–Oct Mon, Tues, Thurs 8 a.m.–5 p.m., Fri 8 a.m.–5 p.m., Sat 9 a.m.–6 p.m., Sun 11 a.m.–6 p.m.*

Marblehead

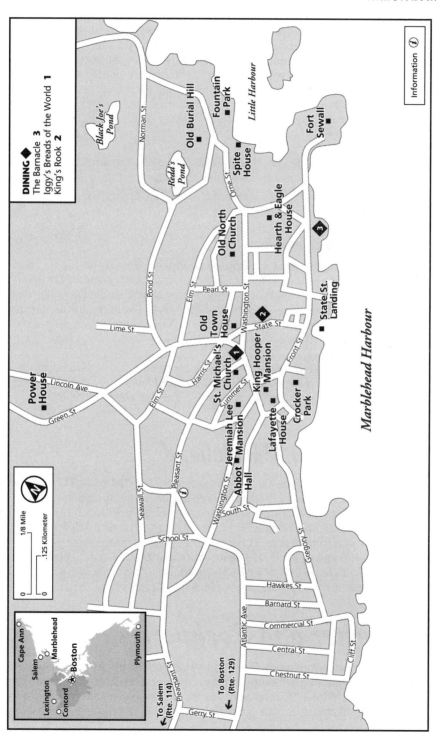

Information ⓘ

DINING ◆
The Barnacle **3**
Iggy's Breads of the World **1**
King's Rook **2**

Black Joe's Pond

Redd's Pond

Norman St.

Old Burial Hill ■

Fountain Park ■

Little Harbour

Spite House ■

Orne St.

Fort Sewall ■

Old North Church ■

Hearth & Eagle House ■

3

Pond St.

Elm St.

Pearl St.

Washington St.

State St. Landing ■

Lime St.

Old Town House ■

Washington St.

2

State St.

Front St.

Power House ■

Lincoln Ave.

Green St.

Elm St.

Harris St.

St. Michael's Church ■

1

King Hooper Mansion ■

Marblehead Harbour

Summer St.

Crocker Park ■

Jeremiah Lee Mansion ■

Lafayette House ■

Abbot Hall ■

Pleasant St.

Seawall St.

Washington St.

South St.

Gregory St.

School St.

N

0 ___ 1/8 Mile
0 ___ .125 Kilometer

Cape Ann ○
Salem ○
Marblehead ○
Lexington ○
Concord ○ ✦ Boston
Plymouth ○

Hawkes St.

Barnard St.

Atlantic Ave.

Commercial St.

Central St.

Cliff St.

Chestnut St.

To Salem (Rte. 114) ←

To Boston (Rte. 129) ↓

Gerry St.

Pleasant St.

Jeremiah Lee Mansion

For a house with an apparently obscure claim to fame, the 1768 Lee Mansion is surprisingly appealing. The original hand-painted wallpaper is the headliner, and the house is an excellent example of pre-Revolutionary Georgian architecture. The Marblehead Historical Society's informative guides bring the history to life with stories about the home and its renovations. The society's headquarters, 170 Washington St., contain several galleries and is open weekdays year-round, Saturdays mid-May to December, and summer Sundays; admission is free.

161 Washington St. ☎ 781-631-1069. Follow Washington St. until it runs uphill toward Abbot Hall; mansion is on the right. Admission: Free; guided tours: $5 adults, $4.50 students, free for children under 11. Open: Mid-May–Oct Mon–Sat 10 a.m.–4 p.m.; Sun 1–4 p.m. Closed Nov–mid-May.

King Hooper Mansion

Robert Hooper was a shipping magnate who earned his nickname by treating his sailors well. His 1728 mansion, which gained a Georgian addition in 1747, now contains period furnishings. Though these pieces aren't originals, they give a sense of upper-crust life in the 18th century. The building houses the Marblehead Arts Association, which stages monthly exhibits.

8 Hooper St. ☎ 781-631-2608. Look for the colorful sign off Washington St. at the foot of the hill near the Lee Mansion. Guided tours: Free; donations requested. Open: Mon–Sat 10 a.m.–4 p.m.; Sun 1–5 p.m. Call ahead; no tours during private parties.

Dining in Marblehead

Iggy's Bread of the World, 5 Pleasant St. (☎ 781-639-4717), serves coffee and some of the best baked goods in the Boston area. Iggy's is a great place to pick up a snack to enjoy while you watch the action on the harbor. **The Barnacle,** 141 Front St. (☎ 781-631-4236), has a water view, but from inside. This restaurant serves moderately priced fresh seafood and doesn't take reservations or credit cards. The **King's Rook,** 12 State St. (☎ 781-631-9838), is a wine bar and café that serves excellent soup, pizza, sandwiches, and desserts.

Gloucester and Rockport

Gloucester, Rockport, Essex, and Manchester-by-the-Sea make up Cape Ann, a dizzyingly beautiful peninsula that gained international attention with the 2000 release of the movie *The Perfect Storm.* Gloucester is a city in transition, a sightseeing and whale-watching center that's also

Gloucester and Rockport

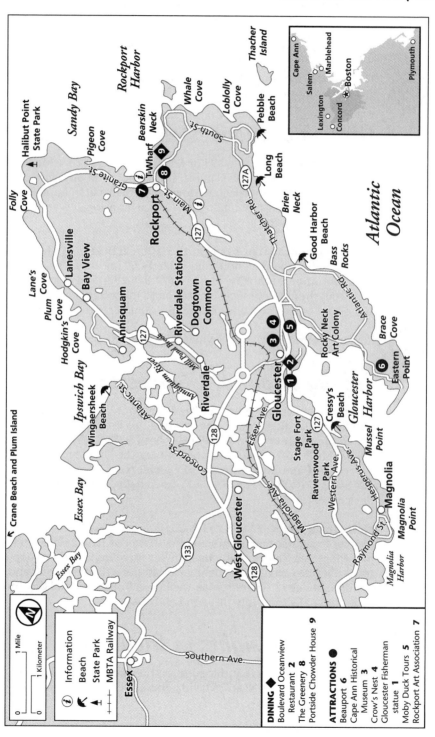

Thacher Island

Cape Ann
Marblehead
Salem
Boston
Lexington
Concord
Plymouth

Rockport Harbor

Sandy Bay

Whale Cove

Loblolly Cove

Pebble Beach

Halibut Point State Park

Pigeon Cove

Bearskin Neck

South St.

Folly Cove

Granite St.

T-Wharf

Long Beach

127A

Main St.

Rockport

Brier Neck

Good Harbor Beach

Bass Rocks

Atlantic Ocean

Lanesville

Bay View

127

Riverdale Station

Dogtown Common

Thatcher Rd.

Lane's Cove

Plum Cove

Hodgkin's Cove

Annisquam

Rocky Neck Art Colony

Brace Cove

127

Mill Pond Brook

Annisquam River

Riverdale

Gloucester

Eastern Point

Gloucester Harbor

Atlantic Rd.

Ipswich Bay

Atlantic St.

Wingaersheek Beach

Essex Bay

128

Essex Ave.

Stage Fort Park

Cressy's Beach

Mussel Point

Magnolia Point

West Gloucester

Magnolia Ave.

Ravenswood Park

Western Ave.

Hesperus Ave.

Magnolia

Magnolia Harbor

Concord St.

133

128

Raymond St.

Crane Beach and Plum Island

Essex Bay

Southern Ave.

Essex

DINING ◆
Boulevard Oceanview Restaurant **2**
The Greenery **8**
Portside Chowder House **9**

ATTRACTIONS ●
Beauport **6**
Cape Ann Historical Museum **3**
Crow's Nest **4**
Gloucester Fisherman statue **1**
Moby Duck Tours **5**
Rockport Art Association **7**

i Information
Beach
State Park
MBTA Railway

1 Mile
1 Kilometer

one of the few commercial fishing ports remaining in New England. The fading industry traces its roots even further back than the city's first European settlement, in 1623. Rockport, at the tip of the cape, is nearly as old but has a less hardscrabble history. Rockport enjoys a reputation as a summer community overflowing with gift shops and galleries.

The contrast of Gloucester and Rockport makes for an enjoyable one-day trip; exploring either can also fill a day.

Getting to Gloucester

To drive from Boston, take I-93 or Route 1 to Route 128, which ends in Gloucester; total mileage: 33 miles. Exit 14 puts you on Route 133, a longer but prettier approach to downtown than exits 11 and 9. Plenty of on-street parking is available, and a free lot is located on the causeway to Rocky Neck.

The commuter rail runs from North Station in Boston to Gloucester. The trip takes about an hour and costs $4.50 one-way. The **Cape Ann Transportation Authority,** or CATA (☎ 978-283-7916), runs buses on Cape Ann (from the Gloucester station to the waterfront, for example) and operates special routes during the summer; call for schedules.

Remember that *Gloucester* rhymes with *roster*.

Taking a tour of Gloucester

Pick up a "Gloucester Maritime Trail" brochure, which describes four excellent self-guided tours. You can find this brochure at the **Visitors Welcoming Center** (☎ 800-649-6839 or 978-281-8865), open summer only at Stage Fort Park, off Route 127 near the intersection with Route 133; or the **Cape Ann Chamber of Commerce,** 33 Commercial St. (☎ 800-321-0133 or 978-283-1601), open daily in summer and weekdays in winter.

Moby Duck Tours (☎ 978-281-3825; Internet: www.mobyduck.com) are 55-minute sightseeing excursions that travel on land before plunging into the water. The amphibious vehicles leave from Harbor Loop downtown. Tickets (cash only) cost $14 for adults, $12 for seniors, and $8 for children under 12. Tours run on weekends from Memorial Day through June, and daily from July through Labor Day.

Seeing the sights in Gloucester

Tourism officials say that the question they field most often lately is "Where's the Crow's Nest?" The fishermen's bar that gained fame through the book and movie versions of *The Perfect Storm* is at 334 Main St. (☎ 978-281-2965), just east of downtown. The Crow's Nest is just what it seems to be — a local hangout.

On Stacy Boulevard just west of downtown, the statue that symbolizes the city testifies to the danger of the seafaring life. More than 10,000 fishermen lost their lives in Gloucester's first three centuries; Leonard Craske's bronze Gloucester Fisherman, "The Man at the Wheel," memorializes them.

To reach East Gloucester, follow signs from downtown or use Exit 9 from Route 128. On East Main Street, follow signs to the Rocky Neck Art Colony, the oldest continuously operating art colony in the country. Park in the lot on the tiny causeway and follow the crowds to Rocky Neck Avenue and its studios, galleries, and restaurants. Most galleries are open daily in the summer from 10 a.m. to 10 p.m.

Beauport (Sleeper–McCann House)

Henry Davis Sleeper decorated his "fantasy house" to illustrate literary and historical themes, which you can learn about during the fascinating house tour. Sleeper, an interior designer, drew on huge collections of American and European art and antiques to create his home from 1907 to 1934. The entertaining tour visits 26 of the 40 rooms. Note that the house, operated by the Society for the Preservation of New England Antiquities, is not open on summer weekends.

75 Eastern Point Blvd. ☎ 978-283-0800. Internet: www.spnea.org. *Follow East Main St. south to Eastern Point Blvd. (a private road), drive ½ mile to house, and park on the left. Guided tours: $6 adults, $5.50 seniors, $3 students and children 6–12. Open: Tours on the hour May 15–Sept 15 Mon–Fri 10 a.m.–4 p.m.; Sept 16–Oct 15 daily 10 a.m.–4 p.m. Closed summer weekends and Oct 16–May 14.*

Cape Ann Historical Museum

Cape Ann's history and artists dominate the displays at this lovely museum. The American Luminist painter Fitz Hugh Lane, a Gloucester native, has his own gorgeous gallery. Other spaces hold contemporary works, and the maritime and fisheries galleries contain fascinating exhibits, models, photographs, and even entire boats (you won't believe how small some of them are).

27 Pleasant St. ☎ 978-283-0455. Follow Main St. west through downtown and turn right onto Pleasant St.; the museum is 1 block up on the right. Parking: Metered street parking or in pay-lot across street. Admission: $4 adults, $3.50 seniors, $2.50 students, free for children under 6. Open: March–Jan Tues–Sat 10 a.m.–5 p.m. Closed Feb.

Dining in Gloucester (and nearby Essex)

The **Boulevard Oceanview Restaurant,** 25 Western Ave., on Stacy Boulevard (☎ **978-281-2949**), serves inexpensive sandwiches and ocean-fresh seafood, including superb Portuguese specialties, in a dinerlike atmosphere; you should make a reservation for dinner in the summer. Another dining option: Follow the locals to the Stage Fort Park snack bar for fried seafood.

Going to or leaving Cape Ann on Route 128, turn away from Gloucester on Route 133 and head west to Essex. This beautiful little town is an important culinary landmark: the birthplace of the fried clam. According to legend, that took place at **Woodman's of Essex,** Main Street (☎ **800-649-1773** or 978-768-6451). Woodman's draws locals and out-of-towners for lobster, steamers, onion rings, and, oh yeah, fried clams. This dining spot is mobbed year-round, but the line moves quickly. An ATM is on the premises; no credit cards are accepted.

Getting to Rockport

By car from Boston, take I-93 or Route 1 to Route 128. Just before Route 128 ends, follow signs to Route 127, and go north into Rockport. Or continue to the very end (Exit 9), turn left onto Bass Avenue, and go about a ½-mile to Route 127A north. From Gloucester, follow Main Street to Eastern Avenue (Route 127) or Bass Avenue. Route 127A is more scenic but longer than Route 127. In downtown Rockport, circle once to look for parking, and then try the back streets. Or use the parking lot on Upper Main Street (Route 127) on weekends. Parking is free; the shuttle bus downtown costs $1.

The commuter rail runs from North Station in Boston to Rockport. The 60- to 70-minute trip costs $5 one-way. The station is off Upper Main Street, less than a mile from the center of town.

Seeing the sights in Rockport

Pick up the pamphlet "Rockport: A Walking Guide" from **The Rockport Chamber of Commerce and Board of Trade,** 3 Main St. (☎ **978-546-6575;** Internet: www.rockportusa.com). The chamber office is open daily in summer and weekdays in winter; the chamber operates an information booth from mid-May to mid-October about a mile from downtown on Upper Main Street (Route 127), just before the WELCOME TO ROCKPORT sign.

Rockport boasts no must-see attractions, but there's more to the town than knickknack shopping. The knickknack shopping is excellent, though — wander around downtown, making sure to detour onto Bearskin Neck, which has more gift shops than some whole cities. (And an interesting name — read the plaque at the entrance to the street to learn the story.) All over downtown, shops sell jewelry, gifts, toys, clothing, novelties, handmade crafts, paintings, and sculpture.

Opposite Bearskin Neck, you'll see a red wooden fish warehouse on the town wharf called Motif No. 1. The warehouse exerts a mysterious totemic power over Rockport residents — or is a testament to the fact that *anything* can become a tourist attraction. Motif No. 1 is famous for being famous. No, I don't know what the big deal is, but there it is.

More than two dozen art galleries display the works of local and nationally known artists. In addition, the **Rockport Art Association,** 12 Main St. (☎ **978-546-6604**), sponsors major exhibitions and special shows throughout the year. The association is open daily, year-round.

To get a sense of the power of the sea, take Route 127 north of town to the tip of Cape Ann. **Halibut Point State Park (☎ 978-546-2997;** Internet: www.state.ma.us/dem/parks/halb.htm) has a staffed visitor center, walking trails, tidal pools, and water-filled quarries — but no swimming. This park is great place to wander around and admire the scenery. On a clear day, you can see Maine.

Dining in Rockport

Woodman's of Essex (see "Dining in Gloucester [and nearby Essex]," earlier in this chapter) will serve you a drink, but Rockport is a dry town. I suggest a picnic, if it's not too windy. Head to Halibut Point (see "Seeing the sights in Rockport"), the end of Bearskin Neck, or another agreeable spot. Stop for provisions at the **Greenery,** 15 Dock Sq. (☎ **978-546-9593**), or the **Portside Chowder House,** on Bearskin Neck (☎ **978-546-7045**), and then sit back and admire the scenery.

Where to watch whales

Whale watching is even more popular in Gloucester than in Boston (turn to Chapter 16 for a full description of whale watching). Prices run about $26 for adults, less for seniors and children; most tour companies will match any competitor's offer, including guaranteed sightings, AAA discounts, or coupons. Downtown, you'll find **Cape Ann Whale Watch (☎ 800-877-5110** or 978-283-5110; Internet: www.caww. com), **Capt. Bill's Whale Watch (☎ 800-33-WHALE** or 978-283-6995; Internet: www. cape-ann.com/captbill.html), and **Seven Seas Whale Watch (☎ 800-238-1776** or 978-283-1776; Internet: www.7seas-whalewatch.com). At the Cape Ann Marina, off Route 133, is **Yankee Whale Watch (☎ 800-WHALING** or 508-283-0313; Internet: www.yankee-fleet.com/whale.htm).

Plymouth

The Pilgrims reside in our national memory, wearing tall black hats and buckled shoes. A visit to their town may cause elementary school flashbacks, but it may also leave you with a new sense of the difficulties those early settlers overcame. Best of all, it's a *real* sense — the attractions that are replicas are faithful reproductions, but many of them are genuine 17th-century relics.

Plymouth is a reasonable day trip that's especially popular with children. The town also makes a good stop between Boston and Cape Cod.

Getting there

By car from Boston, follow I-93 south about 9 miles and bear left onto Route 3. Take Route 3 to Exit 6 (Route 44 east), and then follow signs to the historic attractions. Or continue on Route 3 to the Regional Information Complex at Exit 5 for maps, brochures, and information. To go directly to Plimoth Plantation, use Exit 4. The trip from Boston to Plymouth is about 40 miles and takes 45 to 60 minutes if it's not rush hour. The downtown area is compact, so park where you can. The waterfront meters are particularly convenient.

The commuter rail serves Plymouth (at peak commuting times service is to nearby Kingston) from Boston's South Station during the day on weekdays and all day on weekends; the trip takes 1 hour and the one-way fare is $5. **Plymouth & Brockton buses (☎ 617-773-9401 or 508-746-0378; Internet: www.p-b.com) leave from South Station and take about the same time. The bus is more expensive than the commuter rail ($9 one-way, $17 round-trip) but runs more often. The Plymouth Area Link bus connects the train stations with downtown and other destinations. The fare is 75 cents.

Taking a tour

A narrated tour with **Plymouth Rock Trolley,** 22 Main St. (☎ 508-747-3419), includes unlimited on-and-off privileges. The trolley operates daily from Memorial Day to October, and on weekends through Thanksgiving. Trolleys serve each stop every 20 minutes (except the plantation, where they stop once an hour). Tickets cost $7 for adults and $3 for children 3 to 12.

To get a Pilgrim perspective, take a 90-minute Colonial Lantern Tour with **New World Tours,** 35 North St. (☎ 800-698-5636 or 508-747-4161; Internet: www.lanterntours.com). Participants carry pierced-tin lanterns as they walk around the original settlement under the direction of a knowledgeable guide. Tours run nightly from April through

Thanksgiving. The standard history tour leaves the New World office at 7:30 p.m. The "Ghostly Haunts & Legends " tour leaves from the lobby of the John Carver Inn, 25 Summer St., at 9 p.m. Tickets are $9 for adults and $7 for children.

Narrated cruises run from April or May through November. One-hour **Splashdown Amphibious Tours** (☎ **508-747-7658;** Internet: www.ducktoursplymouth.com) take you around town on land and water. The trips leave from Water Street — either Harbor Place, near the Governor Bradford motor inn, or Village Landing, near the Sheraton — and detour through the harbor. These tours cost $15 for adults, $9 for children under 12, and $3 for children under 3.

Seeing the sights

The **Visitor Center,** 130 Water Street (across from the town pier; ☎ 508-747-7525), distributes information on Plymouth's attractions.

The sight to see is (ask the kids) Plymouth Rock, which history tells us was the landing place of the *Mayflower* passengers. Originally 15 feet long and 3 feet wide, the rock is now much smaller, having been moved (and broken) several times. Yes, it's just a rock, but the descriptions are absorbing, and the sense of history that surrounds the enclosure is curiously impressive.

Mayflower II

A stone's throw from Plymouth Rock, Mayflower II is a full-scale reproduction of the type of vessel that brought the Pilgrims from England to Plymouth in 1620. Full scale is a mere 106½ feet — you may want to remind the kids that it's not a model. Costumed guides provide first-person narratives about the voyage and the vessel, and displays illustrate the Pilgrims' experiences and the history of the ship, which was built in England from 1955 to 1957. Plan to spend at least an hour.

State Pier. ☎ *508-746-1622. Internet:* www.plimoth.org. *Admission: $6.50 adults, $4 children 6–12, and free for children under 6. Admission for both Mayflower II and Plimoth Plantation: $19 adults, $17 seniors, $11 children 6–12, free for children under 6. Open: Apr–Nov daily 9 a.m.–5 p.m.*

Pilgrim Hall Museum

This museum illustrates the daily lives of Plymouth's first white residents with unbeatable props — original possessions of the Pilgrims and their descendants. Displays include one of early settler Myles Standish's swords, an uncomfortable chair that belonged to the Pilgrim's original leader William Brewster (you can sit on a modern-day model, not on the original), and Governor Bradford's Bible. Allow at least an hour.

Plymouth

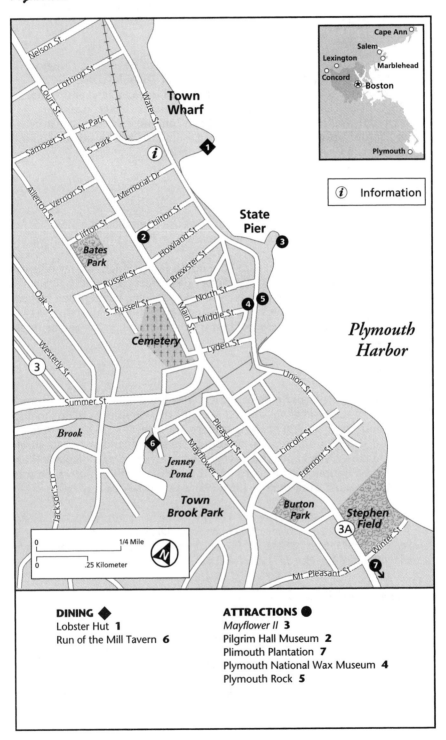

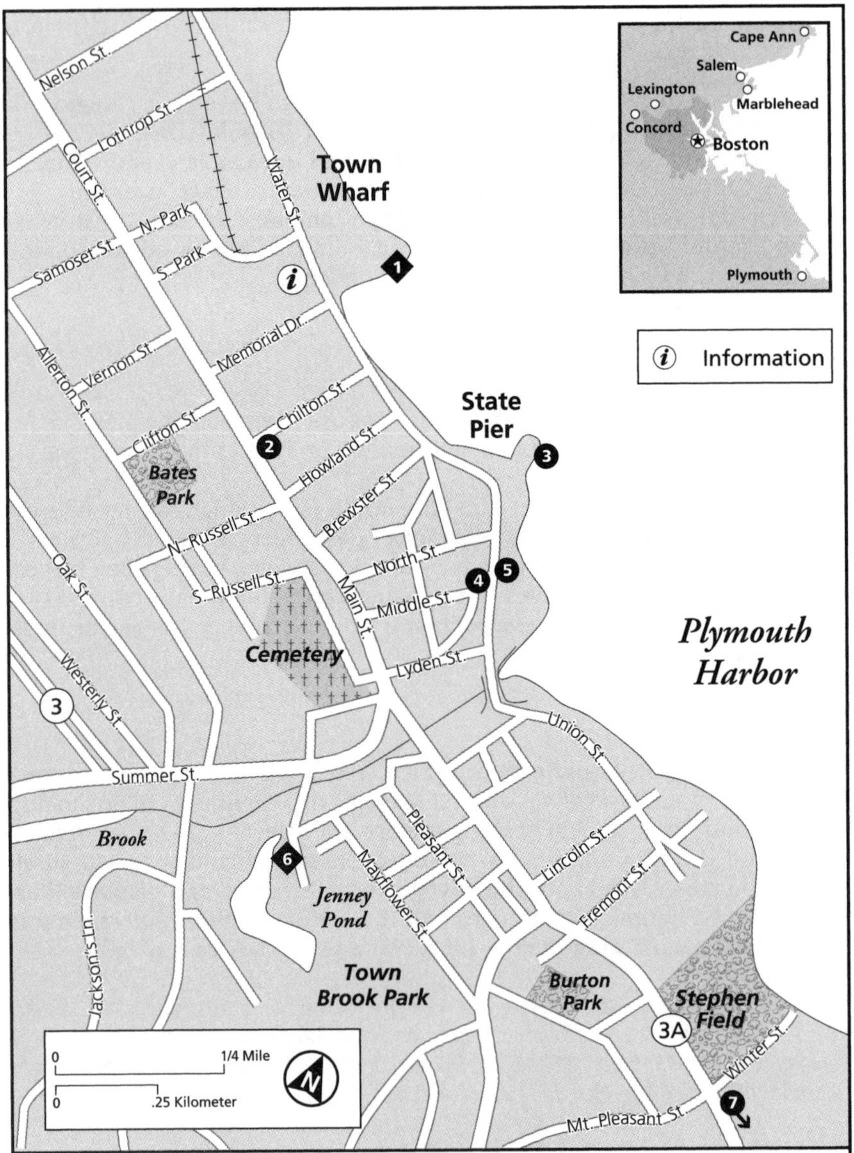
Cape Ann
Salem
Lexington
Marblehead
Concord
Boston
Plymouth
Information
Nelson St.
Lothrop St.
Court St.
Water St.
Town Wharf
N. Park
S. Park
Samoset St.
Memorial Dr.
Vernon St.
Allerton St.
Chilton St.
Clifton St.
State Pier
Howland St.
Bates Park
Brewster St.
N. Russell St.
North St.
S. Russell St.
Oak St.
Middle St.
Main St.
Plymouth Harbor
Cemetery
Lyden St.
Westerly St.
3
Union St.
Summer St.
Brook
Pleasant St.
Mayflower St.
Lincoln St.
Jenney Pond
Fremont St.
Town Brook Park
Burton Park
Stephen Field
Jackson's Ln.
3A
Winter St.
0
1/4 Mile
0
.25 Kilometer
N
Mt. Pleasant St.
1
2
3
4
5
6
7

DINING ◆
Lobster Hut **1**
Run of the Mill Tavern **6**

ATTRACTIONS ●
Mayflower II **3**
Pilgrim Hall Museum **2**
Plimouth Plantation **7**
Plymouth National Wax Museum **4**
Plymouth Rock **5**

75 Court St. ☎ *508-746-1620. Internet:* www.pilgrimhall.org. *From Plymouth Rock, walk north on Water St. and up the hill on Chilton St. Admission: $5 adults, $4.50 seniors and AAA members, $3 children 5–17, free for children under 5. Open: Feb–Dec daily 9:30 a.m.–4:30 p.m. Closed Jan.*

Plimoth Plantation

Allow at least half a day to experience this re-creation of the 1627 Pilgrim village. The "settlers" are actors who assume the personalities of members of the original community; if you chat them up, they'll pretend not to know anything contemporary, which many kids enjoy. The settlers also take part in typical activities, using only the tools and cookware available at the time; you may be able to join them in activities such as harvesting or witnessing a trial. Wear comfortable shoes, because you'll be walking all over, and the plantation isn't paved.

Route 3. ☎ *508-746-1622. Internet:* www.plimoth.org. *From Route 3, take Exit 4, "Plimoth Plantation Highway." Admission: $16 adults, $9 children 6–12, free for children under 6. Admission for both Plimoth Plantation and Mayflower II: $19 adults, $17 seniors, $11 children 6–17, free for children under 6. Open: Apr–Nov daily 9 a.m.–5 p.m. Closed Dec–March.*

Plymouth National Wax Museum

This museum illustrates the Pilgrim story in vivid detail that makes it both informative and memorable. If time is tight and kids are along, this is the stop to make (after the Rock, of course). The galleries hold more than 180 life-sized figures, arranged in striking dramatic scenes, with soundtracks narrating the stories. The scenes include the Pilgrims' move to Holland, the harrowing trip to the New World, the first Thanksgiving, and the tale of Myles Standish, Priscilla Mullins, and John Alden, which you may remember from the Longfellow poem you studied in third grade social studies. Allow 60 to 90 minutes.

16 Carver St. ☎ *508-746-6468. From Plymouth Rock, turn around and walk up the hill or the steps. Admission: $5.50 adults, $5 seniors, $2.25 ages 5–12, free for children under 5. Open: Mar–June and Sept–Nov daily 9 a.m.–5 p.m.; July–Aug daily 9 a.m.–9 p.m. Closed Dec–Feb.*

Dining

On Town Wharf, off Water Street, the **Lobster Hut** (☎ 508-746-2270) is a self-service seafood restaurant with a sensational view. Try the soups and the excellent "rolls" (hot dog buns with your choice of seafood filling). You can order beer and wine, but only with a meal. The **Run of the Mill Tavern** (☎ 508-830-1262) is near the water wheel at Jenney Grist Mill Village, in Town Brook Park off Summer Street. Although it doesn't overlook the ocean, this tavern serves tasty bar fare and seafood in an attractive setting; the clam chowder is great.

Part VI

Living It Up after the Sun Goes Down: Boston Nightlife

The 5th Wave   By Rich Tennant

"For tonight's modern reinterpretation of Carmen, those in the front row are kindly requested to wear raincoats."

In this part . . .

*B*oston offers patrons of the performing arts a cornu-
copia: an internationally renowned symphony
orchestra, the beloved Boston Pops, a top-notch ballet
company, theaters a step away from Broadway, and student performances of every imaginable type. The next two
chapters outline your choices and steer you toward
sources that can tell you more.

You may notice that I'm not rushing to tout the nightlife
options. These choices are nowhere near as encyclopedic,
though they can be just as entertaining. This city loves its
bars, and it embraces clubs that schedule everything from
comedy to folk to jazz to rock. True, the post-midnight
scene may be sparse, but that's not to say that you can't
howl at the moon into the wee hours. You just may not
have a lot of company.

Chapter 22

The Performing Arts

*M*aybe you make your nightlife plans months ahead and don't worry about them again. Perhaps you prefer to wait until just after dinner before deciding what to do next. Boston ably accommodates both strategies. In this chapter, I help you lay the groundwork, and then direct you toward the resources you need to keep up on the classical and popular music scenes as well as the theater and cinema worlds.

For the locations of the venues that I recommend, see the maps in this chapter. (Also, bars and clubs that are described in Chapter 23 appear on the maps in this chapter.)

Planning Ahead

To take a broad look at what types of performing arts events Boston has to offer, check a general resource such as the *Boston Globe*'s Web site: **Boston.com** (http://ae.boston.com). This site includes *Boston* magazine's listings as well. Major pop and rock performers play at the **FleetCenter** (☎ 617-624-1000; Internet: www.fleetcenter.com), and many smaller venues, listed later in this chapter, also host Web sites that list upcoming shows. If you have a favorite performer or group, visit its Web site to check schedules. Or, go right to the performing arts companies if you already know who or what you want to see (for a particular guest artist with the Boston Pops, say, or Boston Ballet's *Nutcracker,* see "The Performing Arts" later in this chapter for contact information on these and other companies).

A hotel package that includes tickets to a show can be a terrific convenience. The ticket price may not reflect a great savings, but knowing for sure that you secured seats for *The Nutcracker* will save a lot of worrying.

Some companies and venues sell tickets by phone or Web; many use an agency. The major Boston ticketing agencies are:

- ✔ **Ticketmaster** (☎ **617-931-2000**; Internet: www.ticketmaster.com)

- ✔ **Next Ticketing** (☎ **617-423-NEXT**; Internet: www.nextticketing.com)

- ✔ **Tele-charge** (☎ **800-447-7400**; Internet: www.telecharge.com, click "across the USA")

The service charge can be hefty, and it applies per ticket, not per order. If your plans may change, double-check the refund policy before you hand over your credit card info.

Venues list their major events months (sometimes years) in advance on their Web sites; check ahead to see whether your favorite group, show, play, or ballet is scheduled to perform in Boston. Discovering this information in advance may influence your travel plans.

The Spur-of-the-Moment Approach

The "Calendar" section of the Thursday *Boston Globe,* the "Scene" section of the Friday *Boston Herald,* and the Sunday arts sections of both papers overflow with possibilities. If you can handle a tiny bit of planning, call your hotel and ask the concierge or front desk to hang on to "Calendar" for you. Other good resources are the weekly *Boston Phoenix* and biweekly *Improper Bostonian* — available free all week from newspaper boxes all over town.

Once you find something appealing, call the box office to see whether the event is sold out. If something jumps out at you and you're looking for a deal, check at a BosTix booth (see "Saving Money on Tickets" later in this chapter) for discounted same-day tickets. If a show sounds great, but it's sold out, ask your concierge for help — sometimes he or she has ticket connections. Finally — this is a long shot, but worth a try — visit the box office in person. Patrons sometimes return tickets (good ones, too), and some venues block seats before configuring the performance space, and then release the extras.

Saving Money on Tickets

Perhaps the best arts resource in town is BosTix, which operates booths at Faneuil Hall Marketplace (on the south side of Faneuil Hall) and in Copley Square (at the corner of Boylston and Dartmouth Streets). BosTix sells same-day theater and concert tickets for half price, subject to availability. No credit cards, refunds, or exchanges are allowed. Check the board for the day's offerings.

Stepping out — Boston-style

Like your trip to Boston, your big evening out can turn into a festival of untied loose ends — if you let it. You already know where you're going, but that doesn't mean the planning is over. Here are a few other issues to address before heading out:

- ✔ **What to wear:** Just about anything clean and neat will suffice. You won't be out of place in something dressy, but for most events, anything short of a sweatsuit is fine. If you insist on wearing jeans to the symphony, theater, or ballet, I doubt I can stop you. But I will suggest that a big evening out feels a lot splashier if you're dressed for it.

- ✔ **Where to dine:** Most restaurants in and near the Theater District can accommodate the beat-the-clock dining style of patrons with an 8 o'clock curtain to catch, but you must remember to alert (and, if necessary, remind) the staff. Two of my favorite destinations before or after a show are **Brew Moon Restaurant & Microbrewery**, 115 Stuart St. (☎ **617-742-2739**), for sophisticated bar-style food, and **Finale**, 1 Columbus Ave. (☎ **617-423-3184**), which specializes in desserts. Turn to Chapters 14 and 15 for restaurant reviews.

- ✔ **When to arrive:** Be on time for the performance or bear the consequences. If you're not in your seat when the curtain goes up, you'll have to wait for a break in the action, and that may take a while.

- ✔ **How to get there:** Walk or take the T, especially if your destination is in the Theater District. If you take a cab or (heaven help you) drive, leave plenty of time for gridlock. To reach the Theater District, go to Boylston or Arlington (Green Line), or New England Medical Center or Chinatown (Orange Line). South Station (Red Line) is about 15 minutes away on foot. Symphony Hall has its own T stop: Symphony (Green Line E). Or get off at Hynes/ICA (Green Line B, C, or D), and then walk 10 minutes on Mass. Ave. The FleetCenter is at North Station (Green or Orange Line).

BosTix (☎ **617-482-2849;** Internet: www.boston.com/artsboston) also sells full-price advance tickets and offers discounts on theater, music, and dance events. Half-price tickets go on sale at 11 a.m. The booths are open Tuesday through Saturday 10 a.m. to 6 p.m., and Sunday 11 a.m. to 4 p.m. The Copley Square booth is open Monday 10 a.m. to 6 p.m.

The Performing Arts

Before plunging into specifics of venues and companies, I want to recommend two eclectic series. The first is summer only, outdoors, and free. From early June to early September, the **Hatch Shell** amphitheater (T: Charles/MGH [Red Line] or Arlington [Green Line]; ☎ **617-727-9547**, ext. 450) on the Esplanade, located on the Boston side of the Charles River, between Storrow Drive and the water, books music and dance performances and films. (If you've seen the Boston Pops' Fourth of July concert on TV, you've seen the Hatch Shell.) Seating is on the grass or on a blanket if you have one. Check ahead for schedules.

Boston Performing Arts and Nightlife

The Atrium **36**
Avalon **4**
Axis **3**
The Bar at the Ritz **29**
The Bay Tower **38**
Berklee College of Music **11**
The Black Rose **37**
Blue Man Group **20**
BosTix **13 37**
Boston Ballet **23**
Boston Center for the Arts **18**
Boston Pops **10**
Boston Symphony Orchestra **10**
Brew Moon Restaurant
   & Microbrewery **24**
Bristol Lounge **27**
Bull & Finch Pub **30**

Charles Playhouse **20**
Club Café **16**
Colonial Theatre **26**
Comedy Connection
   at Faneuil Hall **37**
Cornwalls **2**
Emerson Majestic Theatre **25**
FleetBoston Pavilion **42**
FleetCenter **35**
Fritz **17**
The Good Life **40**
Hard Rock Café **15**
Hatch Shell **32**
Hill Tavern **34**
Huntington Theatre Company **9**
Isabella Stewart Gardner
   Museum **6**
Jacques **19**

Jillian's Boston **5**
Mr. Dooley's Boston Tavern **39**
Museum of Fine Arts **7**
New England
   Conservatory of Music **8**
Oak Bar **14**
Paradise Rock Club **1**
Parish Café and Bar **28**
Radius **41**
Screen on the Green **31**
Sevens Ale House **33**
Shear Madness **20**
Shubert Theatre **21**
Symphony Hall **10**
Top of the Hub **12**
Wang Theatre **23**
Wilbur Theater **22**

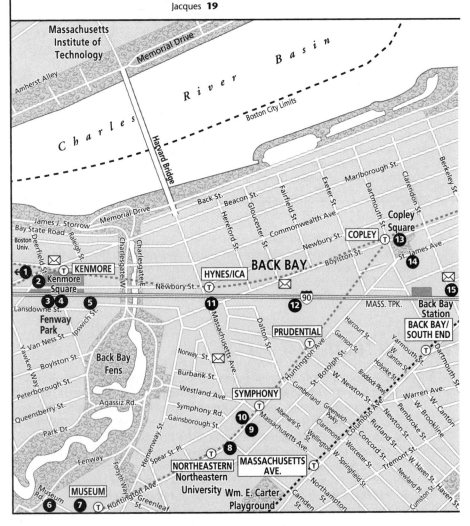

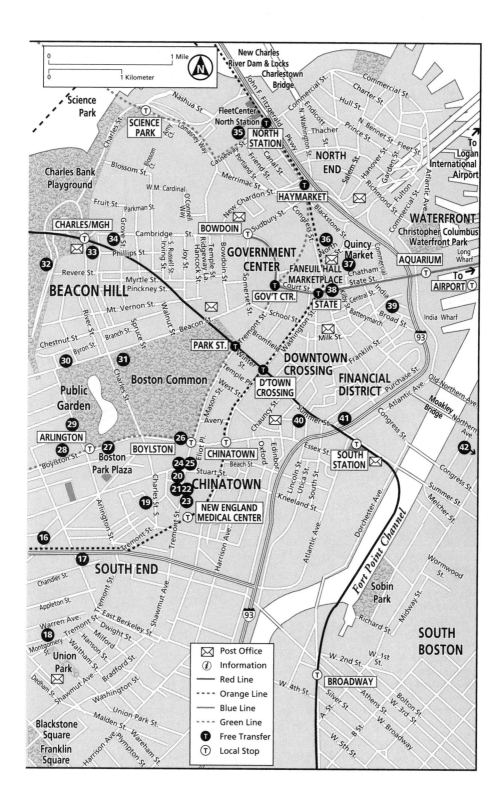

0 _____ 1 Mile
0 _____ 1 Kilometer

New Charles
River Dam & Locks
Charlestown
Bridge
John F. Fitzgerald Pkwy.

Science Park

SCIENCE PARK (T)

Charles Bank Playground

Charles St.

Nashua St.

Lomasney Way

Amy Ct.

Blossom Ct.

Blossom St.

W.M. Cardinal

O'Connell Way

Fruit St.

Parkman St.

Grove St.

CHARLES/MGH

34 (T)

33

32

Revere St.

Phillips St.

S. Russell St.

Irving St.

Myrtle St.

BEACON HILL

Pinckney St.

Mt. Vernon St.

Chestnut St.

Byron St.

Branch St.

Spruce St.

Walnut St.

Beacon St.

River St.

30

31

Charles St.

Public Garden

Boston Common

29

ARLINGTON

28 (T) 27

Boylston St.

Boston Park Plaza

BOYLSTON

26 (T)

Eliot Pl.

CHINATOWN

24 25

20

21 22

23

19

16

17

SOUTH END

Chandler St.

Appleton St.

Warren Ave.

18

Union Park

Montgomery St.

Tremont St.

Waltham St.

Hanson St.

Milford

Dwight St.

East Berkeley St.

Dedham St.

Shawmut Ave.

Bradford St.

Washington St.

Union Park St.

Blackstone Square

Franklin Square

Malden St.

Wareham St.

Harrison Ave.

Plympton St.

FleetCenter
North Station (T)

35

NORTH STATION (T)

Causeway St.

Friend St.

Portland St.

Canal St.

Merrimac St.

New Chardon St.

Congress St.

Sudbury St.

HAYMARKET

BOWDOIN (T)

Cambridge St.

Temple St.

Ridgeway La.

Hancock St.

Bowdoin St.

GOVERNMENT CENTER

Somerset St.

Court St.

GOV'T CTR. (T)

Temple Pl.

PARK ST. (T)

Tremont St.

Bromfield St.

Winter

West St.

Avery

Mason St.

Chauncy St.

Washington St.

School St.

Milk St.

DOWNTOWN CROSSING (T)

D'TOWN CROSSING

Summer St.

40

41

Oxford

Edinbor

Essex St.

Beach St.

Stuart St.

CHINATOWN

NEW ENGLAND MEDICAL CENTER (T)

Harrison Ave.

Tremont St.

Arlington St.

Charles St. S.

Commercial St.

Charter St.

Hull St.

N. Bennet St.

Fleet St.

Prince St.

Salem St.

Hanover St.

Garden St.

Richmond St.

Endicott St.

N. Washington St.

Thacher

NORTH END

Commercial St.

Atlantic Ave.

Fulton

WATERFRONT

Christopher Columbus Waterfront Park

Long Wharf

AQUARIUM (T)

36

Quincy Market

FANEUIL HALL MARKETPLACE

37

38

STATE (T)

State St.

Chatham St.

Kilby St.

Central St.

Batterymarch

Broad St.

India

39

India Wharf

93

Franklin St.

FINANCIAL DISTRICT

Purchase St.

Atlantic Ave.

Old Northern Ave.

Moakley Bridge

Northern Ave.

42

Congress St.

Summer St.

Melcher St.

Lincoln St.

Utica St.

South St.

Kneeland St.

SOUTH STATION (T)

Dorchester Ave.

Fort Point Channel

Sobin Park

Richard St.

Midway St.

Wormwood St.

SOUTH BOSTON

W. 1st St.

W. 2nd St.

W. 3rd St.

BROADWAY (T)

W. 4th St.

Silver St.

Athens St.

Bolton St.

W. Broadway

A St.

B St.

W. 5th St.

To Logan International Airport

To AIRPORT (T)

☒ Post Office
ⓘ Information
—— Red Line
----- Orange Line
—— Blue Line
----- Green Line
🅣 Free Transfer
(T) Local Stop

Cambridge Performing Arts and Nightlife

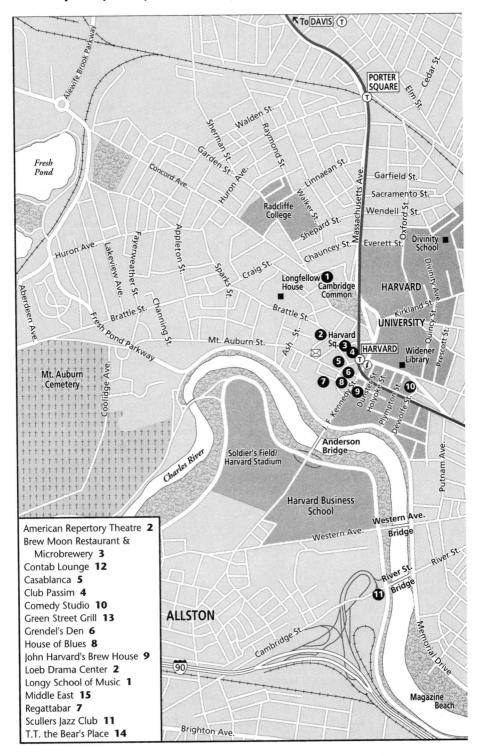

American Repertory Theatre **2**
Brew Moon Restaurant & Microbrewery **3**
Contab Lounge **12**
Casablanca **5**
Club Passim **4**
Comedy Studio **10**
Green Street Grill **13**
Grendel's Den **6**
House of Blues **8**
John Harvard's Brew House **9**
Loeb Drama Center **2**
Longy School of Music **1**
Middle East **15**
Regattabar **7**
Scullers Jazz Club **11**
T.T. the Bear's Place **14**

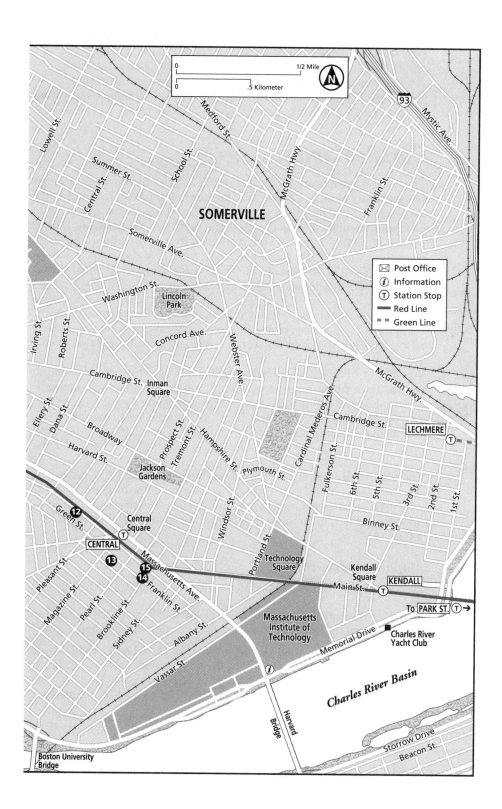

The other top series coordinates performances by international stars of classical music, dance, theater, jazz, and world music. The **FleetBoston Celebrity Series,** 20 Park Plaza, Boston, MA 02116 (☎ 617- 482-2595, or 617-482-6661 for Celebrity Charge; Internet: www.celebrityseries.org), takes place at different performance venues throughout the Boston area. Tickets are available to individual performances or in packages to three or more events.

Classical music

The **Boston Symphony Orchestra (BSO)** and the **Boston Pops** perform at **Symphony Hall,** 301 Mass. Ave. (at Huntington Ave.; T: Symphony [Green Line E]). The hall, known around the world for its perfect acoustics, turned 100 in 2000; when the main tenants are away, it books other companies. The BSO is in residence from September to April, the Pops from May to early July. Tickets start at $25 and top out at $80-plus. Call ☎ 617-266-1492, 617-CONCERT for program information, or 617-266-1200 for tickets; or check www.bso.org.

The Pops also schedule holiday programming in December (it sells out quickly) and a week of *free* outdoor performances, including the renowned Fourth of July concert, in early summer at the Hatch Shell.

Visit the box office 2 hours before a BSO or Pops show time, when returns from subscribers go on sale (at full price). A limited number of symphony "rush" tickets (one per person, same-day only) go on sale for $8 at 9 a.m. Friday, and 5 p.m. on Tuesday and Thursday. Wednesday evening and Thursday morning rehearsals are sometimes open to the public; call to see if rehearsal tickets ($14.50) are available.

The highly regarded **Handel & Haydn Society** (☎ 617-266-3605; Internet: www.handelandhaydn.org) schedules "historically informed" concerts, often with a choir, year-round. The ensemble uses period instruments and techniques in interpreting baroque and classical music.

Museum productions

For music with art, investigate these options at Boston museums:

- ✔ The **Museum of Fine Arts** (☎ 617-267-9300) schedules courtyard concerts on Wednesday evenings from June through September.

- ✔ The **Isabella Stewart Gardner Museum** (☎ 617-734-1359) books music on weekend afternoons from September through April.

You can also check out Chapter 16 for more info about these museums.

College concerts

Students and faculty members at three prestigious institutions perform frequently during the academic year; admission is usually free or cheap. Contact the following for specifics:

- ✔ **Berklee College of Music** (☎ 617-747-2261; Internet: www.berklee.edu);

- ✔ **New England Conservatory of Music** (☎ 617-585-1122; Internet: www.newenglandconservatory.edu);

- ✔ **Longy School of Music** (☎ 617-876-0956; Internet: www.longy.edu).

Pop and rock music

The major arena for touring groups and artists is the **FleetCenter** (off Causeway Street; T: North Station [Orange or Green Line]; ☎ 617- 624-1000; Internet: www.fleetcenter.com). Built in 1995, FleetCenter is a top-of-the-line facility, but the seating is at a pretty shallow angle; bring binoculars.

The **FleetBoston Pavilion,** 290 Northern Ave., South Boston (T: South Station [Red Line]; ☎ 617-374-9000; Internet: www.bankbostonpavilion.com), is a huge white tent open only in the summer. The pavilion books pop, jazz, folk, country, and some rock and rap artists. The airy outdoor setting makes it especially enjoyable. The venue is a 25-minute walk from the T station; call ahead for shuttle-bus and water-transportation info.

Turn to Chapter 23 for listings of smaller places to hear live rock and pop.

Dance

If you've heard of **Boston Ballet** (☎ 617-695-6955; Internet: www.bostonballet.org), it's probably because of *The Nutcracker* — an excellent reason, but not the only one. The company presents classic and modern works from October through May. Most performances are at the Wang Theatre, 270 Tremont St., and the Shubert Theatre, 265 Tremont St.

Built as a movie palace in the 1920s, the Wang presents certain difficulties for the ballet audience — namely awkward sight lines and the sensation that you're about to fall out of the balcony. Spend as much as you can on tickets for *The Nutcracker* (the highest price tops $70), especially if you're introducing your kids to this holiday spectacle. And remember your opera glasses.

If contemporary dance is more your style, check in with **Dance Umbrella** (☎ 617-482-7570; Internet: www.danceumbrella.org). Performances take place at venues in Boston and Cambridge, most often at the Emerson Majestic Theatre, 219 Tremont St.

The Theater Scene

Pre-Broadway tryouts still play in Boston, as do touring national companies of shows that do well in New York. The Theater District is a tiny area that centers on the intersection of Tremont and Stuart streets, between Chinatown and the Back Bay. With the recent flourishing of the Boston theater scene, it's not unusual for shows to be up at all five major professional stages. Two noted repertory companies and dozens of colleges also contribute to the growing theatrical buzz.

See "Saving Money on Tickets," earlier in this chapter, for information on BosTix and its half-price-ticket operation. Full-price tickets for legitimate theaters seldom go for less than $20; smaller companies and college performances are considerably cheaper.

Big-time theater

Most Broadway shows play in the Theater District at the following locations:

- ✔ **Colonial Theatre,** 106 Boylston St. (☎ 617-426-9366)
- ✔ **Shubert Theatre,** 265 Tremont St. (☎ 617-482-9393)
- ✔ **Wang Theatre,** 270 Tremont St. (☎ 617-482-9393)
- ✔ **Wilbur Theater,** 246 Tremont St. (☎ 617-423-4008)

To reach the Theater District take the T to Boylston or Arlington (Green Line), or New England Medical Center or Chinatown (Orange Line).

University performances

The **Huntington Theatre Company** plays at the Boston University Theatre, 264 Huntington Ave. (T: Symphony [Green Line E]; ☎ 617-266-0800; Internet: www.huntington.org). The **American Repertory Theatre (ART)** performs at Harvard University's Loeb Drama Center, 64 Brattle St., Cambridge (T: Harvard [Red Line]; ☎ 617-547-8300; Internet: www.amrep.org).

The Huntington and the ART tend to be more adventurous than their Theater District counterparts; for something even more audacious, head to the South End. The **Boston Center for the Arts,** 539 Tremont St. (between Berkeley and Clarendon Streets; T: Back Bay [Orange Line]; ☎ 617-426-2787), boasts five performance spaces, with more under construction, and an apparent willingness to try just about anything.

Family-friendly theater

Children old enough to be interested in the theater can enjoy a good introduction at either of two long-running shows: Blue Man Group and *Shear Madness.* How old should your child be to attend these shows? I'd say 10 or so — this is a lot of money to spend on someone who may not last until the curtain falls — but that's your call. **Blue Man Group** (Internet: www.blueman.com) consists of three cobalt-colored performance artists and a rock band. The show incorporates goofy props (including food), music, and willing spectators who become participants — one even gets painted. In its third decade, **Shear Madness** (Internet: www.shearmadness.com) is a "comic murder mystery" set in a hair salon. The audience helps solve the crime; the details have been different at every performance since the show opened in Boston in 1980.

Both shows run (on different stages) at the Charles Playhouse, 74 Warrenton St., off Stuart Street, in the Theater District. Tickets for Blue Man Group cost $39 and $49; for *Shear Madness* tickets run $34. Buy them at the box office or through Ticketmaster.

At the Movies

Two free outdoor series make summer evenings fly. Starting in early June, **Screen on the Green** (Internet: www.screenonthegreen.com) shows classic pictures such as *The Philadelphia Story.* Show times are Tuesday at dusk on Boston Common, near Beacon and Charles Streets. **Free Friday Flicks** (☎ 617-727-9547, ext. 450; Internet: www.wbz.com) projects films on a large screen in the amphitheater at the Hatch Shell on the Esplanade. These are family movies, with a tendency to lean toward the last couple of Disney releases rather than the classics. However, the season is long — a couple of gems usually sneak in.

Chapter 23

Hitting the Clubs and Bars

. . . .

In This Chapter

▶ The bars and lounges

▶ The clubs — music, dance, and comedy

▶ The gay and lesbian scenes

. . . .

*E*ven if you know nothing about Boston except what you saw on the TV show "Cheers," you already know something important: The neighborhood bar is a big deal. A spell in a local watering hole is a great way to get to know any new city, and Boston is no exception. Many nightspots schedule live music; if you'd rather shake your bon-bon than bend your elbow, you'll find a number of places to do that, too. In this chapter, I guide you toward some congenial spots to indulge in your recreation of choice.

For the locations of my recommended nightspots, see the maps in Chapter 22.

The Basics

The state drinking age is 21; you must have a valid driver's license or passport. Have an ID ready if you look younger than 35 or so, especially near college campuses. The skeptical bouncer is all that stands between the management and a liquor-license suspension; he probably doesn't want to hear any lame jokes.

A club that advertises a "21-plus" show means that only persons 21 years of age or older may enter the club; "18-plus" means 18-, 19-, and 20-year-olds may enter but can't drink alcohol.

 By law, bars close at 1 a.m. or earlier, clubs at 2 a.m. The T shuts down by 1 a.m. systemwide, with the last car from some stations running shortly after 12:30. Be ready to spring for cab fare.

Unless otherwise noted, the establishments in this chapter don't impose a cover charge; of course, that's subject to change, depending on the entertainment on a particular night.

Making the Scene: Bars and Lounges

The most famous tavern in town is the **Bull & Finch Pub,** 84 Beacon St. (T: Arlington [Green Line]; ☎ 617-227-9605; Internet: www.cheersboston.com), better known as the "Cheers" bar. Somewhat improbably, it retains a loyal neighborhood clientele, but most patrons are out-of-towners looking for souvenirs and snapshots. This popular spot is open daily 11 a.m. to 1 a.m.

To capture the memory of your visit to this pub, take your photos outside — the interior bears no resemblance to the "Cheers" TV-show set.

Another fun tourist magnet is the **Hard Rock Cafe,** 131 Clarendon St. (T: Back Bay [Orange Line] or Copley [Green Line]; ☎ **617-424-ROCK;** Internet: www.hardrock.com). The Hard Rock is a huge, noisy space lavishly adorned with rock 'n' roll memorabilia. The food is better than average, and the downstairs room sometimes schedules live music. And guess what? You can buy a souvenir. The Hard Rock is open daily 11 a.m. to 1 a.m.

Sky-high lounges

The romantic lounge at **The Bay Tower,** on the 33rd floor of 60 State St. (T: State [Orange or Blue Line]; ☎ 617-723-1666; Internet: www.baytower.com), offers splendid city views, live music, and dancing. Note: You can't enter in denim or athletic shoes. The lounge is open Monday to Thursday 5 p.m. to midnight, Friday and Saturday 5 p.m. to 1 a.m., and closed Sunday.

Top of the Hub, 800 Boylston St. (T: Prudential [Green Line E]; ☎ 617- 536-1775), occupies the 52nd floor of the Prudential Tower. Sunset shows off the panoramic view best, but any non-foggy time is good. The lounge schedules music and dancing nightly; dress is casual but neat. The lounge is open Sunday to Wednesday until 1 a.m., and Thursday to Saturday until 2 a.m.

Brew pubs

The microbrew fad, thankfully, seems to be on the wane. The surviving breweries specialize in deftly crafted creations and, as a bonus, tasty food.

My favorite is **Brew Moon Restaurant & Microbrewery,** a small chain that serves award-winning brews and remarkable house-made root beer. The Theater District branch, 115 Stuart St. (T: Boylston [Green Line] or Chinatown [Orange Line]; ☎ **617-742-2739**), is open daily 11:30 a.m. to 2 a.m. The Harvard Square location, 50 Church St. (T: Harvard [Red Line]; ☎ **617-499-2739**), is open 11:30 a.m. to 1 a.m. Monday to Saturday, and until midnight Sunday.

Also in Harvard Square, **John Harvard's Brew House,** 33 Dunster St. (T: Harvard [Red Line]; ☎ **617-868-3585;** Internet: www.johnharvards. com), attracts a boisterous student crowd with English-style brews made on the premises and reasonably priced pub grub. The pub is open daily 11:30 a.m. to 1:30 a.m.

Classy cocktail spots

The top-shelf martini shakers reside in hotel bars, those elegant, expensive destinations where you can channel Nick and Nora Charles. (Don't think of it as more expensive than a regular bar; think of it as cheaper than taking a room.) Dress up a little. All stay open into the early morning.

The Bar at the Ritz, in the Ritz-Carlton, 15 Arlington St. (T: Arlington [Green Line]; ☎ **617-536-5700**), was famous long before "Cheers" was even a pilot episode. The Ritz retains the crown with a combination of Brahmin atmosphere and killer martinis.

The Bristol Lounge, in the Four Seasons Hotel, 200 Boylston St. (T: Arlington [Green Line]; ☎ **617-351-2000**), is a refined destination for cocktails, luscious American food, afternoon tea, and (on weekend nights) the decadent Viennese Dessert Buffet. Enjoy live piano music every night.

The clubbiest place in town is the **Oak Bar** at the Fairmont Copley Plaza Hotel, 138 St. James Ave. (T: Copley [Green Line]; ☎ **617-267-5300**). Wood paneling and nightly live entertainment set the scene; cigar smoke and the raw bar tickle your senses. Proper dress is required. The Oak Bar is open daily at 4:30 p.m.

The Atrium lounge in the lobby of the **Bostonian Hotel,** 40 North St. (at Faneuil Hall Marketplace; T: Government Center [Green or Blue Line] or Haymarket [Orange Line]; ☎ **617-523-3600**), has less of a hideaway feel than many hotel bars. The wraparound windows afford a great view of the scene at the marketplace. Hear live piano music on weeknights.

Hibernian hangouts

That's a snappy way to say "Irish bars," which occupy an honored place in the Boston bar pecking order. Ponder which came first — the bartending job or the brogue — while you sip a Guinness.

My favorite is **Mr. Dooley's Boston Tavern,** 77 Broad St. (T: State [Orange or Blue Line]; ☎ 617-338-5656), a popular Financial District spot. World-class bartenders, hearty food, music, and imported draught beer in an authentic atmosphere — what more could you want? A cover of $3 is charged on weekend nights.

Considerably larger and rowdier is **The Black Rose,** 160 State St. (at Faneuil Hall Marketplace; T: State [Orange or Blue Line]; ☎ 617-742-2286; Internet: www.irishconnection.com/blackrose). The Black Rose books live entertainment to the delight of huge crowds who often sing along. The location makes it popular with tourists, but you'll find plenty of clued-in locals, too. You'll pay a cover of $3 to $5 at night.

Neighborhood bars

As promised, I point you toward some places where you can mingle with the locals. This list was strenuously edited, and it comes with a suggestion: If your wanderings take you past an agreeable-looking establishment, pop in.

Start with Cambridge (T: Harvard [Red Line]), where the colorful mix of patrons makes for peerless eavesdropping. In Harvard Square, you'll see professors, students, and more colorful types at **Casablanca,** 40 Brattle St. (☎ 617-876-0999), and **Grendel's Den,** 89 Winthrop St. (☎ 617-491-1160).

In Central Square (T: Central [Red Line]), the **Green Street Grill,** 280 Green St. (☎ 617-876-1655; Internet: www.2nite.com/greenstreet), has an amazing blues and jazz jukebox. Live music plays on weekends (with a cover charge, usually less than $10), and excellent food is served every night.

Beacon Hill (T: Charles/MGH [Red Line]) in Boston caters to the postcollegiate set. Check out the clean-cut types swilling beer at the **Sevens Ale House,** 77 Charles St. (☎ 617-523-9074), and the **Hill Tavern,** 228 Cambridge St. (☎ 617-742-6192).

The Good Life, 28 Kingston St. (off Summer Street; T: Downtown Crossing [Red or Orange Line]; ☎ 617-451-2622), is a madly popular after-work stop. The retro, lounge-y feel is a welcome holdover from the swing-dancing craze of the late '90s, without the zoot-suited poseurs at the bar.

A family-friendly pleasure dome

Imagine an establishment that incorporates a dance club, five full bars, and a restaurant. You can shoot pool (on one of the 52 tables), take a virtual-reality movie "ride," or play slot machines (for fun, not money). You can tackle a classic or contemporary game in the 250-game video midway, play darts or table tennis, or just watch your kids have a ball. That's **Jillian's Boston,** 145 Ipswich St. (at Lansdowne Street; T: Kenmore [Green Line B, C, or D]; ☎ **617/437-0300;** Internet: www. jilliansboston.com), a 70,000-square-foot complex at the end of the Lansdowne Street nightclub strip.

Jillian's is open Monday to Saturday 11 a.m. to 2 a.m., and Sunday noon to 2 a.m. The complex admits children under 18, who must be with an adult, before 7 p.m. Valet parking is available Wednesday to Sunday after 6, except during Red Sox games.

Nearby, **Radius,** 8 High St. (T: South Station [Red Line]; ☎ **617-426-1234**), attracts a chic Financial District crowd (no, that's not a contradiction). The restaurant is the headliner here, but the sleek bar is almost as much of a see-and-be-seen spot.

In the Back Bay (T: Arlington [Green Line]), indoor and outdoor seating is available at the **Parish Café and Bar,** 361 Boylston St. (☎ 617- 247-4777). Another after-work hot spot, this place is also a popular lunch stop because of its terrific sandwich menu.

In Kenmore Square (T: Kenmore [Green Line B, C, or D]), **Cornwalls,** 510 Commonwealth Ave. (☎ **617-262-3749**), is an English-lovers paradise that encourages loitering. A good place to visit if you're feeling old — the years fall away when you have to show an ID, even if you haven't needed one in years.

Checking Out the Clubs

The information in this section is the most volatile in the whole book. I steer you toward some reliable places and neighborhoods, but I can't promise that what's hot tonight will even be there next month. Dance clubs that usually book DJs sometimes feature live music; live-music clubs rarely restrict themselves to one genre. Check the "Calendar" section of the Thursday *Globe,* the *Phoenix,* the *Improper Bostonian,* or the "Scene" section of the Friday *Herald* when you're making plans.

Throughout this section, I note specific hours for a few places. For the others, keep in mind that most clubs open between 7 and 10 p.m. and must close at 2 a.m. These hours can change, however, depending on who's playing, who's booking, and whether a show is all-ages or 21-plus. If you really need to know the specifics, call ahead.

The original **House of Blues,** 96 Winthrop St., Cambridge (T: Harvard [Red Line]; ☎ **617-491-BLUE,** or 617-497-2229 for tickets; Internet: www. hob.com), rises above its chain status by being so darn cool. This hot spot books everyone from promising locals to international superstars for evening and weekend-matinee shows. The food is good, the crowds enthusiastic, and the music the real thing. Advance tickets ($7 to $30; matinees $5) are strongly recommended. The House is open Monday to Wednesday 11:30 a.m. to 1 a.m., Thursday to Saturday 11:30 a.m. to 2 a.m., and Sunday 4:30 p.m. to 1 a.m.

One of the liveliest events you'll ever experience is the House of Blues' **Sunday gospel brunch.** Call ahead for tickets (adults $26, children $13); seatings are at 10 a.m., noon, and 2 p.m.

Club-hop 'til you drop

Boston's most popular nightlife destination is Kenmore Square, specifically **Lansdowne Street,** off Brookline Avenue outside the square, across the street from Fenway Park.

Head to Kenmore Square for the city's best dance club, **Avalon,** 15 Lansdowne St. (T: Kenmore [Green Line B, C, or D]; ☎ **617- 262-2424**). This club is probably reinventing some aspect of itself as you read this. The multilevel space expanded in 1999 to accommodate more concerts, but the consistent reason to come here is "Avaland," the Friday night dance party. Management imports the highest-profile DJs it can find and turns the house dancers loose. The cover is usually $5 to $15, more for special events. Avalon is open Thursday to Saturday 10 p.m. to 2 a.m. The dress code forbids jeans and athletic wear, and requires jackets and shirts with collars for men.

Under the same management, **Axis,** 13 Lansdowne St. (T: Kenmore [Green Line B, C, or D]; ☎ **617-262-2437**), boasts a younger (collegiate and post-), looser crowd. Deafening rock, house, and techno music keeps the leather-clad crowds moving. The cover charge is around $7 to $11. Axis is open Tuesday through Sunday 10 p.m. to 2 a.m.

Nearby, you'll find a somewhat more sophisticated clientele at the **Paradise Rock Club,** 967 Commonwealth Ave. (T: Green Line B to Pleasant St.; ☎ **617-562-8804,** or 617-423-NEXT for tickets). Paradise is one of the best-known live-music venues in the area — its medium size allows artists who aren't ready to tour on their own to headline. This club is also famous for tangling with the Boston Licensing Board and losing its license for several months; you *must* have an ID. Tickets run $10 to $30.

Cambridge's **Central Square** (T: Central [Red Line]) draws enthusiastic crowds that go for music-making over scene-making. Many shows are 18-plus, with room for 30-pluses who can keep their fogeyish musings to themselves. (But *boy,* these places are loud.)

The **Middle East,** 472–480 Mass. Ave. (T: Central [Red Line]; ☎ 617-492-9181; Internet: www.mideastclub.com), books rock of all stripes in two rooms every night. The cover ranges from $7 to $15.

The eclectic bookings at **T. T. the Bear's Place,** 10 Brookline St. (T: Central [Red Line]; ☎ 617-492-0082, or concert line 617-492-BEAR; Internet: www.mindspring.com/~ttthebears), run the musical gamut. This place is a little crowded; expect to get to know your neighbors. The cover runs from $3 to $15, but usually under $10.

Three blocks away is the **Cantab Lounge,** 738 Mass. Ave. (T: Central [Red Line]; ☎ 617-354-2685). The Cantab is a neighborhood bar that happens to book great music — usually R&B or rock, sometimes jazz. The cover seldom tops $7.

For jazz fans

The two biggest local clubs are two of the best in the country — an enjoyable dilemma for devotees, a great opportunity for novices. You simply can't go wrong at either place.

The **Regattabar** is in the Charles Hotel, 1 Bennett St., Harvard Square (T: Harvard [Red Line]; ☎ 617-661-5000, or 617-876-7777 for Concertix). Regattabar is a large space where the crowd sometimes gets a little distracted (and chatty). Tickets run $6 to $25. Regattabar is open Tuesday to Saturday, and some Sundays.

Scullers Jazz Club is in the Doubletree Guest Suites hotel, 400 Soldiers Field Rd. (☎ 617-562-4111; Internet: www.scullersjazz.com). The room overlooks the Charles. The difficulty of getting to the hotel (it's not near the T) means the crowd includes fewer casual fans — a plus if your favorite artist is playing. Ask about dinner packages, which include preferred seating. Show tickets cost $10 to $35.

Just for laughs

The best comedy club around is the **Comedy Connection at Faneuil Hall,** on the upper level of Quincy Market (T: Government Center [Green or Blue Line] or Haymarket [Orange Line]; ☎ 617-248-9700). Promising locals and big-name visitors have packed the spacious room since 1978. Tickets run from $8 (for unknowns) to as much as $30 (for sitcom stars and the like).

You'll find fewer famous names but more potential in Cambridge at the **Comedy Studio,** in the Hong Kong restaurant, 1236 Mass. Ave. (T: Harvard [Red Line]; ☎ 617-661-6507). This place is good for improv, inspired sparring with the audience, and even sketch comedy.

Two more names you need to know

Johnny D's Uptown Restaurant & Music Club, 17 Holland St. (north of Cambridge, near Mass. Ave.), Somerville (T: Davis [Red Line]; ☎ 617-776-2004, or concert line 617-776-9667; Internet: www.johnnyds.com), schedules a wild assortment of musical genres and styles. No matter what your taste, the schedule is worth checking out. Cover $2 to $16, usually $10 or less. Open daily 11:30 a.m. to 1 a.m.

Club Passim, 47 Palmer St. (T: Harvard [Red Line]; ☎ 617-492-7679), is one of the few remaining legends in Harvard Square, and it actually lives up to its international reputation as a folk-music proving ground. The coffeehouse (which does not serve alcohol) has been around for over 30 years; your favorite artist has almost certainly played here. The cover charge is usually $5 to $12 or so; for big names, it might top $20. Open Sunday through Thursday 11 a.m. to 11 p.m. and Friday through Saturday 11 a.m. to 4 a.m.

Gay and Lesbian Clubs and Bars

Some dance clubs schedule a weekly gay night; the largest and best known is Sunday at Avalon and Axis (see earlier in this chapter). For entertainment listings, check *Bay Windows* (Internet: www.baywindows.com) and the *Phoenix* (Internet: www.bostonphoenix.com).

Club Café, 209 Columbus Ave., South End (T: Arlington [Green Line] or Back Bay [Orange Line]; ☎ 617-536-0966), is a lively spot that serves drinks and food, but not so noisy that you can't strike up a conversation. Club Café attracts men and women with live music and video entertainment. Thursday is see-and-be-seen night. The club is open daily until 1 a.m.

Jacques, 79 Broadway, in the Theater District (T: Arlington [Green Line]; ☎ 617-426-8902), is Boston's only drag venue. Jacques attracts a mixed (gay and straight) clientele with live music and performance art, too. The club is open daily until midnight.

Fritz, in the Chandler Inn Hotel, 26 Chandler St. (at Berkeley Street; T: Back Bay [Orange Line]; ☎ 617-482-4428), will make you feel right at home: It's a regular old sports-mad neighborhood bar. Fritz is open daily until 1 a.m.

Part VII
The Part of Tens

The 5th Wave   By Rich Tennant

"I want a lens that's heavy enough to counterbalance the weight on my back."

In this part . . .

People love top-ten lists — just ask Moses. The lists in this section aren't exactly biblical prophecy, but they do offer some inside information about blending in. You can do this in two ways: With your behavior and with a traditional thrifty Yankee attitude.

Chapter 24

The Top 10 Ways Not to Look Like a Tourist

In This Chapter

▶ Dressing like a local

▶ Keeping in step

▶ Talking the talk

---

*O*n a brief visit to Boston, you probably won't blend in — and you probably won't want to. One of the best ways to acquaint yourself with a new city is to plead ignorance and seek directions and advice from the locals. This chapter offers suggestions for fitting in without becoming so assimilated that people are asking *you* for directions. Just remember that if you insist on leaving the conference without removing your name tag, it might as well say, "Hi, I'm from out of town."

Always Dress in Layers

Even on the steamiest summer day, a midafternoon change in wind direction (or a stop at an enthusiastically air-conditioned store) can mean a sharp drop in temperature. You'll be glad to pull on a long-sleeved T-shirt or light sweater. And a spring or fall day that starts with a foggy morning can become toasty once the haze burns off — not a good time to have nothing on under your sweatshirt.

Keep Moving

Bostonians reputedly walk and talk faster than any other Americans — even New Yorkers. While sightseeing, step to the curb to check your map, count heads, or admire the architecture. Remember that the neighborhoods that attract hordes of tourists are also places where regular people live and work. When you block their paths while you get your bearings, you're forcing them off the sidewalks and into the paths of (scary sound effect) Boston traffic.

Stay in Touch with the Freedom Trail

Distinguished by red paint or red brick, smack in the middle of the sidewalk, the Freedom Trail won't steer you wrong. If you lose track of where you are, follow the trail to an intersection or landmark. You don't need to keep to it religiously; in fact, I strongly suggest a bit of wandering. One observation to note: if you're standing right on it as you tangle with your map, you'll look like a big ol' tourist.

Don't Exclaim, "That Must Be the Old North Church"

As you follow the Freedom Trail away from the Paul Revere House, you'll come to a house of worship on Hanover Street. This is St. Stephen's, the last remaining Boston church designed by legendary architect Charles Bulfinch. The Old North Church is across the street, a block beyond the Paul Revere statue that faces St. Stephen's.

Be in Your Party Clothes Early . . .

Bars close at 1 a.m. or earlier, clubs wrap it up at 2 a.m., and the line between "fashionably late" and "shut out" is all too thin. If the only admirers of your hot new outfit are the other people at the pancake house, don't say I didn't warn you.

. . . and Bring Cab Fare

Should you manage to scout out some late-night action, don't expect to jump on the T when you're through; it closes by 1 a.m. (every station posts the time of the last train in either direction). After the T closes, you'll be at the mercy of friends and cabbies.

Watch What You Say about Baseball

In cities that take sports less seriously, you can start a casual conversation with "How 'bout those (insert name of local nine)?" In Boston, just mentioning the Red Sox can land you on the business end of a lecture about Babe Ruth, Johnny Pesky, Carlton Fisk, Bucky Dent, Bill Buckner, and a bunch of other guys you couldn't pick out of a lineup. If you're up for that, great; if not, the weather is a reliable icebreaker.

Likewise, Chowder

This issue is less contentious than it once was, but still a divisive one. This disputed matter concerns a certain red ingredient found in the clam chowder in a big city some 200 miles south of the right-thinking people of Boston. You can sidestep it by ordering the version Legal Sea Foods attributes to Rhode Island (*never* Manhattan). In short, New England clam chowder does not contain tomatoes. Deal with it.

Pack the Right Shoes

Especially if you visit downtown, think twice before strapping on sandals. The Big Dig acts as a sort of gravel farm, and the closer you get to the site, the likelier you are to wind up with something uncomfortable in your shoe. Stick to closed footwear. And if you think that wearing socks with your sandals is an acceptable alternative, I'm sorry, but I'm going to have to pretend that we've never met.

Save the "I Pahked My Cah" Jokes

Everybody has an accent, even you (you just can't hear your own). The Boston accent isn't exactly poetic, but making fun of someone who speaks with one is both provincial and rude. That doesn't mean you can't enjoy it, though. Use your curious ear for discreet eavesdropping — the T is great for this — and you'll soon hear English being mangled in ways that will curl your hair.

Chapter 25

The Top 10 Free (Or Almost Free) Activities

- -

In This Chapter

▶ Finding free — or nearly free — cultural events

▶ Touring Boston on the cheap

▶ Rewarding people-watching spots

- -

*W*hether your budget resembles an impoverished student's or a Texas tycoon's, a few extra bucks are always welcome. In this chapter, I point you toward activities that can help create financial wiggle room. For general information, turn to Chapter 3, "Planning Your Budget."

Music Outdoors

In warm weather, musicians take to the streets and outdoor venues in droves. The free performances range from impromptu jam sessions to huge concerts that promote local radio stations. One congenial series brings jazz to Christopher Columbus Park, on the waterfront across the street from Faneuil Hall Marketplace, at 7 p.m. on summer Fridays. City Hall Plaza and the Hatch Shell on the Charles River Esplanade book larger events. Check around (in the papers or at the front desk) when you arrive — you'll definitely find something that appeals to you.

Music Indoors

Colleges and churches take up the slack when cold weather drives tunesmiths indoors. Students and instructors at local universities as well as prestigious conservatories perform throughout the school year.

The big academic names are **Berklee College** (Internet: www.berklee.edu), the **New England Conservatory** (Internet: www.newenglandconservatory.edu), and **Cambridge's Longy School** (Internet: www.longy.edu), but there's no telling what you might find while in Boston. Churches schedule secular performances as well as religious works; the best-known series runs year-round at historic Trinity Church, in Copley Square, Fridays at 12:15 p.m.

Check listings in the *Globe* "Calendar" section or the *Phoenix* before or when you arrive for more information about the Boston area's abundant free and cheap activities.

National Park Service Tours

Your tax dollars pay off like lottery tickets at the Park Service sites that dot eastern Massachusetts. Free or (at some locations) inexpensive tours complement and interpret the historic and cultural attractions. Check the Web site: www.nps.gov. Or drop into the **Boston National Historic Park Visitor Center,** 15 State St. (☎ 617-242-5642).

Movies

The **Screen on the Green** (Internet: www.screenonthegreen.com) and **Free Friday Flicks** (Internet: www.wbz.com) film series bring classic and family movies to Boston Common and the Esplanade, respectively. Screen on the Green, on Tuesdays in the early summer, tends to draw an after-work crowd; Free Friday Flicks, which runs later in the season, is more kid-friendly. Either makes a splendid way to spend an evening.

Theater

This area is another with a substantial college component, and the usual potential and pitfalls of amateur stagecraft. Again, local listings can point you in the right direction. For the less adventurous (or more discriminating, if you prefer), professionals perform free on Boston Common in July and early August with the **Commonwealth Shakespeare Company** (Internet: www.commonwealthshakespeare.org). The top-notch troupe mounts one production per season with a cast that's about half Equity actors.

Museums

Your low-budget options are few but fun. Free: The Institute of Contemporary Art on Thursday from 5 to 9 p.m., the Harvard University museums on Saturday before noon, and the university art museums all day Wednesday. Cheap: The Children's Museum charges $1 per person on Friday from 5 to 9 p.m., and the Museum of Fine Arts schedules pay-what-you-wish hours ($5 suggested for adults) on Wednesday from 4 to 9:45 p.m. Potentially expensive: If you're just in this for the shopping (and believe me, you're not alone), remember that every museum will let you into its gift shop without paying an admission fee.

People Watching

For the price of a cup of coffee or a drink, you can camp out and enjoy the passing parade just about anywhere. Three favorite destinations: the Hanover Street *caffès* in the North End, sidewalk tables and window seats on Newbury Street in the Back Bay, and the outdoor tables at the Harvard Square Au Bon Pain.

Haymarket

The Haymarket could fall under "People Watching," but it is such an unusual experience that it deserves special attention. This open-air market consists of stalls piled high with fruits, veggies, and fish. Located on Blackstone and North streets, near Faneuil Hall Marketplace, the market operates only on Friday and Saturday. If you're on the Freedom Trail, slow down and have your camera ready — the gregarious vendors, fanatical bargain-hunters, and colorful produce make a perfect photo op.

Street Fairs

From fashion shows to pony rides — you'll find alfresco diversions all over town, on weekends throughout the summer and fall. The North End, the Back Bay, and Harvard Square stage notable multiple-block parties; check the newspapers or ask at your hotel's front desk for details of festivities during your visit.

Hydrotherapy

Check out a map of Boston and Cambridge — both of which abound with waterfront property. Pack a lunch, a camera, or just a craving for a little down time, and head toward the harbor or the river to kick back. Abundant maritime traffic crisscrosses the harbor, which lies within view of Logan Airport's flight patterns. Recreational craft on the Charles River include graceful sailboats and college crew shells.

You'll find excellent spots for a water break in downtown Boston on Long Wharf (follow State Street to the end) and off Commercial Street at Fleet Street and Hull Street, in Charlestown near the harbor ferry dock, and in the Back Bay on the Charles River Esplanade. The Cambridge side of the river is essentially one long park, with particularly enjoyable spots near Harvard and Kendall squares.

Appendix

Quick Concierge

● ●

American Automobile Association (AAA)

Road service ☎ 800-222-4357; other services ☎ 800-222-8252. The Boston office is in the Financial District at 125 High St., off Pearl Street.

Ambulance

Call ☎ 911. This call is free from pay phones.

American Express

The main local office is at 1 State St. (☎ 617-723-8400); it's open weekdays from 8:30 a.m. to 5:30 p.m. The Back Bay office, 222 Berkeley St. (☎ 617-236-1334), is open weekdays 9 a.m. to 5:30 p.m. The Cambridge office, 39 John F. Kennedy St., Harvard Square (☎ 617-661-0005), is open weekdays 8:30 a.m. to 7:30 p.m., Saturday 11 a.m. to 5:30 p.m., Sunday noon to 5 p.m.

Area Codes

As of April 2001, eastern Massachusetts has eight area codes (four old codes "overlaid" with four new ones), and every phone number is 10 digits (11 if you count dialing 1 first). Even if you're calling next door, you must dial the area code first. In Boston proper, the area codes are **617** and **857**; in the immediate suburbs, **781** and **339**; to the north and west, **978** and **351**; to the south and east, **508** and **774**.

ATMs

Widely available throughout Boston and Cambridge at banks, on the street, in convenience stores and supermarkets, and in some subway stations. (See Chapter 12.)

Baby-Sitters

Check with your hotel's front desk or concierge for suggestions. See Chapter 4 for information about the agency Parents in a Pinch (☎ 800-688-4697 or 617-739-KIDS).

Camera Repair

Try Bromfield Camera & Video, 10 Bromfield St. (☎ 800-723-2628 or 617-426-5230), near Downtown Crossing; or the Camera Center, 107 State St. (☎ 800-924-6899 or 617-227-7255), in the Financial District.

Convention Centers

Hynes Convention Center, 900 Boylston St. (☎ 617-954-2000 or 617-424-8585 for show info; Internet: www.jbhynes.com). World Trade Center, 164 Northern Ave. (☎ 800-367-9822 or 617-385-5000, or 617-385-5044 for show info; Internet: www.wtcb.com). Bayside Expo Center, 200 Mt. Vernon St., Dorchester (☎ 617-474-6000; Internet: www.baysideexpo.com).

Credit Cards

The toll-free emergency number for Visa is ☎ 800-847-2911. The number for Master-Card is ☎ 800-307-7309. American Express cardholders should call ☎ 800-221-7282 for all money emergencies.

Dentists

Check with the front desk or concierge at your hotel, or try the Massachusetts Dental Society (☎ 800-342-8747 or 508-651-7511; Internet: www.massdental.org).

Doctors

Check with the front desk or concierge at your hotel, or try a referral service. Every hospital in town has one, including Massachusetts General (☎ 800-711-4MGH) and Beth Israel Deaconess (☎ 617-667-5356). Before seeking medical treatment, be sure you understand your insurance carrier's policy on emergency care and preapproval.

Emergencies

Call ☎ 911 for the police, a fire, or an ambulance. This call is free from pay phones.

Hospitals

Closest to downtown are Massachusetts General Hospital, 55 Fruit St. (☎ 617-726-2000), and New England Medical Center, 750 Washington St. (☎ 617-636-5000). At the Harvard Medical Area on the Boston– Brookline border are Beth Israel Deaconess Medical Center, 330 Brookline Ave. (☎ 617- 667-7000); Brigham and Women's Hospital, 75 Francis St. (☎ 617-732-5500); and Children's Hospital, 300 Longwood Ave. (☎ 617-355-6000), among others. In Cambridge: Mount Auburn Hospital, 330 Mount Auburn St. (☎ 617-492-3500), and Cambridge Hospital, 1493 Cambridge St. (☎ 617-498-1000).

Hotlines

AIDS Hotline (☎ 800-235-2331 or 617-536-7733); Poison Control Center (☎ 617-232-2120); Rape Crisis (☎ 617-492-7273); Samaritans Suicide Prevention (☎ 617-247-0220); Samariteens (☎ 800-252-8336 or 617-247-8050).

Information

Greater Boston Convention & Visitors Bureau, ☎ 800-SEE-BOSTON or 617-536-4100. Telephone directory assistance, ☎ 411. (Also see "Where to Get More Information" later in this Appendix.)

Internet Access

It's not your imagination: Kinko's is everywhere. Locations include 2 Center Plaza, Government Center (☎ 617-973-9000); 10 Post Office Sq., Financial District (☎ 617-482-4400); 187 Dartmouth St., Back Bay (☎ 617-262-6188); and 1 Mifflin Place, off Mount Auburn Street near Eliot Street, Harvard Square (☎ 617-497-0125).

Liquor Laws

The legal drinking age is 21. Always be ready to show identification. At sporting events, everyone buying alcohol must show ID. Liquor stores and a few supermarkets and convenience stores sell alcohol. Liquor stores (and the liquor sections of other stores) close on Sundays, but restaurants and bars may serve alcohol. Some smaller restaurants don't have full liquor licenses; ask when you make your reservations.

Maps

Pick up a map at any visitor information center (see " Where to Get Information in Person," in Chapter 10), at most hotels, and from the clerks in most T token booths.

Newspapers/Magazines

The *Boston Globe* and *Boston Herald* are the city's daily papers. The free weekly *Boston Phoenix* and free biweekly *Improper Bostonian* carry arts coverage and entertainment and restaurant listings. Newspaper boxes around Boston and Cambridge distribute both. *Boston* magazine is a lifestyle-oriented monthly. (See "Information on the web" later in this Appendix for the *Boston Globe* and *Boston Phoenix* Web site information.)

Pharmacies

At least one CVS is in every neighborhood. Downtown Boston has no 24-hour drugstore. The CVS in the Porter Square Shopping Center, off Mass. Ave. in Cambridge (☎ 617-876-5519), is open

24 hours, 7 days a week. The pharmacy at the CVS at 155–157 Charles St. in Boston (☎ 617-523-1028), next to the Charles/MGH T stop, is open until midnight. Some emergency rooms can fill your prescription at the hospital's pharmacy.

Police

Call ☎ **911** for emergencies. The nonemergency number is ☎ 617-343-4200.

Radio Stations

WBUR-FM, 90.9, is the local National Public Radio affiliate. WBZ-AM, 1030, carries news, sports, and weather with traffic reports every 10 minutes on weekdays.

Rest rooms

The visitor center at 15 State St. has a public rest room, as do most tourist attractions, hotels, department stores, and public buildings. Most Starbucks locations and large chain bookstores have rest rooms. If you're walking the Freedom Trail, especially with children, be sure to use the rest rooms at Faneuil Hall Marketplace before venturing into the North End, which has no public facilities. Restrooms are available at the CambridgeSide Galleria, Copley Place, and Prudential Center shopping areas.

Safety

Boston and Cambridge are generally safe for walking. As in any city, stay out of parks (including the Esplanade) at night, unless you're in a crowd. Use common sense: Walk confidently, try not to use ATMs at night, and avoid dark, deserted streets. Specific areas to avoid at night include Boylston Street between Tremont and Washington Streets, and Tremont Street from Stuart to Boylston Streets. Watch your step near the Big Dig (that is, most of downtown), where walking surfaces can be uneven. Public transportation in the areas you're likely to visit is busy and safe, but service stops between 12:30 and 1 a.m.

Smoking

All public buildings and many restaurants ban smoking. Boston and Cambridge restaurants that do permit smoking must, by law, confine it to the bar. Brookline bans smoking in all restaurants and bars.

Taxes

The 5 percent state sales tax doesn't apply to food, prescription drugs, newspapers, or clothing worth less than $175. The state meal tax (which also applies to take-out food) is 5 percent. The lodging tax is 12.45 percent in Boston and Cambridge.

Taxis

To call ahead in Boston, try the Independent Taxi Operators Association (☎ 617-426-8700); Boston Cab (☎ 617-536-5010); or Town Taxi (☎ 617-536-5000). In Cambridge, call Ambassador Brattle (☎ 617-492-1100) or Yellow Cab (☎ 617-547-3000). For more information, see "Cab Session: Taxis," in Chapter 11.

Time Zone

Boston is in the eastern time zone. Daylight saving time begins on the first Sunday in April and ends on the last Sunday in October.

Tipping

The average tip for most service providers, including waiters and cab drivers, is 15 percent, rising to 20 percent for particularly good service. Tip bellhops $1 or $2 a bag, hotel housekeepers at least $1 per person per day, and valet parking and coat-check attendants $1 to $2.

Transit Information

For T information, call ☎ 617-222-3200. For airport transportation information, call ☎ 800-23-LOGAN.

Weather Updates

Call ☎ 617-936-1234 for forecasts.

Toll-Free Numbers and Web Sites

Major North American carriers

Air Canada
☎ 888-247-2262
www.aircanada.ca

America West Airlines
☎ 800-235-9292
www.americawest.com

American Airlines
☎ 800-433-7300
www.aa.com

Canadian Airlines International
☎ 800-426-7000
www.cdnair.ca

Continental Airlines
☎ 800-523-3273
www.continental.com

Delta Air Lines
☎ 800-221-1212
www.delta.com

Frontier Airlines
☎ 800-432-1359
www.frontierairlines.com

Northwest Airlines
☎ 800-225-2525
www.nwa.com

Southwest Airlines
☎ 800-435-9792
www.iflyswa.com

Trans World Airlines (TWA)
☎ 800-221-2000
www.twa.com

United Airlines
☎ 800-241-6522
www.ual.com

US Airways
☎ 800-428-4322
www.usairways.com

Car-rental agencies

Alamo
☎ 800-327-9633
www.goalamo.com

Avis
☎ 800-831-2874
☎ 800-TRY-AVIS in Canada
www.avis.com

Budget
☎ 800-527-0700
www.budgetrentacar.com

Dollar
☎ 800-800-4000
www.dollar.com

Enterprise
☎ 800-325-8007
www.enterprise.com

Hertz
☎ 800-654-3131
www.hertz.com

National
☎ 800-CAR-RENT
www.nationalcar.com

Rent-A-Wreck
☎ 800-535-1391
rent-a-wreck.com

Thrifty
☎ 800-847-4389
www.thrifty.com

Major hotel and motel chains

Best Western International
☎ 800-528-1234
www.bestwestern.com

Clarion Hotel
☎ 800-CLARION
www.hotelchoice.com

Comfort Inn
☎ 800-228-5150
www.comfortinn.com

Courtyard by Marriott
☎ 800-321-2211
www.courtyard.com

Crown Plaza Hotel
☎ 800-227-6963
www.CrownePlaza.com

Days Inn
☎ 800-325-2525
www.daysinn.com

Doubletree Hotel
☎ 800-222-TREE
www.doubletreehotels.com

Econo Lodge
☎ 800-55-ECONO
www.hotelchoice.com

Fairfield Inn by Marriott
☎ 800-228-2800
www.fairfieldinn.com

Hampton Inn
☎ 800-HAMPTON
www.hampton-inn.com

Hilton Hotel
☎ 800-HILTONS
www.hilton.com

Holiday Inn
☎ 800-HOLIDAY
www.holiday-inn.com

Howard Johnson
☎ 800-654-2000
www.hojo.com

Hyatt Hotels & Resorts
☎ 800-228-9000
www.hyatt.com

Marriott Hotel
☎ 800-228-9290
www.marriott.com

Quality Inn
☎ 800-228-5151
www.hotelchoice.com

Radisson Hotels International
☎ 800-333-3333
www.radisson.com

Ramada Inn
☎ 800-2-RAMADA
www.ramada.com

Residence Inn by Marriott
☎ 800-331-3131
www.residenceinn.com

Ritz-Carlton
☎ 800-241-3333
www.ritzcarlton.com

Sheraton Hotels & Resorts
☎ 800-325-3535
www.sheraton.com

Super 8 Motel
☎ 800-800-8000
www.super8motels.com

Travelodge
☎ 800-255-3050
www.travelodge.com

Westin Hotels & Resorts
☎ 800-937-8461
Internet: www.westin.com

Wyndham Hotels & Resorts
☎ 800-996-3426
www.wyndham.com

Where to Get More Information

Cambridge Office for Tourism

Request a free guide to the place the tourist office insists on calling Boston's "Left Bank."

18 Brattle St., Cambridge, MA 02138. ☎ *800-862-5678 or 617-441-2884. Internet:* www.cambridge-usa.org.

Greater Boston Convention & Visitors Bureau

The bureau offers a comprehensive visitor information kit for $6.25; the kit includes a travel planner, guidebook, map, and coupon book with shopping, dining, attractions, and nightlife discounts. The "Kids Love Boston" guidebook costs $3.25. Call the main number to gain access to the "Boston by Phone" service, which provides information on lodging, attractions, dining, nightlife, shopping, and travel services.

2 Copley Place, Suite 105, Boston, MA 02116-6501. ☎ *888-SEE-BOSTON or 617- 536-4100. Internet:* www.bostonusa.com.

Massachusetts Office of Travel and Tourism

Request the free *Getaway Guide* magazine, which includes information about attractions and lodgings, a map, and a seasonal calendar. Because this office covers travel and tourism for the whole state, it has less Boston-specific material than the Convention & Visitors Bureau. But the material offered is still useful (and free!). The online "lobster tutorial" makes an excellent cheat sheet.

100 Cambridge St., 13th floor, Boston, MA 02202. ☎ *800-227-6277 or 617-727-3201. the free Getaway Guide Internet:* www.mass-vacation.com.

Information on the Web

www.Boston.com

The *Boston Globe*'s city guide is the most complete and up-to-date resource around. It includes everything from weather forecasts to movie reviews, plus enough links and listings to keep you busy for hours.

http://boston.citysearch.com

Copious lifestyle and entertainment listings, including restaurant reviews. (Ticketmaster owns CitySearch, which took over Microsoft Sidewalk in 1999.)

www.bostonphoenix.com

The alternative weekly offers abundant arts and entertainment coverage (listings and reviews), plus excellent listings for the gay, lesbian, and bisexual community.

www.massport.com/logan

The Massachusetts Port Authority, which runs the airport, constantly updates its site with the latest in weather and air-traffic info. The visitor-information area includes many useful links.

www.mayorsfoodcourt.com

Results of restaurant inspections (and rein-spections), with numerical scores and pop-up windows that explain the regulations. Gross, but addictive.

www.boston-online.com/wicked.html

The "Wicked Good Guide to Boston" is the decoder ring you need to untangle that incomprehensible Boston accent.

www.bigdig.com

The Big Dig — see what all the fuss is about.

Information in print
Frommer's Boston

A comprehensive look at "the Hub," with more hotel, restaurant, and attraction list-ings than this book can accommodate. I have it on very good authority that the author wishes you well.

Frommer's New England

The perfect accessory on a multiple-state or -city visit to this appealing region.

Boston magazine

The slick monthly covers the arts, entertain-ment, and politics; gives the annual *Best of Boston* awards; and runs the city's best money-is-no-object ads. You can also check it out online at www.bostonmagazine.com.

Making Dollars and Sense of It

Expense	Amount
Airfare	
Car Rental	
Lodging	
Parking	
Breakfast	
Lunch	
Dinner	
Babysitting	
Attractions	
Transportation	
Souvenirs	
Tips	
Grand Total	

Notes

Fare Game: Choosing an Airline

Travel Agency:_____ Phone:_____

Agent's Name:_____ Quoted Fare:_____

Departure Schedule & Flight Information

Airline:_____ Airport:_____

Flight #:_____ Date:_____ Time:_____ a.m./p.m.

Arrives in:_____ Time:_____ a.m./p.m.

Connecting Flight (if any)

Amount of time between flights:_____ hours/mins

Airline:_____ Airport:_____

Flight #:_____ Date:_____ Time:_____ a.m./p.m.

Arrives in:_____ Time:_____ a.m./p.m.

Return Trip Schedule & Flight Information

Airline:_____ Airport:_____

Flight #:_____ Date:_____ Time:_____ a.m./p.m.

Arrives in:_____ Time:_____ a.m./p.m.

Connecting Flight (if any)

Amount of time between flights:_____ hours/mins

Airline:_____ Airport:_____

Flight #:_____ Date:_____ Time:_____ a.m./p.m.

Arrives in:_____ Time:_____ a.m./p.m.

Notes

Sweet Dreams: Choosing Your Hotel

Enter the hotels where you'd prefer to stay based on location and price. Then use the worksheet below to plan your itinerary.

Hotel	Location	Price per night

Menus & Venues

Enter the restaurants where you'd most like to dine. Then use the worksheet below
to plan your itinerary.

Name	Address/Phone	Cuisine/Price

Places to Go, People to See, Things to Do

Enter the attractions you would most like to see. Then use the worksheet below to plan your itinerary.

Attractions	Amount of time you expect to spend there	Best day and time to go

Going "My" Way

Itinerary #1

- ☐ _____
- ☐ _____
- ☐ _____
- ☐ _____

Itinerary #2

- ☐ _____
- ☐ _____
- ☐ _____
- ☐ _____

Itinerary #3

- ☐ _____
- ☐ _____
- ☐ _____
- ☐ _____

Itinerary #4

- ☐ _____
- ☐ _____
- ☐ _____
- ☐ _____

Itinerary #5

- ☐ _____
- ☐ _____
- ☐ _____
- ☐ _____

Itinerary #6

- ☐ _____
- ☐ _____
- ☐ _____
- ☐ _____

Itinerary #7

- ☐ _____
- ☐ _____
- ☐ _____
- ☐ _____

Itinerary #8

- ☐ _____
- ☐ _____
- ☐ _____
- ☐ _____

Itinerary #9

- ☐ _____
- ☐ _____
- ☐ _____
- ☐ _____

Itinerary #10

- ☐ _____
- ☐ _____
- ☐ _____
- ☐ _____

Notes

Making Dollars and Sense of It

Expense	Amount
Airfare	
Car Rental	
Lodging	
Parking	
Breakfast	
Lunch	
Dinner	
Babysitting	
Attractions	
Transportation	
Souvenirs	
Tips	
Grand Total	

Notes

Fare Game: Choosing an Airline

Travel Agency:_____ Phone:_____

Agent's Name:_____ Quoted Fare:_____

Departure Schedule & Flight Information

Airline:_____ Airport:_____

Flight #:_____ Date:_____ Time:_____ a.m./p.m.

Arrives in:_____ Time:_____ a.m./p.m.

Connecting Flight (if any)

Amount of time between flights:_____ hours/mins

Airline:_____ Airport:_____

Flight #:_____ Date:_____ Time:_____ a.m./p.m.

Arrives in:_____ Time:_____ a.m./p.m.

Return Trip Schedule & Flight Information

Airline:_____ Airport:_____

Flight #:_____ Date:_____ Time:_____ a.m./p.m.

Arrives in:_____ Time:_____ a.m./p.m.

Connecting Flight (if any)

Amount of time between flights:_____ hours/mins

Airline:_____ Airport:_____

Flight #:_____ Date:_____ Time:_____ a.m./p.m.

Arrives in:_____ Time:_____ a.m./p.m.

Notes

Sweet Dreams: Choosing Your Hotel

Enter the hotels where you'd prefer to stay based on location and price. Then use the worksheet below to plan your itinerary.

Hotel	Location	Price per night

Menus & Venues

Enter the restaurants where you'd most like to dine. Then use the worksheet below to plan your itinerary.

Name	Address/Phone	Cuisine/Price

Places to Go, People to See, Things to Do

Enter the attractions you would most like to see. Then use the worksheet below to plan your itinerary.

Attractions	Amount of time you expect to spend there	Best day and time to go

Going "My" Way

Itinerary #1

- ☐ _____
- ☐ _____
- ☐ _____
- ☐ _____

Itinerary #2

- ☐ _____
- ☐ _____
- ☐ _____
- ☐ _____

Itinerary #3

- ☐ _____
- ☐ _____
- ☐ _____
- ☐ _____

Itinerary #4

- ☐ _____
- ☐ _____
- ☐ _____
- ☐ _____

Itinerary #5

- ☐ _____
- ☐ _____
- ☐ _____
- ☐ _____

Itinerary #6

☐ _____
☐ _____
☐ _____
☐ _____

Itinerary #7

☐ _____
☐ _____
☐ _____
☐ _____

Itinerary #8

☐ _____
☐ _____
☐ _____
☐ _____

Itinerary #9

☐ _____
☐ _____
☐ _____
☐ _____

Itinerary #10

☐ _____
☐ _____
☐ _____
☐ _____

Notes

Index

FOR DUMMIES
BOOK REGISTRATION

Register This Book and Win!

We want to hear from you!

Visit **dummies.com** to register this book and tell us how you liked it!

- ✔ Get entered in our monthly prize giveaway.

- ✔ Give us feedback about this book — tell us what you like best, what you like least, or maybe what you'd like to ask the author and us to change!

- ✔ Let us know any other *For Dummies* topics that interest you.

Your feedback helps us determine what books to publish, tells us what coverage to add as we revise our books, and lets us know whether we're meeting your needs as a *For Dummies* reader. You're our most valuable resource, and what you have to say is important to us!

Not on the Web yet? It's easy to get started with *Dummies 101: The Internet For Windows 98* or *The Internet For Dummies* at local retailers everywhere.

Or let us know what you think by sending us a letter at the following address:

For Dummies Book Registration
Dummies Press
10475 Crosspoint Blvd.
Indianapolis, IN 46256

BESTSELLING
BOOK SERIES